AN EPISTLE OF COMFORT

THE ORCHARD BOOKS
Uniform with this volume

AN EPISTLE OF COMFORT

TO THE REVEREND PRIESTS,
AND TO THE
HONOURABLE, WORSHIPFUL, AND
OTHER OF THE LAY SORT,
RESTRAINED IN DURANCE FOR THE
CATHOLIC FAITH

by

ROBERT SOUTHWELL, S.J.

Edited by

MARGARET WAUGH

With a Foreword by

PHILIP CARAMAN, S.J.

LONDON: BURNS & OATES

BURNS & OATES LIMITED

25 Ashley Place, London S.W.1

This Edition first published 1966

NIHIL OBSTAT: IOANNES M. T. BARTON, S.T.D., L.S.S.

CENSOR DEPUTATUS

IMPRIMATUR: PATRITIUS CASEY

VICARIUS GENERALIS

WESTMONASTERII: DIE 2 APRILIS 1965

272
50e

MADE AND PRINTED IN GREAT BRITAIN BY
THE BROADWATER PRESS LTD, WELWYN GARDEN CITY, HERTFORDSHIRE
SET IN 'MONOTYPE' PERPETUA

FOREWORD

ALL who have read Robert Southwell's *Epistle of Comfort* in the typescript of this edition agree that it may well establish itself as a classic of Christian literature. It is more than a hundred years ago that the historian Richard Simpson last published the work in monthly instalments in *The Rambler*. Since then it has been read by a few recusant historians, though a larger public has come to know of it through extracts printed in my Elizabethan anthology, *The Other Face*.

Simpson saw in the *Epistle* the finest literary expression of the persecuted Catholic community, and rightly judged it comparable, and in many ways superior, to the recognized masterpieces of Elizabethan prose. In Southwell's *Epistle* and in Campion's heroic life, Simpson saw the bravest embodiment of the Catholic spirit. While he was republishing Southwell's text in *The Rambler*, he was engaged also on his classic biography of Edmund Campion. Only in 1935 was Campion's life re-written by Mr Evelyn Waugh with a grace of style that matched Campion's own. Now, just thirty years later, Southwell's *Epistle* has been re-edited by Mr Waugh's daughter in a manner designed to overcome the linguistic difficulties that account for the failure of Simpson to popularize Southwell's message as he had done Campion's.

Since I first read the *Epistle*, I became impatient to present it again to Catholics who, after the passage of a century, were perhaps more capable of appreciating both its stylistic perfection and message of surpassing nobility. When other commitments made this impossible, I suggested the task to Margaret Waugh. The principles that have guided her are explained in the Introduction, and are unexceptionable both to the sympathetic scholar and to the general reader. Moreover, all who are acquainted with the first edition will admit that she has brought to the work a reverence for enduring language and an awareness both of past achievement and present needs. By making the *Epistle* available again in this fluent, comprehensible and faithful edition, she has placed the Catholic, indeed the Christian, community in her lasting debt. This might appear extravagant commendation only to those who have not read this book.

PHILIP CARAMAN, S.J.

Feast of Edmund Campion, 1 December 1964.

INTRODUCTION

ROBERT SOUTHWELL, the second son of Sir Richard Southwell, was born in 1561 at Horsham St Faith, one of three ecclesiastical properties awarded to his grandfather for his services as a commissioner for the suppression of the monastic houses. This grandfather had been an eminent courtier in the reign of Henry VIII, and ironically had sat on the Bench at the trial of Henry Howard, Earl of Surrey, the grandfather of Philip Howard, to whom Robert addressed the letters of comfort which he later expanded into this book. Through his mother, Bridget Copley, Southwell claimed cousinship with Sir William Cecil, Sir Francis Bacon and Sir Edward Coke.

Robert was brought up a Catholic and sent to school at Douai, where he boarded at the English seminary and attended classes at the neighbouring school of the Flemish Jesuits. At the seminary he became acquainted with Cardinal Allen, leader of the English Counter-Reformation. At the Jesuit school he knew Father Lessius, then a young master, not yet ordained, later to become one of the leading theologians of Europe. From Douai Southwell was sent to the famous Jesuit school, Clermont, in Paris. There he came under the influence of one of the first English Jesuits, Father Thomas Darbyshire, nephew of Bishop Bonner of London. At Paris, at the age of seventeen, he sought admission into the Society of Jesus but was refused owing to his youth. This rebuff elicted from him his first verses that have survived. To prove his determination he walked to Rome and there was received into the novitiate of Sant' Andrea on the Quirinal on 17 October 1578.

Both before and after his ordination (1584) he lived at the English College, where he acted as tutor to the students, whom later he championed against the slanders of the government in his *Humble Supplication*. On 8 May 1586, at the request of Cardinal Allen and Father Robert Persons, Southwell set out from Rome to England with Father Henry Garnet. Aquaviva, the General of the Jesuits, was heard to murmur that he was "sending lambs to the slaughter"; Southwell spoke of himself and his companion as "two arrows shot at the same mark". On 17 June they stepped ashore about a mile east of Folkestone.

From his first days in England Southwell devoted much of his time to the prisons of London. His appearance there among the Catholics, who for years had suffered deprivation and dirt, inspired them with fresh hope. His first recorded sermon, later printed as *St Mary Magdalene's Funeral Tears*, was preached on her feast day, 22 July, in the Clink, just over a month after his arrival in England. Henceforth, and especially during his first years on the mission, his principal work was among prisoners; they were his peculiar flock. Young, debonair, imaginative and poetic though he was, it was the sordid grime of prisons, with their depth of despair and human suffering, that attracted him more than the conspiratorial, adventurous, falconing life of disguise and escape of such dashing Jesuits as John Gerard. Southwell saw suffering as the noblest fate of humanity.

When in the spring of 1587 Southwell took up residence at Arundel House in the Strand, he began a series of letters to his hostess's husband, Philip Howard, who had already spent two years of the eleven he was to spend imprisoned in the Tower. These letters are not extant, though Southwell must have kept copies or rough drafts. He writes: "Having written this *Epistle of Comfort* to an especial friend of mine, and not thinking at first to let it pass any further, not only the time, which it principally serveth, but the entreaty of divers, enforced me so far, that I could not but condescend to the publishing of the same, though it cost me much labour in altering the style."

Southwell never met Philip Howard, but these letters, the basis of the *Epistle of Comfort*, began a great spiritual friendship between the two future martyrs, and to Philip Howard, cut off from all spiritual comforts, they were of incalculable help in his lonely school of sanctity. Later when Southwell himself was imprisoned in the Tower, Philip's dog once found its way to Southwell's cell. Philip used to say he loved the dog the better for it.

In July 1592 Southwell was betrayed and arrested at Uxenden Manor, near Harrow, Middlesex, and was tortured in a most savage manner by his captor, Richard Topcliffe, in his private dwelling attached to the Gatehouse prison, Westminster. Father Garnet spoke of Southwell as a "Goliath of fortitude"; Robert Cecil, who saw him in his agony, later told a friend: "They boast about the heroes of antiquity, but we have a new torture which is not possible for a man to bear. And yet I have seen Robert Southwell hanging by it, still as a tree-trunk, and none able to drag one word from his mouth."

What Southwell wrote in the *Epistle* he was prepared, indeed called upon, to practise. It is this that helps to make his book a spiritual classic, comparable in fervour to the *Imita-*

tion of Christ and surpassing it both in use of imagery and in poetic content.

After nearly two years of solitary confinement in the Tower, Southwell was executed at Tyburn on 22 February 1595.

The *Epistle of Comfort* is Southwell's earliest considerable prose work written in English. It follows close on *Mary Magdalene's Funeral Tears*, which is no more than sermon length. In altering the Epistle for a general readership, Southwell would have erased many personal allusions, understood only by the recipient of the original letters; also exhortations applicable only to a man of his position, and probably also several autobiographical reminiscences. To a man of Southwell's impulsive temperament this work of revision, as he himself confessed, was laborious.

The first edition bears no date: on the title-page are the words "imprinted at Paris", but this was only a cover for the secret press set up by Garnet and Southwell in London within the first twelve months of their reaching England. The false imprint also served to excuse the numerous printing errors, inevitable in the first major production of a hastily established press: "faults in orthography or printing" were attributed to the "French printers' ignorance of our language".

From a sentence at the beginning of Chapter 15 it is possible to date the completion of the *Epistle*, if not the printing of the first edition. Addressing the "persecutors" of the Church, Southwell writes: "Our constancy forceth men to look more into our cause, and then by seeking they find, by finding they believe, and by believing are as ready to die as we ourselves. Our prisons preach, our punishments convert, our dead quarters and bones confound your heresy. You have laboured to suppress us *this thirty years*; and yet from our ashes spring others, and our dead bones, as Ezechiel prophesied, are come to be a 'huge army'."

The beginning of the persecution was commonly reckoned from the opening of the first Parliament of Elizabeth, which introduced the changes in worship. On this calculation the *Epistle* was completed shortly before the end of 1587; and there is confirmation of this in the references Southwell makes to contemporary events. While he speaks by name of several English martyrs, he mentions none who suffered in or after 1588, the worst year of executions. This probable date of publication also has particular interest for the lexicographer, for it places the first usage of several words earlier than at present recorded in the *Oxford English Dictionary*.

In the *Epistle* Southwell developed the theme of suffering and transfiguration that was the subject of the *Funeral Tears*; but already, after less than six months in England, it is possible to see an advance in his prose style. Under the stress of heart-rending missionary experience, he writes with greater urgency. The stylized manner, the precocities of phrase and artifacts give way to more direct speech; his approach is more immediate. The brilliant choice of metaphor and balance of phrase remain but the impact is greater. Southwell was writing with an urgent purpose, namely, to fortify the spirit of Catholics who had lost everything in their adherence to the old faith. The greater part of the book develops the motives that should inspire their endurance, and sets out the prizes that await the unyielding combatant. The old lessons are illustrated by new similes: each paragraph instils encouragement: every comparison is illuminating. One example must suffice in this introduction. Addressing the persecutors, he writes: "When the red hot iron is put into the water, it maketh a great noise and seemeth to do the water great harm, whereas in the end we find that the fire thereof is quenched, the force of burning lost, and the water little the worse. Like this is your triumph over us. God will show you by rueful experience that the martyrs' estate was not hurt."

The similarity of Southwell's title to St Thomas More's *Dialogue of Comfort against Tribulation* is an accident of circumstance. The two books are totally dissimilar in their plan and execution. St Thomas More writes as a philosopher, musing and meditating in a heavenly manner on his fate; Southwell as a passionate pastor of souls. Although he sets out his chapter titles as propositions (perhaps a relic of his recent Roman training), he does not attempt to prove a thesis. He is practical and poetical by turns, devotional and polemical; his argument and metaphors merge with a natural fluency; he is stern and sweetly comforting. On the example of the imprisoned Catholics the survival of "true religion" depended. He represents suffering as the highest privilege and the surpassing mystical experience of the true Christian. "As the paperer of old rotten shreds, oftentimes gathered out of unclean dunghills, by his industry maketh so fine, white and clean paper that it is apt to receive any curious drawing, painting or limning; so our scattered parts . . . cast into dunghills [God] will restore to such purity of per-

fection that they shall be more capable of his glorious ornaments than they were before."

Here and throughout his work he manifests the outlook
of contemporary theologians. While he is severe, he is not
unkind. He is always serene and free from ranting. He ad-
monishes his enemies with charity, and shows the confidence of a protagonist secure in his stand and assured of ulti-
mate triumph. "The priests and Catholics whom you persecute", he tells his adversaries, "are stones that God throweth at you to make you, by their example and exhortation,
stop feeding on the carrion of sin and heresy. But like enraged hounds, you break your teeth, not considering the
hand that threw it."

In addressing both Catholics and non-Catholics Southwell
makes no attempt to soften the sharper edges of dogma. But
it must be remembered that his message is always spiritual.
Partly for this reason the book has permanent value; partly
also because it is an original and individualistic work utterly
free from the clichés of ascetical writers. It is difficult to
explain its comparative neglect in modern times.

The Protestants had appealed to the Fathers of the Church
for support of their position; Southwell uses the Fathers,
principally St Cyprian, to refute them. A persecuted
Church was something that had parallels only in the early
Christian centuries; and both in Southwell's judgement,
and Allen's, the Christians of North Africa in the time of
Cyprian offered the nearest analogy to the position of
Catholics in England in the last decades of the sixteenth
century.

In preparing Southwell's text for publication, I have omitted the Latin of the Fathers and have retained only Southwell's translations. These are gracefully done and fuse so intimately with his own prose style that it is difficult, on hearing the book read, to determine where Augustine, Tertullian or Basil ends and Southwell resumes.

A fascinating curiosity of the *Epistle* is the number of metaphors Southwell draws from natural history. He was not a countryman; what he knew of hunting and falconry he learnt later from Father John Gerard. The greater part of the knowledge he shows here is derived from books. At the time Southwell wrote his *Epistle* there was a widespread interest in animals, stimulated partly by the zoo, then housed in the Tower of London, but still more by a popular work compiled by John Maplet, *A Greene Forest or Naturall Historie*, which appeared in 1567. The third of the three parts of this lexicon (the entries are arranged alphabetically) deals with beasts, fishes and fowls. The detailed preface to this part distinguishes the behaviour and characteristics of male and female, fierce and tame animals. Maplet himself drew his information mainly from Pliny and from the medieval encyclopedia of Bartholomaeus Anglicus, *De Proprietatibus Rerum*. There are indications that Southwell at times went behind Maplet to his sources. Bartholomaeus' work, printed in 1535 and again in 1583, is likely to have been in the library of Arundel House or in the larger mansions that Southwell visited during his first twelve months in England. Writing of the beaver Maplet says (p. 74): "When they are hunted, they, espying the huntsman earnestly pursuing them . . . the male is reported to bite off his own stones and to geld himself, and by that means becometh very swift."

Bartholomaeus (Lib. 18, cap. 29) has: "they ransom themselves with that part of the body for which they be most pursued." Southwell, in Chapter 10 of the *Epistle*, uses this story thus: "When the beavers are hunted and see themselves straitened, they bite off their own stones, for which by kind they know themselves to be chiefly pursued, so that the hunter having his desire may cease to follow them any further. Now, if nature hath taught these brute things so painful a means to save themselves from bodily danger, how much more ought reason and faith teach us to forgo willingly not only liberty and living, but even our very life, and purchase thereby the life of our souls, and deliver ourselves from eternal perdition."

It was from these sources, also, that Shakespeare drew; but Southwell cast further afield and used much animal lore found in the writings of the Fathers, particularly in St John Damascene, who was well informed on the unicorn. Other animal lore Southwell took direct from the Scriptures.

However, most of the similes which are found in profusion in every chapter of this book are Southwell's own. There are long passages that read like a poet's scrapbook: indeed, much of his imagery is found again in his poems, which he wrote at intervals during the years following the completion of the *Epistle*. It would be hard to point to a book of this period in which there are so many passages of sustained poetic and spiritual appeal. Here and there it is possible to trace his own personal experience. When in Chapter 5 he writes of the leper hospital, he is probably recalling his days as a novice in Rome, where he worked among the sick and dying of the city. "Do but cast your eyes into one hospital of lazars. See the cankers, fistulas, ulcers and rottings, the wolls, sores and festered carbuncles. Weigh the miseries of the frenzy, palsy, lethargy, falling sickness and lunacy. Consider the diseases of the eyes, ears, mouth, throat and every parcel of man's body. . . ." In the Introduction he would seem to be recapturing his feelings on his recent ride from Rome to the French coast on his way back to England. "For as to the wayfaring pilgrim, wandering in the dark and misty night, every light (though never so little) is comfortable, and to the stranger that travelleth in a land of divers languages, any that can (though it be but brokenly) speak his country's tongue, doth not a little rejoice him; so peradventure in this foggy night of heresy, and the confusion of tongues which it hath procured here in our island, this dim light, which I shall set forth before you . . . will not be altogether unpleasant." Again his own observation in the houses of his noble friends is reflected in a fine passage on Elizabethan courtly love:

> We see that an enamoured knight hath no greater felicity than to do that which may be acceptable to his paramour. And the fading beauty of a fair lady's countenance is able to work so forcibly in men's minds that neither loss of riches, danger of endurance, menacings of torments, no not present death is able to withhold where she inviteth, or make the bark ride at anchor that is wafted in her streams. Every peril undertaken for her seemeth pleasant, every reproach honourable, all drudgery delightsome, yea the very wounds that come from her or are suffered for her are void of smart: and the wounded wretch rejoices more with the hope that his hurt will purchase favour than feels aggrieved that his

body hath received such a maim. Her colours seemeth the fairest, the meat that fitteth her taste seemeth the sweetest, the fashion agreeable to her fancy seemeth the comeliest; her faults are virtues; her sayings, oracles; her deeds, patterns. Finally, whatsoever pleaseth her, be it never so unpleasant, seemeth good, and whatsoever cometh from her, be it ever so dear bought and of little value, is deemed precious and a cheap pennyworth. O unspeakable blindness of man's heart, that so easily traineth to senses' lure, and is so soon caught with the beauty of an image and hath not grace to remember whom it resembleth.

As he proceeds it can be seen how every aspect of English life in Elizabethan England provided material for his meditations: there are similes drawn from the marble-quarries and foundries, from the lives of husbandmen, embroiderers, portrait-painters and sea-faring captains. Both the choice and handling of his metaphors are scintillating.

The unequal length of the chapters suggests that the basis of each was a letter of greatly different length. In the first draft that Southwell sent to Philip Howard, he would seem to have written on until he had exhausted in each letter the "cause of comfort" that was its theme. He did not revise the scheme, but merely added the last two chapters before publication.

In this edition the chapter divisions are unaltered from the first printed version of the Epistle. For easier reading new paragraphs have been made. Since my purpose has been to present the text, not for scholars, to whom it is available in one sixteenth- and two seventeenth-century editions, but to a wider Catholic public, who, after reading it, may well adopt it as a spiritual classic, I have everywhere modernized the spelling, punctuation and syntax. Archaic grammar and constructions have been made intelligible; and some alterations of phrase have been made that leave the sense and savour of the original unimpaired. All archaisms that can be immediately understood are retained; care has been taken that no alteration in the text should modify the sense in the smallest measure.

It is impossible to track down more than an occasional reference Southwell makes to the Fathers: often he gives no chapter reference; and there is never an indication of the edition he is using; frequently the references are wrongly given. It would seem that for the benefit of Philip Howard he quoted without references and then later attempted to supply them; but either the pressing demand for the book or the risk in delaying to check his references made him publish the work without revising and ordering them. Since I have been able to check only one in three, it seemed more consistent to print them at the end of the book in the form he gave them. On the other hand all his references to Scripture have been corrected and regularized. Here and there I have added notes at the foot of the page, to explain either an allusion or the usage of an English word.

Finally, in the last paragraph I have used the first person singular in reference to various alterations made to the text of the *Epistle of Comfort*. This I have little right to do since the work of editorship is less mine than that of Father Philip Caraman, who helped, guided and encouraged me throughout. I can only express my humble gratitude. I should also like to thank Audrey von Lintzgy who typed the manuscript.

A history of the editions of the *Epistle* is given in James H. McDonald's *The Poems and Prose Writings of Robert Southwell, S. J., A Bibliographical Study* (Oxford, 1937). Pierre Janelle's *Robert Southwell, the Writer* (London, 1935) gives the work its place in the development of Southwell's prose style. Christopher Devlin's *Robert Southwell, Priest and Poet* (London 1956), provides the historical setting of the *Epistle*.

M. W.

CONTENTS

CONTENTS

PREFACE

Having written this Epistle of Comfort to an especial friend of mine,* and not thinking at first to let it pass any further, not only the time, which it principally serveth, but the entreaty of divers, enforced me so far that I could not but condescend to the publishing of the same, though it cost me much labour in altering the style. Accept therefore, gentle reader, my goodwill and hearty desire for thy comfort. And albeit (as thou wilt easily perceive by the reading) neither the style nor the concept answereth to the weight and importance of the subject, yet I hope that thou shalt not find it so barren and fruitless but that therein thou mayest glean some ears of comfort and pick some few crumbs for thy spiritual repast.

And if through thy good disposition and tenderness of mind thou find any further contentment thereby than it would yield of itself, whatsoever thou deemest praiseworthy attribute it to the spirit of that body, whereof I am an unworthy member, and to which next unto God, I owe what good soever is in me. But if anything be amiss, impute that to mine own error or ignorance. Thus wishing thee the full effect, which by reading thereof thou desirest, I cease to withhold thee with any longer Preface. Thy hearty wellwiller in Christ Jesus,

R. S.

* Blessed Philip Howard: see Introduction.

AN EPISTLE OF COMFORT

To the Reverend Priests, and to the Honourable, Wor-
shipful, and other of the Lay sort, restrained in durance
for the Catholic Faith

IT hath been always a laudable custom in God's Church
for such as were afflicted in time of persecution to comfort one another, not only by continual prayer and good
works but also by letters and books. And although the estate
of imprisoned confessors or (as the Fathers call them[1]) designed martyrs, hath been so honourable, and they evermore presumed to be so especially lightened and assisted by
the Holy Ghost, that the fountain of spiritual delights was
thought always to lie open unto them; yet because inward
helps are nothing prejudiced, yea rather abetted by external motives, I thought it no presumption to show my
reverent affection towards God's prisoners by presenting
unto them this Epistle of Comfort. And though others have
largely treated of the same subject, and that in very forcible
sort, yet because where the same calamities are still continued, the remedies against them cannot be too often repeated, I deemed it not unprofitable in this heat and severity
of molestations to employ some labour in a thing of the like
tenour. For as to the wayfaring pilgrim, wandering in the
dark and misty night, every light (though never so little) is
comfortable, and to the stranger that travelleth in a land of
divers languages, any that can (though it be but brokenly)
speak his country's tongue, doth not a little rejoice him; so
peradventure in this foggy night of heresy, and the con-

fusion of tongues which it hath procured here in our island, this dim light, which I shall set forth before you, and these my Catholic, though broken, speeches which I shall use unto you, will not be altogether unpleasant. And though I may say with Tertullian,[2] that as the sickest are most willing to talk of health, not for that they enjoy it, but because they desire it, so I exhort you to patience as one that would have it rather than as one that possesseth it. Yet because sometimes a diseased physician may prescribe healthsome physic, and a deformed engraver carve a fair image, I hope no man will blame me if for my own good and your comfort I have taken upon me to address unto you this short Treatise, wherein I will enlarge myself but in a few points, which seem unto me the principal causes of consolation to those that suffer in God's quarrel.

THE FIRST CHAPTER

The first cause of Comfort in Tribulation is that it is a great presumption that we are out of the devil's power

IT must greatly comfort all who have been reclaimed from schism or heresy or from a dissolute life to a constant profession of the Catholic faith, to be persecuted for that cause by the devil and his instruments. For it is a very sure sign that they have been delivered out of his power and are now accounted sheep of God's flock, since otherwise he would never pursue them so heavily.

While the poor cripple lay long at the pond of Probatica, none would say a word of rebuke unto him (Jn 5), but as soon as he was cured by Christ both in body and in soul and began joyfully to execute His commandments, he was straightway reproved for carrying his bed on a Sabbath day. The like we read of the seelie* blind man (Jn 9). So long as he continued in his blindness, he was never called in question, but so soon as his eyes were opened, not only he himself, but his parents also were presently converted. When Mary Magdalen (Lk. 3) came to wash Christ's feet with tears and anoint them with precious ointment, there was a Simon to murmur at her for the one, and a Judas to reprehend for the other, although they did not speak against her whilst she held to her lewd course.

* *seelie*: can mean *harmless* or *enjoying the blessing of God*. R. S. might be using it here in either sense.

5

The devil desireth *to dash our little ones against the rock* (Ps. 136.9), that is, to blast virtue in the bud before it grows either to fruit or flower. So he began with Eve in Paradise, insomuch as the forbidden apple is thought by the Fathers to have been the very first that she tasted (Gen. 3). So did Pharaoh procure to root out the Hebrews by killing their babes (Ex. 1); as Herod also thought to do with Christ, when he murdered the innocents (Mt. 2).

The devil hath his mastiffs to guard his fold so that if any escape, they may presently bark and bite him with detractious slanders; and if that will not serve, with heavier afflictions. Of these persons the Scripture says, *the children of men, their teeth are like swords and arrows and their tongue a sharp blade* (Ps. 56.5). And though they be very ugly monsters that instead of teeth and tongue carry such murderous weapons, yet such are the instruments of the devil who persecute those who recoil from his service. These men St Cyprian well describeth in the person of Novatian, saying that a man of that office is a *forsaker of the Church, an enemy of mercy, a murderer of penance, a preacher of pride, a corruptor of the truth and a spoiler of charity*.[1]

But they that leave their journey for such are like horses that are frightened by shadows, since they fear the pains and troubles of this world, which indeed are but shadows in respect of those of the world to come.[2] *There they trembled for fear where there was no just occasion thereof* (Ps. 52.6). It is not for us to be concerned with the slanders of men or to abandon the service of God for them, seeing that it is but a very slender excuse to allege the fear or words of a vassal as a just impediment of not performing our duty towards our Sovereign. *The friendship of this world is an enemy to God*

6

(Jas. 4. 4); and St Paul himself said, *that if he would have pleased men, he could not have been the servant of Christ* (Gal. 1. 10).

It were a great folly for the blind to revile or scorn others because they see, or for the lame to contemn those that are sound of limbs; and much more sottishness were it for a man that seeth to go blindfold, or to put out his eyes for the blind wretches' scoffing, or to limp or maim himself for the cripples' sayings. *He that walketh an upright way and feareth God is despised of him that treadeth an infamous path* (Prov. 14. 2). But, *He that dwelleth in the heavens shall laugh such to scorn* (Ps. 2. 4), knowing how much better they deserve it, than those whom they make their stales.* It is no disgrace to the sun to be hated of the owl and night birds, nor to the jewel to be trodden on and not esteemed of the beasts. Aristippus,† when one told him that men despised him, answered, so do the beasts despise men, making as little account of their contempt as they did to be contemned of the beasts.

Lo, my witness, saith Job, *is in heaven, and in the highest he that is privy to my doings* (Job 16. 20). We must not esteem how we are judged by men, but how acceptable we are unto God, who is the only umpire to whom we must look for the final verdict upon all our actions. St Bernard[3] compareth such as are influenced by the words of men's mouths unto the moon, which because it hath but a borrowed light some-

---

* *stale*: This word has many meanings but R. S. is probably using it in the sense of *a lover or mistress whose devotion is turned into ridicule for the amusement of a rival*—hence a laughing-stock.

† Aristippus was a citizen of Cyrene and a friend of Socrates. He was a teacher of rhetoric and for a time a courtier of Dionysius I. He was also noted for his high living.

7

times waxeth and sometimes waneth and otherwhiles is not seen at all. So, saith he, they that rely their consciences in other men's lips are sometimes of great, otherwhiles of little, and full often of no account, as it pleaseth the flattering tongues to set forth or suppress their praise. But he that with the sun carrieth his light within him, may say with St Paul, *our glory is the testimony of our conscience* (2 Cor. 1.12); although he may be covered from men's eyes in a cloud of disgrace and malicious slanders, yet can his light be never so darkened, but that *thy Father which seeth in secret, will reward you* (Mt. 6.4), *and in the day of judgment shall he shine like the sun itself, in the view of the whole world, agreeably to that saying, The just like the sun shall blaze out their brightness* (Wis. 3.7).*

You must not think, when you are come out of the whale's belly, to sit with Jonas in the shadow (Jon. 4),† but that you shall have some envious worm to gnaw the ivy root asunder. And if you were changed from a thorn or briar into an odoriferous cedar, the worm that cannot breed in you, would be gnawing about you. It is the property of the devil and his instruments to feed like storks upon the venomous and evil actions of men. They only take pleasure to see us in sin, and rejoice at the calamities which follow if we amend.

And as vultures or ravens, though they straightway smell a dead corpse when it is corrupted, and are drawn to it by

* R. S. is quoting from memory. The verse is: *The just shall shine and shall run to and fro like sparks among the reeds.*

† God caused an ivy to grow in order to give Jonah shade but then caused a worm to appear who gnawed through the ivy, so Jonah was unprotected from the sun and when he complained God replied, *Thou art grieved for the ivy, for which thou hast not laboured, nor made it to grow, which in one night came up and in one night perished.*

8

the unsavoury stench in which they delight; yet the sound bodies they neither scent nor seek out. So the wicked are ready to flock about us while we are in the stench of sin and corrupted with vice, because they themselves delight therein: yet if we be sound and whole, and have cast from us that carrion whereof they were eager, they neither smell us nor seek us, yea rather avoid us and hate us. The savour of virtue striketh them dead; and though in the winter when the vine was bare, they could lie under it, yet in the spring when it beginneth to flower, they, like serpents, are stricken dead with its scent, and therefore no marvel that they mortally hate it.

In our storm is their time of singing, as is usual with the sirens, and they are most sad in our calm and sorry in our welfare.* And as the ship, while it is upon the main sea, is in a manner a castle or commonwealth by itself, and having all the sails hoisted up and swollen with the wind, and the banners displayed, danceth with a very lofty shew upon the waves and allureth every eye to behold its pride; but when it is come into the haven, it is straightway ransacked by the searcher, forced to pay custom; and the sails being gathered, the banners taken in, the anchors cast, it lieth quietly at ride and is little regarded. So they, who while they sailed upon the surges of worldly vanities and followed the tide of a conscienceless course might range uncontrolled, and having the favourable gale of authority to waft them forward, and honours and pomp to set them forth, were admired of the people; but if they chance, by God's calling, to retire them-

---

* R. S. appears to be comparing the rejoicing of the wicked over the sufferings of Catholics with the singing of the sirens as they lure mariners to their death.

9

selves into the port of true faith and virtuous life to work their salvation, they are straightway searched and sacked, their sails gathered, the accustomed wind set, their glory disgraced, and they little or nothing esteemed. *If you were of the world, the world would love you: but because I have chosen you out of it, it beareth you malice* (Jn 15.19).

St Basil[4] recounteth of his own experience that the leopard beareth such a furious hatred to man that, at the sight of him, it suddenly flieth in his face; and so to avoid its rage, the custom is to shew unto it a man's picture on a paper, which it presently rendeth and teareth asunder, shewing thereby how eagerly it is bent against man himself, whose image it cannot abide. Even so, the devil and his followers, not being able to wreak their malice against Almighty God whom they especially hate, turn their spite against God's image, that is man's soul, and so much the more enviously seek the overthrow of it, the more they see it wax like unto God, not only in nature but also in goodness.

When we come to the service of Christ, we come to a rough profession, which is bound to have continual defiance and enmity with the pleasures, vanities, and praises of this world. Therefore we can look for nothing else at their hands, that are friends of the world, but only trouble, hatred, and persecution. *Let every one that cometh to the service of God*, saith St Augustine, *persuade himself that he is come like a grape to the wine press, he shall be crushed, squeezed and pressed, not so much to procure his death to the world, as his reservation in God's cellar.*[5]

A thief, as St Chrysostom observed,[6] when he entereth into a house to rob, first putteth out the light, according to the text: *He that doth evil hateth the light* (Jn 3.20), and therefore the devil and his imps, seeing those that were once darkness now become *light in our Lord* (Eph. 5. 8), seek to disgrace and blemish their virtues so that they may the more freely continue their wicked purposes. *Let us circumvent the righteous*, say the wicked, *because he is contrary to our works* (Wis. 2. 12). *But*, saith Origen, *as it is a dispraise and abasement for one to be honoured and praised by the impious only, so is it a great honour to be persecuted and disgraced by them, because it is a pregnant proof that we are enemies of their lewd behaviour.*[7]

Howsoever the dogs bark, yet dogs remain they, and we men: so the bad remain wicked, and we for all their slanders no whit the less virtuous. The more the waves and billows, how boisterous soever they be, beat against a stony rock, the more are they broken and turned into a vain foam and froth, and yet the rock nothing the weaker. Let the malicious fume and fret against us, our rock is impregnable if we cleave unto it; hurt themselves they may, but harm us they cannot. So it appeareth in St Stephen's persecutors, of whom it is written that *they were cut in their hearts, and they gnashed with their teeth at him* (Ac. 7. 54); and yet was he nothing moved or terrified with their furious spite. His example should be unto us a pattern of constancy, and teach us to make the same account of the obloquies of our adversaries that he did of the malice of the Jews. For how can it move any of God's servants to be evil spoken of, especially by heretics? *As though*, saith St Cyprian, *amongst the lapsed and profane persons, who are out of the Church and out of whose breasts the Holy Ghost is departed, there could be anything looked for except a depraved mind, a deceitful tongue, cankered hatreds and sacrilegious lies, to which whosoever giveth credit must needs be numbered with them in the day of judgement.*[8]

Wherefore, whosoever have entered a virtuous course let them prepare their minds to all kinds of temptation, both by words and wicked endeavours of the bad, since assuredly we know that the devil will never agree with those that in God's cause are his enemies, howsoever he fawned upon them while they were in his power. As long as the lion hath the prey in his paws he can dally and play with it, but if he see any chance of it escaping from him, he forthwith fixeth his claws into its flesh. Pharaoh never so fiercely did persecute the Israelites as when they were going out of Egypt (Ex. 14). Laban never pursued Jacob till he departed from him (Gen. 31). So the devil little careth to bark or bite at those that are his household servants until such time as they begin to wax strangers unto him. Of this the Scripture giveth us warning: *He which forsook wickedness, lay open to the spoil* (Is. 59. 15). And St Gregory saith to the same effect, *Our enemy, the more he seeth us to rebel against him, the more he endeavoureth to overcome us. For those of whom he findeth himself in quiet possession he little careth to molest.*[9] So may we understand the words of Holofernes unto Judith (Jdt. 11. 1): *I have never hurt a man who was willing to serve the king.* Young Tobias (Tob. 6), so long as he walked in the mire and dirt, went quietly and was never troubled; but when he went to wash his feet in the clear river, there was presently a fish ready to devour him.

The pirates, when they know the ship to be empty, let it quietly pass; but when it cometh laden with rich merchandise, their manner is to assail it with all violence. So, saith St Chrysostom,[10] while men are void of virtue, the devil letteth not their voyage, but when they are enriched with grace and have taken in their freight of the gifts of God's spirit, he straight giveth the onset with tribulation. He cometh not in styes and kennels to seek his prey, for he knoweth that there is nothing to be found but mire and filth. His haunt is to the rich coffers and chests of jewels and plate. Those that have nothing in them but sin and wickedness lie always open unto him, and well he knoweth that they are not worth the robbing: but those that begin to fill their coffers with the jewels of virtue, and cleanse their souls from vice to give room to God's heavenly treasures are a prey that he longeth to get, as the same saint observeth.[11]

The devil well knoweth that such as are out of God's favour may be won without strokes, and he is able with every push to lay them grovelling in what sin he listeth; but when he findeth one returned to grace and armed with godliness against his encounters, he cometh upon him with sad blows and by all slights and violence endeavoureth to overcome him. A paper wall he breaketh with one knock, but when he findeth a strong rampart or bulwark, he straight planteth his battery and useth all possible engines to overthrow it. But alas his force is but feeble, his engines weak to batter down the adamant rock of virtue, and therefore, as St Chrysostom saith, [12] therein he doth but spurn against a thorn; and while he seeketh to hide the fire in his garments, he doth but burn himself and give the fire matter to work upon and shew itself the more.[13]

God will always defend a Moses, and praise him most when Aaron and Mary murmur against him (Num. 12); and Christ will take upon him the patronage of a Magdalen, though Judas might try to control her good works (Mt. 26). Yea, if men oppress them, the very senseless and unreasonable creatures will fight in their defence and witness their innocency. The sea will honour a true Israelite, by giving dry passage (Ex. 14). The hungry lions will be lambs to Daniel (Dan. 6). The crows will feed an Elias (3 Kgs 17. 4): and the flames of fire withhold their force from burning a Sidrach, Misrach, and Abdenago (Dan. 3).

THE SECOND CHAPTER

The second cause of Comfort in Tribulation is that it sheweth us to be God's children, tenderly beloved by him

ANOTHER reason why we should willingly suffer tribulation is that *whom God loveth he chastiseth, and scourgeth every child that he receiveth* (Heb. 12.6). And St Paul calleth those that are without correction base born and not true children of Christ (Heb. 12.8). When David was reviled of Semei, he acknowledged it as coming from God who treated him as his child: *Our Lord hath commanded him to rail at me* (2 Kgs 16.10). God knoweth how easily in the vanities of this life we revolt from him, and therefore restraineth our licentious humour with the snaffle of affliction and with trouble curbeth our affections.

The falconer that hath a hawk of great price on his fist, be he never so fond of it, yet will he not let it loose. Yea the more he loveth it, the more care he hath to keep it hooded, to have good jesses at the legs and to hold it fast.* So dealt God with David, whom though he advanced to succeed Saul in his kingdom and gave him not only the victory over Goliath but bound unto him the good will of Saul's son and family, yea of the whole people, yet put he jesses to his legs, unwilling to lose so choice a piece; and for this end he was so persecuted by Saul that he was miserably tossed and tur-

* R. S. was instructed in falconry by John Gerard (cf. *John Gerard*, trans. Philip Caraman, S.J., p. 218).

moiled, and suffered famine, thirst and other great distresses.

St Paul, a great favourite of God, soared so high that he came to the third heaven, and some Divines and Fathers hold that he had the view of the very essence of God, and yet he had his jesses: *Lest the greatness of revelation should puff me up, there is allotted unto me an angel of Satan to buffet me* (2 Cor. 12.7).

Benjamin of all the brothers was most tenderly loved of Joseph, and therefore was Joseph's cup found in Benjamin's sack (Gen. 44). So is the chalice which Christ drank of, that is the chalice of tribulation, found in the sacks of those whom Christ most loveth. The new pieces are tried whether they be good by fire and gunpowder, which if they can bear without breaking, they are much esteemed.

God is very choice whom he adopteth for his child. His inheritance is so great that he meaneth to give it to such only as shall well deserve it. Therefore not only beginners are tried to the proof before he make any reckoning of them, but even those to whom he hath given honourable entertainment in his service, and maketh great account of, are put in continual proof of their perseverance. So when Abraham seemed to be most in God's favour, he was tried and bidden to offer his own son (Gen. 22). When God himself praised Job he was straight assaulted with most grievous temptations (Job 1). Yea, and Christ after that voice, *This is my beloved Son* (Mt. 3. 17), was presently led by the Spirit into the desert to be tried with temptation. And it was said to Tobias: *Because thou wert acceptable unto God, it was necessary that temptation should prove thee* (Tob. 12.13).

Such patients, saith St Gregory,[1] as be not past cure, God giveth bitter medicines unto, because he mindeth to restore them to perfect health; but such as are so far gone that by ordinary course of physic they are not likely to be recovered, he suffereth to do what best liketh their fantasy without controlment. When David numbered his people, God scourged him with a great mortality (2 Kgs 24); but Augustus committed the same sin, yea and a greater, making all to pay tribute, yet was not once touched. When Jonas fled by sea from going to Ninive (Jon. 4), doubtless in the ship there were divers more grievous sinners than he, being all Gentiles; and yet at the trial of whose sins caused the tempest to be raised the lot fell upon Jonas; and when he was cast into the sea the storm ceased, which is a token that the wicked, though they be full freight with sin, shall sail with a calm tide and prosperous gale: but those whom God loveth shall have their storms and be cast into a sea of afflictions for that little which they have offended.

This language of the Holy Ghost is not understood by the worldlings, who, like fleshworms, only feed upon the pleasures of this life and dream of no other felicity. Alas poor wretches! full little understand they their own misery, carrying under the names of Christians the hearts of Pagans, preferring pleasure and the future pains due unto it before the Cross of Christ and the eternal felicity ensuing after it. But such men carry their sins to hell to be punished with everlasting torments, while the afflicted souls, being purged here, shall after their decease enjoy their heavenly inheritance. This is signified in Leviticus: *He that blasphemeth God shall carry his sin, but he that taketh his name in vain shall die the death* (Lev. 24. 15). Compared to blaspheming God or reviling him, it is but little to take his name in vain; and yet it is punished in this life with present death, the other not, because (as Origen understandeth it) the other is so great that it deserveth a more grievous revenge and therefore shall the offender carry it with him into hell.

So it befell to the rich glutton (Lk. 16) whose offences, not being purged with any tribulation, were reserved to the flames of hell wherein he was buried; whereas Lazarus, in life full of miseries, went without any stop into the bosom of Abraham. The Machabees foretold the same punishment would fall on Antioch when he put them to death: *We suffer this for our own faults, having offended our God, but think not thou that it shall pass unrevenged that thou hast presumed to fight against God; (for to thee shall be no resurrection unto life)* (2 Mac. 7. 18–19, 14). And this manner and fatherly kind of proceeding used Paul with that sinful Corinthian of whom he said: *I have given him over to Satan for the destruction of his flesh so that his soul may be saved* (1 Cor. 5.5).

To be suffered to enjoy continually all sorts of delight and to have no cross to traverse our comforts is in truth a most rueful scourge of God and a token of a reprobate soul. This scourge did God threaten upon the people of Jerusalem, for when reckoning the enormities committed by them, he subjoineth presently: *For which I will not chastise your daughters for their fornications* (Jer. 5. 9): as who would say, this shall be part of your punishment for this.

St Basil,[2] expounding those words of Isaias, *I will leave my vineyard desolate, it shall neither be pruned nor digged* (Is. 5. 6), understandeth them to mean that a soul that sinneth without scourge thereby waxeth wild, fruitless and full of weeds.

A more plain saying for this purpose we have in the second

book of Machabees, where the Holy Ghost in these words warneth us of it: *I beseech them that shall read this book not to be terrified by these adversities but deem those things which have happened to be rather to the amendment than destruction of our nation* (2 Mac. 6. 12). For not to suffer sinners to enjoy long their designments but straightway to send them revenges is a token of a great benefit. For God dealeth not with us as with other nations whose sins he leaveth to the last day to be punished together; for though he chastiseth us, he never removeth his mercy from us and never forsaketh us in our trouble. Well therefore saith St Augustine: *Why weepest thou? That which thou sufferest is a medicine, not a punishment; it is a correction, not a condemnation. Reject not the whip, if thou wilt not be rejected from the inheritance; regard not what pain thou sufferest in the scourge but what place thou hast in thy Father's will.*[3]

The calves of oxen, as St Gregory noteth, *that are designed for the slaughter house are suffered to run and range at their will in pleasant pastures; but those that are appointed to live are put in the plough, yoked, tyered* and whipped.*[4] Of this St Augustine useth these words: *How many be there that run dallying like oxen to the stall and prepare their way to hell with singing and dancing?*[5] And David saith: *He hath given them over to their own hearts' desires, they shall go according to their own counsels* (Ps. 30.18). But howsoever they prosper here in all their attempts and worldly ways, *they carry their sin with them*, and in them is that saying of Job verified: *They pass their days in jollity, and in a moment they tumble into hell* (Job 21. 13). True it is that in this life they are not partakers of the toils of other men, and they shall not be scourged with them, and therefore they are

* Probably an old form of *attired*—prepared, equipped.

puffed up with pride and overwhelmed in their own sin and impiety. But sure it is that *they shall feed on the fruits of their own way* (Prov. 1. 31) in the world to come. These fruits are thus described in Deuteronomy: *Their grape is full of gall and their clusters extreme bitter: the gall of dragons is their wine, and the uncurable poison of cockatrices** (Deut. 32. 32). The thieves, says St Chrysostom,[6] till they come before the judge, live in delights and enjoy abundance of other men's spoil and calamity and plenty of all pleasures. So the world-lings live till their time of account come, but then shall they be thrown into floods of fire. And, as St Augustine warneth, *There shall come a judgement, that shall make the wicked wither and the faithful flourish.*[7] Better therefore it is to be chastised here with God's children than spared and pampered with the vassals of Satan. Better to be dashed with the fruitful plants than to flourish with barren trees and in the end be quite cut down to make fuel for hell fire. For according to the saying of St Augustine: *The good toil because they are scourged as children, the bad triumph because they are condemned as aliens.*[8] And, as St Gregory observeth, *Let us then account sinners most miserable, when we see them left in their sins without correction.*[9]

There is a people, saith David (Ps. 143. 12-15), *whose sons are like flourishing young spires, their daughters decked and trimmed like temples, their granaries and cellars full of provisions, their sheep and cattle fat and fertile, no ruins in their houses, no noise or cry in their streets.* But for all this, do not say, *Blessed is the people that hath these things.* The oak is stately of growth, full of fair leaves, and casteth a pleasant shadow, but the fruit

---

* *cockatrice*; a fabulous reptile, said to blast by its breath or look; identified with the *basilisk*.

thereof serveth for nothing but for swine to feed upon.

And Clement of Alexandria[10] compareth such to the profane temples of the Egyptians. If you look on them you shall first see very sumptuous and stately buildings, garnished about with variety of marbles, portraitures and curious works. Within, the first rooms are adorned and decked with gorgeous furniture and great majesty, but if you go into the most secret chapels to view the god for whose honour all this solemnity and preparation is used, you shall find some ugly viper or crocodile or some other venomous serpent. So is it with those that enjoy prosperity in this world. If you consider their houses, they are costly and glorious; if you mark their attire, it is fair and precious; if you view their bodies, they are personable and comely; but if you enter into their inmost room and consider what is harboured in all this bravery, you shall not find a clean image of God, but in place thereof a monstrous, ugly and sinful soul in the state of damnation. Therefore be not deceived with their vain external gloss.

Though you see the fish merrily catch the bait, and with fleeting and turning to and fro, seem to rejoice at it, marvel not, saith St Augustine,[11] neither deem it happy: the fisher hath not yet fastened in the fish's gills; but surely it will be one day verified in such: *As the fishes are caught with the hook and the birds with the snare so are men taken in time of misery* (Eccl. 9. 12). And in the end, howsoever they now dally and play in pleasure, the fisher, as Habacuc foretold, *shall draw all up with his hook, and shall bale and gather it into his net* (Hab. 1. 15). And then, alas, for their liberty they shall reap restraint, and for one dainty bite be an eternal prey of the worrying and devouring hell-hounds.

And for this cause doth God chastise his children in this life, and if they cannot be won with easier remedies, whom he seeth ready to run astray, he holdeth them back with a hard bit of adversity and hedgeth them in with the thorns of tribulation. *I will hedge in thy way with thorns*, saith God to the sinful soul, *and I will enclose it with a wall* (Os. 2. 6).

First, like a most faithful paramour of our soul, hanging in most rueful manner naked, wounded and ready to die upon the cross, he hath often sent us embassies of love, saying, *Tell my beloved that I languish for love* (Cant. 5. 8): and we most ungratefully have refused his messengers. He hath shewed us his feet nailed to attend our coming,[12] his side open to give us entrance, his arms stretched forth ready to embrace us, his head inclined to afford us the kiss of peace, his eyes shut to all our offences, his ears unstopped to hear our petitions, his hands open to enrich us with his gifts, finally a multitude of bleeding wounds to shew us how entirely he loved us and how dearly he bought us. But we, like the stiff-necked Jews, nothing moved with his excessive love, have contemned all his invitings. Yea, when uttering his most ardent desire for our souls, he said, *I thirst* (Jn 19. 28), we answered him with a draught of vinegar and gall. And when yielding up the ghost to conclude our redemption, he said, *It is consummated* (Jn 19. 30), we with most brutish and savage hearts fought with his dead corpse, not sparing with one, yea with a thousand spears of our sins, to wound him to a second, yea to many deaths. Yet all this ungratefulness hath not altered his affection. But, seeing that he cannot move us with so many griefs sustained in our behalf, he obscureth the sun of our comforts, he sendeth earthquakes of tribulations, he maketh the graves open and setteth death before our eyes, to win in a manner by force, since by love he could not, and to make us confess him even among the midst of his enemies, with the Centurion, and say: *Undoubtedly this was the Son of God* (Mt. 27. 54).

The vanities of this world cast the soul into such a delightsome frenzy and lull it so dangerously asleep that many in a frantic fit of licentiousness run headlong to perdition: *And while they rejoice they rave* (Wis. 14. 28); and others in a careless and remiss kind of life sleep themselves to death: *like wounded wretches sleeping in their graves* (Ps. 87. 6). And therefore God holdeth over his children the rod of tribulation both to temper and stay the raging mood of the frantic and to rouse the dead sleepers out of their lethargy. And as it must be construed in good part by any reasonable man to bind and keep in awe, yea to whip and beat the mad man when he falleth into his rage;* likewise to pinch, nip, and wring, yea and with red hot irons to burn the sick of a lethargy when he entereth into his dead sleep: so for God to correct our former, or to prevent our future infirmities by the scourges or hot irons of affliction cannot but be thought the part of a merciful and provident Father. For, as St Augustine noteth: *Not every one that spareth is a friend, nor every one that striketh, our enemy. Better are the wounds of a friend than the flattering kisses of a foe. Better is it to love with sincerity than to deceive with lenity:†* he that bindeth the frantic or waketh the sick of the lethargy, though to both troublesome, yet to both is very friendly.[13]

To wean us from an unnatural nurse, God anointeth her teat with the bitterness of tribulation. And as a mother, de-

---

* This was the normal treatment of the mad in the sixteenth century.
† *lenity*: leniency.

sirous to affectionate her child to herself above all others, maketh all of her household use it crossly in show so that it findeth good entreaty of none but her and so may more willingly repair unto her, so God, saith St Chrysostom,[14] suffereth us to be molested by the world, flesh, and devil so that we may only acknowledge him and come unto him as our chief succour and refuge.

The devil kisseth where he meaneth to kill. He giveth us a draught of poison in a golden cup, and in a sumptuous and stately ship wafteth his passengers upon the rocks of eternal ruin: *while with pleasures without he delighteth us*, saith Eusebius of Emesa, *inwardly he deceiveth us and killeth our soul while he flattereth our fancy*.[15] For when he moveth us to labour our wits and settle our affection on these inferior things, what doth he persuade us, but with a golden hook, to fish in a filthy puddle and sink where nothing can be gotten but venomous and unsavoury vermin. With syrens' sweet notes he wooeth us into the salt sea of perdition. With crocodiles' tears he endeavoureth to entrap us, and when he sheweth a man's face and glorious locks adorned with a crown of gold, as the locusts of the Apocalypse did (Apoc. 9), then he meaneth, even like the same, to bite us with his lion's teeth and sting us with his scorpion's tail. Because all his favours and friendly countenance are but kisses of an enemy. *He shroudeth his bitter poison under a deceitful sweetness: the pleasant savour of the cup inviteth, but the sweet taste of the poison choketh: it is honey that cometh up to our lips, but gall and poison that goeth down into our bowels*.[16]

And although the devil with a smooth flight and an even wing hovereth in the air, as though he were an eagle that delighted to view the sun and look towards heaven, he yet beareth a ravening mind, and in truth is but a greedy kite that hath his eyes always fixed on the earth, and maketh only such a fair show in the air the better to watch a fit time when he may best seize upon his prey.

For this St Basil[17] compareth him to a thief that, when he cannot catch his booty by open violence, seeketh by shrouding himself in the valleys, bushes and darkness of the night to take the poor traveller unprovided, and so to spoil him. For so the devil, when he seeth that by open pursuit he cannot overthrow us, covertly covereth himself in the shadows and briars of worldly vanities and delightsome allurements, thereby to entrap us ere we prevent his trains.*

But God taketh a contrary course.[18] The husbandman doth lop the vine lest all the force be unprofitably spent in leaves and the root thereby weakened and the fruit neither so much, nor so pleasant, as it would be otherwise. So God, like a careful keeper of our soul, lest our whole mind should be employed in vain and superfluous pleasures, cutteth them from us so that our wits which would have been diffused in them without profit, being kept in compass by troubles, may be fitter to work and bring forth fruits of eternal salvation.

Where God purposeth to heal, he spareth not to lance. He ministereth bitter syrups to purge corrupt humours, and sendeth embassies of death and revenge where he meaneth to afford eternal life and felicity. Good Raguel prepared a grave for young Tobias (Tob. 7) and yet desired heartily his long life. Joseph accused his brothers as spies when he meant them least harm, and restrained little Benjamin as guilty of theft (Gen. 44), whom he knew full well to be a guiltless innocent. But these accusations were but like

* *trains*: tricks or stratagems.

25

water in a smith's forge (to kindle not to quench), a rough entrance to a most kind usage, and an outward shew of suspicion to utter the more his entire affection. Even so dealeth God with his children.

We have passed through fire and water, saith David, *and he hath led us out into comfort* (Ps. 65. 12). Many go *out of prison and chains*, but their journey's end is *to a kingdom* (Eccl. 4. 14). Many be in a few things vexed, but they shall be well considered* for it in many. *Many are tried like gold in the furnace, but in time there shall be regard paid unto them* (Wis. 3. 6). If the infirmity be grievous, at the least it *maketh the soul sober* (Ecclus. 31. 2). And if God begin with *I have afflicted thee*, he will doubtless end with *I will afflict thee no more* (Nah. 1. 12). And finally, *As we are fellows of his passion, so shall we be of his comfort* (2 Cor. 1. 7): and *If with him we die, with him shall we live, and if we suffer his cross, we shall be partners of his crown* (2 Tim. 2. 11).

God woundeth, but his wounds be wounds of a friend. He sent Jonas to Ninive to threaten to overthrow them (Jon. 1), but his intent was to bring them to repentance so that he might continue towards them his favour. He sent to Ezechias to tell him of his last day (4 Kgs 20), but his meaning was to make him sorry for his offence, that he might adjourn the day. He suffered Daniel to be thrown to the den of lions (Dan. 6), but it was to advance him to greater credit.

Anyone that had seen Joseph undeservedly in prison (Gen. 39), Judith in her enemies' camp (Jdt. 10), Mardocheus in sackcloth with his gibbet before his eyes (Est. 5), and innocent Susanna going to be stoned (Dan. 13), would have lamented their case and feared their further misfor-

* *considered*: recompensed.

26

tune. But had he known that Joseph's prison should end in a princedom, Judith's hazard with a most happy victory, Mardocheus's peril with royal preferment and Susanna's stoning with glory and triumph, he would have thought them much beholden to God for the ensuing felicity rather than greatly to be pitied for their present distress.

The fig-tree hath bitter and rugged leaves, it beareth no flowers, and yet bringeth forth most dainty and sweet fruit. The devil, because indeed he hath no fruit, is fain to feed his followers with leaves that soon wither and flowers that soon fade, and all that he giveth is blown away with a blast. But God, because he loveth us sincerely, and not in shew only but in verity, giveth us the fruit without flower or leaf, that is, his gifts and graces without external and vain solaces. Yea, and sometimes he besetteth his fruits not only with rugged and bitter leaves but also with sharp and pricking thorns so that the hardness to attain them may make them the more prized, and the remembrance of former adversity may make the comforts following more delightsome.

The benefit of calm weather is most desired and best welcome after a boisterous tempest. Health is never so much esteemed as after a great sickness, and all pleasure is most pleasant to those that have been least acquainted with it and most troubled with the contrary, as in the proverb of Solomon: *A full stomach will loath the honeycomb, and one that is hungry will think the bitter sweet* (Prov. 27. 7).

But albeit God affordeth his final reward only to those that have passed through many tribulations, yet when they are in trouble or anguish, he doth not abandon or leave them desolate but watereth their miseries with sundry comforts. *There shall flow a fountain out of the house of our Lord*, saith Joel,

and shall water the torrent of thorns (Joel 3. 18). And David
saith to the same effect, *According to the number of the sorrows
of my heart, thy solaces have rejoiced my mind* (Ps. 93. 19). St
Stephen, when he was stoned, saw heaven open and Christ
standing at the right hand of his Father (Ac. 7). When
Eliseus was beset with the Assyrians he saw a hill of fiery
chariots standing in his defence (4 Kgs 6). And when Elias
was like to die for hunger he was fed and comforted by an
angel (3 Kgs 19). And St Paul noteth it always falleth out
true, that *as the passions of Christ abound in us, so also by Christ
aboundeth our consolation* (2 Cor. 1. 5). As the musician
neither straineth the string of his instrument too high for
breaking, nor letteth it too low for fear of distuning, so God,
saith St Chrysostom,[19] will keep a mean, neither suffering us
to be carelessly secure, nor driving us for want of comfort to
despair. Hilarius fitly expresseth this, saying: *The rod of the
root of Jesse flowered that the sweetness of the flower might mitigate
the severity of the rod.*[20]

For if the potter tempereth his furnace agreeably to the
vessel that he mindeth to frame: if the goldsmith use great
care not to have his fire too great or too little for the quantity
of his metal: if the carrier hath a regard not to load his beast
more than he is well able to bear, how much more wary is
God, said St Macarius,[21] in not suffering us to be tempted
above our force. For, as St Augustine well noteth, *so much
is the Devil permitted to tempt thee, as is for thy benefit, that thou
mayest be exercised, proved and come to knowledge of thyself, that
knewest not thyself before.*[22]

28

THE THIRD CHAPTER

The third cause of Comfort in Tribulation is that
we are moved to suffer Tribulation willingly, both
by the precedent of Christ and the title of a
Christian

THIRDLY, one that understandeth the course of Christian behoof* cannot but think it a most comfortable
thing to suffer adversity for a good cause, seeing it is
not only the livery and cognizance of Christ but the very
principal royal garment which he chose to wear in this life.
And therefore it cannot be taken but well of a soldier to be
clad in his captain's harness, or of a disciple to be like his
master. St Augustine saith: *In vain he claimeth the name of a
Christian that doth not imitate Christ. For what doth it avail thee
to be called that which thou art not, and to usurp another man's
name?*[1]

Aman, a most ambitious and haughty-minded man,
thought the greatest honour that a prince could do to his
subject was to make him ride on his palfrey, attired in his
most royal and stately robes (Est. 6). If, therefore, tribulation be the most precious garment that Christ did wear, and
the Cross his palfrey, we are greatly honoured when he ad-
vanceth us the same prerogative. Of this did St Paul greatly
glory, when he said, *God forbid that I should glory save in the
Cross of our Lord Jesus Christ.* And in the same place, *I bear the
marks of our Lord Jesus in my body* (Gal. 6. 14, 17). This St

* *behoof*: obligation.

29

James accounted a principal cause of joy and comfort, when he said, *Esteem it all joy, when you shall fall into divers temptations* (Jas 1. 2).

It is noted in the Scriptures as a singular proof of Jonathan's good will to David that he gave him his own coat and apparel (1 Kgs 18). Elias departing from Eliseus cast him down his mantle in token of good will (4 Kgs 2). And St Jerome[2] writeth that St Anthony wore St Paul the first Eremite's coat upon high and solemn feasts for love and reverence. And shall we not acknowledge it for a singular favour to be clad with Christ's attire, and to wear the token of his good will towards us? *Christ's garments comfort not those that walk in robes*, saith St Bernard, *the stable and manger comfort not those that love the highest rooms in the synagogues*, but those only that, rightly judging the manifold miseries that they have deserved, wear the mourning weed of sorrow and repentance.

He is an undutiful child that is ashamed to profess who is his father, and a most malapert servant that refuseth to wear his master's livery; but the most ungrateful creature of all is he that doth not willingly accept the livery of his God and maker. If we be Christians, affliction is our coat, and the cross our cognizance.

It was said to Constantine when he became a Christian: *In this sign shalt thou conquer.* When Jacob saw the coat of his son Joseph imbrued with blood, thinking that he had been devoured by a wild beast, as his brothers said, he cut his garments, put on sackcloth, mourning his son a long time: and when his other children that had betrayed Joseph went about to comfort him, he refused to receive any consolation (Gen. 37). Let us look on the sacred coat, not of our son, but of our Father and Redeemer, of whose humanity it is said: *Why is thy garment red and thy apparel like theirs that tread in the wine press? and who is this that cometh from Edom with stained attire* (Is. 63. 2)? Let us cast our eyes upon this coat, dyed in his own innocent blood. Let us consider that not only one beast devoured him but that for our sins he was a prey of many bloody and impious hell hounds. And doubtless it cannot seem much to us to wear patiently the haircloth of tribulation, to cut off the garments of our vain pomp and superfluities, and sit with Jacob comfortless, sorrowing and lamenting, rather than receive any comfort at their hands that betrayed our Father, that is, the vanities, sins and pleasures of this world.

In the Machabees (1 Mac. 6. 34) it is written that, when the elephants went to the field, they shewed them a bloody coloured juice, to sharpen and enrage them the more to the battle. When we go to battle, beside the blood of infinite martyrs, we have Christ our Captain and King, hanging upon the Cross, who openeth five fountains, gushing out with his innocent blood, and sheweth us his whole body all gory with lashes. Shall not all this hearten us constantly to encounter all tribulation and to war against our vain desires and appetites, when they draw us away from the cross towards delight and pleasure?

When we have a thorn in our foot (much more if it be in our head or heart) all the rest of our body is so troubled that no consolation seemeth sweet, and we wish rather for the surgeon to lance us than for any pleasure to delight us. Since Christ is our head and is stuck full and crowned with thorns, if we be true members of his body, how can it be but that we must needs both care little for all comfort and be more willing to sorrow with our head and be lanced for his sake than lain unto the worldly solaces which he contemned? For, as St Bernard saith, *it is an indecent thing to have a dainty member under a thorny head.*

Good Urias, when David bade him go lie in his own house, wash his feet and take his ease like a true Israelite, answered again, *The ark of God and Israel and Juda dwell but in tents, my Lord Joab and the servants of my Lord lie upon the face of the earth: and shall I go into my house to eat, drink, and have the company of my wife? By thy safety, O King, and by the safety of thy life, I will not do it* (2 Kgs 11. 11). He thought it an odious thing to have better lodging than the ark of God and his captain and fellow soldiers. He thought it a great stain to sleep in a soft bed, while they lay on the hard ground, and therefore chose to lie before the King's gate rather than once to enter into his own house. Lo, our Ark lieth not in tents, but in the manger. Our Captain lieth not on the hard ground, but hangeth naked and nailed to a reproachful cross. Our fellow soldiers lie not only upon the face of the earth but some have been cast into dungeons, others into fires, many amongst lions and raging beasts, finally all have tasted of divers and bitter afflictions. And can any true Urias think it much to take like part with all these?

When the King of Ninive mourned in sackcloth and ashes, all his peers and people did the same (Jon. 3). When Jonathan ventured to climb most craggy and dangerous rocks and was ready alone to set upon a whole troop of Philistines, his man said unto him, *Go whither thou wilt, and I will not fail to follow thee which way soever thou goest* (1 Kgs 14. 7). Yea one of Saul's esquires, seeing the King to have run upon his own sword and killed himself, presently (though wickedly) followed his example, choosing rather to spill his life with his prince than to spare it for his enemies (1 Kgs 31). Behold our King mourneth in sackcloth and ashes for divers calamities; our Jonathan climbeth up to the mount of Calvary, laden with a heavy cross upon his torn and wounded shoulders; he alone encountered the devil and all his imps and offereth himself to the troop of his enemies in the garden; yea, our Saul falleth for our sakes on the most rigorous sword of his own justice; and shall we, for whose benefit all this is done, ungratefully refuse to follow his example? Shall he mourn in sackcloth, and we bath in pleasure? Shall he, fighting alone in our defence, be all in a gore of blood with infinite wounds; and shall we disport and solace ourselves with fond and vain delights? Shall he be stricken through with the sword of revenge to suffer for us?

Alas, we are they that deserve rather to sit with Job on the dunghill than in sackcloth only with the Ninivites. We are they that deserve with naked hands and knees to creep upon the most ragged rock of adversity. For us it were fitter, in regard of our trespasses, to hazard our lives among a thousand blades and torments. Finally, it would behove us with repentant hearts and loathsomeness of our former life to embrace the sword of God's just revenge and therewithall to kill old Adam in ourselves, that is, *the old man with his vices, and concupiscences* (Gal. 5. 24).

O most unnatural children, who, having before their eyes the most bloody slaughter of their own father, yea being revived and raised from death with his blood, like pelican's younglings, will not yet learn the excessiveness of his love nor consider how much they ought to do and suffer for themselves, who by their misdeeds have been cause of so intolerable pains unto their heavenly Father.

Far other was the effect of Christ's passion on St Paul, who being enflamed with the force of so unusual an example laboured himself to be a perfect scholar in this doctrine, esteeming it the highest and most needful point of Christian knowledge to understand the value, necessity and manner of patient sufferance. He would have no other university but Jerusalem, no other school but Mount Calvary, no other pulpit but the cross, no other reader but the crucifix, no other letters but his wounds, no other commas but his lashes, no other full points* but his nails, no other book but his open side, and finally no other lesson but *to know Jesus Christ and him crucified* (1 Cor. 2. 2). In this school should be our chiefest study. Here should we learn by Christ's nakedness how to clothe ourselves; by his crown of thorns how to adorn ourselves; by his vinegar and gall how to diet ourselves; by his hanging on the cross how to repose ourselves; and by his painful and bitter death how to esteem the pleasures of this life.

Here may we see the wonderful fruits and miraculous sequels ensuing upon tribulation patiently accepted which pass all natural reach and have been set down unto us, as shores of comfort to uphold us in all our distresses. Here may we see that death reviveth, that sores salve, that blood washeth, that sorrow solaceth, that an eclipse lighteth, that the fast-nailed guideth, the thirsty giveth drink, the weary refresheth, the diseased cureth, the dead bringeth forth. And albeit these principally be the proper effects only of Christ's passion: yet through these merits they are now experienced to follow also the martyrdoms of Christ's ser-

* full points: full stops.

vants, to whom all crosses are comfortable and their bodily death the cause of many a soul's spiritual life.

Now we may truly interpret Sampson's riddle, *Out of the devourer there came meat, and out of the strong issued sweetness* (Jg. 14. 14). For if like fierce Sampson's, our sins most cruelly murdered that lion of the tribe of Juda, so our repentant thoughts, like bees, suck at the flowers of his passion and work a delicious comb of honey. Not only we ourselves taste its sweetness but our example moves others to feed willingly on the same and shows them that the eyesell* and gall of our tribulations in this lion's mouth hath been altered from the wonted bitterness to sweetness; and that the lionish rage of persecutors, accustomed to devour so many souls, doth now rather minister a most pleasant viand to God's servants, yea, and those rigorous judgements of God, which have heretofore been so terrible unto us, are now become *more to be desired than gold and precious stone, and more sweet than honey and the honeycomb* (Ps. 18. 11).

Bitter were the waters of tribulation and so untoothsome to man's taste that few could endure the annoyance thereof, and our squeamish stomachs were rather contented to want health than to procure it by such unsavoury and loathsome physic. And for this did our heavenly physician strain this bitter medicine through the nectared cloth of his sacred humanity, and left therein such a taste of sweetness that what was before so eagerly eschewed hath since been eagerly thirsted. We need not now cry, *Death is in the pot* (4 Kgs 4. 40), because the prophet hath seasoned it, not with a little flour or meal, but with his own blood. We need not murmur against the waters of Mara (Ex. 15. 23) (that is of

* *eysell*: vinegar.

ghostly discomfort) as fit to be drunk, or fear to sink in the tempestuous pool of bodily vexation, for our Moses hath sweetened the one with the sacred wood of his cross, and since our Eliseus cast into the other the wood of life (that is his blessed body), *our iron began to swim* (4 Kgs 6. 6)*, where before it had sunk, and the desolate that said, *I am set fast in the depth of the mud and can find no steady footing* (Ps. 68. 3), may begin to sing, *He hath led me out of the lake of misery, and the mire of filth, and hath brought me upon the water of reflection* (Ps. 39. 3).

Let us not therefore be afraid to say now to Christ, *O Lord, command me to come unto thee upon the waters* (Mt. 14. 28). For be the surges never so boisterous, the water never so deep, the stormy winds never so outrageous, if we run upon them towards Christ, they will either yield dry passage by dividing themselves, as the Red Sea did to the Israelites, or they will uphold us from perishing, as the waves did St Peter. *For faithful is God, who will not suffer you to be tempted more than you are able to bear* (1 Cor. 10. 13).

And surely now is the time that we are called to Christ through fire and water, and now with open voice doth he renew his old proclamation: *Whosoever loveth father, mother, wife, children, house or livings more than me is not worthy of me: and he that taketh not up his cross (and that every day) cannot be my disciple* (Mt. 10. 37).

We must not now seek Christ as our Lady did, *amongst her kinsfolk and acquaintances* (Lk. 2. 44), nor as the spouse did

---

* This refers to the story of Eliseus who, after the head of an axe had fallen into the Jordan and sunk, cut off a piece of wood and threw it after the axe head. Thereupon the iron came to the surface and swam. R. S. means that our Eliseus (i.e. Christ) will take care that we do not sink in the *tempestuous pool of bodily vexation*.

that said, *In my bed in the nights have I sought whom my heart best loved* (Cant. 3. 1): nor as the Israelites did, of whom Osee speaketh: *In their flocks and herds shall they go, to seek our Lord* (Os. 5. 6). For, as St Anselm well noteth, *He lieth not in the delicacy of a gorgeous bed, neither is he found in the land of dainty livers.*[3] Moses saw him in the desert, amidst the fire and thorns (Ex. 3. 2), in the mount amongst lightnings, thunderings, and mists (Ex. 19. 16). Daniel saw him in a fiery throne and amongst fiery wheels, with a swift fiery flood running before him (Dan. 7. 9). Shall we think to be more privileged than our ancient fathers? Think we to find in down and daintiness him that appeared to them so terrible and fearful? Do we think that his rigour and justice, signified by these terrible semblances, is so relented that he should shew himself unto us only in amiable and lovely countenances? Surely we are greatly deceived if we feed ourselves with this vain persuasion?

For albeit the New Testament be fuller of grace, yet is it no less full of agonies. Though Christ's service be *sweet*, and *light*, yet is it a *yoke* and a *burthen* (Mt. 11. 30). And though our champions be of more courage and our foes more enfeebled since our redemption, yet doth *the kingdom of heaven still suffer violence, and the violent bear it away* (Mt. 11. 12); *and none shall be crowned but they that have lawfully fought for it* (2 Tim. 2. 5). If Christ was seen transfigured in Mount Tabor in glorious manner, he was also at the same time heard talking *de excessu* of his bitter passion (Lk. 9. 31). And even Peter who allured by the glory [of Christ transfigured], cried: *It is good for us to be here* (Mt. 17. 4) was yet affrighted with the voice and *fell upon his face, and was in a great fear* (Mt. 17. 6).

If he were in pomp and triumph at his entrance into Jerusalem (Mt. 21. 9), his pomp was of small pleasure and his triumph not without tears; and as fast as the children on the one side did set forth his praises, so fast did the Pharisees on the other side repine and murmur against him (Lk. 19. 39).

There is no reason that Christ should shew himself more favourable to us that have been his enemies than to his own body. Neither can we justly complain if before we find him, he gives us a sip of that bitter chalice of which for our sakes he was content to drink so full a draught. Yea we may be heartily glad if, after long tears and deep sighs, we may in the end find him at all, whether it be in the poverty of the crib and manger or in the agonies of his bloody sweat in the garden or in the midst of blasphemies, reproaches and false accusations at the tribunal or in the torments of a shameful death upon the cross.

And we must think ourselves as much in his favour when we are chosen to be witnesses to his passion as well as his glorious transfiguration. For the same apostles whom he took with him in token of particular love, to Mount Tabor, he afterwards led with him to the heavy conflict of the garden (Mt. 17. 1 and 26. 37).

Whether he foster the weaklings or exercise the stronger or check the unruly, giving divers remedies to divers persons, he tendereth all as his own children.[4] If it is pleasant and glorious for men to have their children resemble them, because they are most delighted to have bred their own features on their offspring, how much more comfort is it to our heavenly Father, saith St Cyprian,[5] when any is so born to spiritual life that his divine prowess and generosity is set forth in his children's acts and praises? Neither doth this comfort consist in seeing in us a shadow of his beauty, a spark of his wisdom or a resemblance of his might, riches or glory, but rather in seeing in us the scars, wens and warts of his vexations and pains: which the more they deface us in outward shew, the more they beautify us in our soul; and the more ugly and odious they make us in the mistaking of man's eye, the more amiable they render us in the sight of God.

For as the scar of a wound in the child's face, which he hath suffered in his father's quarrel, though it make his countenance less eyesome,* and disfigure his favour, yet is it more an edging whetstone of fatherly affection to the parent than if it were absent, because it yieldeth a perpetual testimony of a dutiful and loving mind: so God, more desirous to have us affectionate than fortunate children, delighteth more to see our torturings, rackings, chains and imprisonments for his sake (which are assurances of our love) than to see us swim in his temporal gifts. He praiseth more the Ninivite in his sackcloth and Job disfigured in his dunghill than either of them in all the pomp and glory of their riches.

St Gregory noteth, *The loss of felicity searcheth the force of affection. For neither prosperity proveth a friend nor adversity concealeth an enemy*. [6] And, as St Cyprian also saith, *It is effeminate to boast when there is no peril, the combat in adversity is a trial of the truth*. [7] If therefore God is more delighted with our valour in conflict than with all pleasure in peace, let us say with St Peter, *With thee I am ready to go into prison and to death itself* (Lk. 22. 33), and with St Thomas, *Let us go also and die together with him* (Jn 11. 16).

We read in the book of Kings (2 Kgs 2. 12) that to shew

* *eyesome*: pleasant to the eye.

their captains disport Joab's and Abner's servants entered into so fierce and desperate a game that blood and wounds was the beginning but mutual murder the end of their past-time. And if they at a word's warning ventured themselves to so open a hazard for the vain contentment of their captains and in hope of a sorry reward nothing comparable to their peril, how much more ought we, being challenged to the field by God's enemies, give our heavenly Captain a proof of our loyalty and a perfect remonstrance of our serviceable minds, by waging in spiritual battle with his foes, and most readily encountering them in his quarrel with what danger soever?

We see that an enamoured knight hath no greater felicity than to do that which may be acceptable to his paramour. And the fading beauty of a fair lady's countenance is able to work so forcibly in men's minds that neither loss of riches, danger of endurance, menacings of torments, no not present death is able to withhold where she inviteth, or make the bark ride at anchor that is wafted in her streams. Every peril undertaken for her seemeth pleasant, every reproach honourable, all drudgery delightsome, yea the very wounds that come from her or are suffered for her are void of smart: and the wounded wretch rejoices more with the hope that his hurt will purchase favour than feels aggrieved that his body hath received such a maim. Her colours seemeth the fairest, the meat that fitteth her taste seemeth the sweetest, the fashion agreeable to her fancy seemeth the comeliest; her faults are virtues; her sayings, oracles; her deeds, patterns. Finally, whatsoever pleaseth her, be it never so unpleasant, seemeth good, and whatsoever cometh from her, be it ever so dear bought and of little value, is deemed precious and a cheap pennyworth. O unspeakable blindness of man's heart, that so easily traineth to senses' lure, and is so soon caught with the beauty of an image and hath not grace to remember whom it resembleth.

I will not stay upon Christ's corporal seemliness, though indeed he were *white and ruddy, a choice piece out of thousands* (Cant. 5. 10), and *comely in feature above all the sons of men* (Ps. 44. 3), and in that respect more amiable than any other. But I set before the eyes of our faith the glory, majesty and beauty of his Godhead, wherein whatsoever is in any creature that may breed delight or contentment, either to our sense or soul, is so perfectly united together that there is no more comparison between the delight that his presence yieldeth and that which any worldly thing can afford than between the fairest damsel in the world and her shadow, between the light of a sparkle and of the sun, yea between a most ugly leper and a most beautiful angel. St Augustine considering this said, *God is the true and chiefest life, in whom, from whom, and by whom are all good things that are happy to enjoy whatsoever they be. From whom the revolting is falling, to whom the returning is rising, in whom the staying is sure standing. God from whom to depart is to die, to whom to repair is to revive, in whom to dwell is to live. God whom none leaveth, but deceived; none seeketh but admonished; none findeth but the cleansed.*[8]

If therefore God be so perfectly amiable and the chiefest object of pleasure, why do we not say with David, *What have I in heaven, or what desired I in earth beside thee?* (Ps. 72. 25). Why do we not cry out with St Augustine, *Whatsoever is not God is not pleasant, and whatsoever my Lord will vouchsafe upon me, let him take away all, and give me himself.*[9]

Shall the presence of his picture, wherein he is but rudely

expressed, make us lavish of our wealth, careless of our liberty, and prodigal of our lives? And shall not he, whom the picture representeth, woo us to as much readiness in his affairs? Can we, to please his shadow, delight in danger, embrace dishonour, triumph in our harms, and yet care so little for him that casteth it as not to think him more worthy of the like affection? Are we so eager, liquorous* and pliable to those colours, cates,† and fashions that a base creature of his liketh: and shall not the favours, food and attire of our Creator be as acceptable unto us? Finally, shall we take no exception against the faults, words and deeds of a frail and faulty wretch, and not be as much moved with the virtues, sayings and examples of an infallible truth?

What is the fairest creature in the world but an imperfect counterfeit and vain shadow of God's sovereign beauty and majesty? If, therefore, with the natural poise of affection, we sink so deep into the liking thereof, according to the saying of St Augustine: *My love is my load; with that I am carried whithersoever I am carried*,[10] much more ought we to be deeply ravished with the love of God, and so settle our minds therein that we think it our chiefest happiness in this life to embrace all hazards, disgraces and misfortunes in his quarrel, and find most cause of comfort, when, for his glory, we are in the most bitter pangs.

For, as St Gregory noteth, *The love of God is not idle; it worketh great effects where it is; if it refuse to work, love it is not.* And much the more ought we to rejoice in our passions for

* *liquorous*: liquid. R. S.'s use is about 100 years earlier than the first use in O.E.D.

† *cates*: bought provisions (as opposed to home-made). Hence choice viands or dainties.

42

Christ, because we have been so tenderly beloved of him that whatsoever we suffer for him is less than what he suffered for us. And whatsoever we spend in his behalf, we only restore unto him his own for we are never able to come out of debt, though we had as many lives to spend as drops of blood to shed. For, as St Bernard saith, *If I owe myself wholly for my first making, what can I add more for my redeeming, especially seeing I was not so easily redeemed as I was made? In the first work he gave me myself, in the second himself, and when he gave me himself, he restored unto me myself. Therefore thus given and restored, I owe myself for myself, and I owe myself twice. But now what am I able to repay my Lord for himself? For though I could repay myself a thousand times, what am I in comparison of my Lord?*[11]

O hard and stony heart that is not incensed at the consideration of such inflamed love, and being wooed of so loving a spouse, can reject this offer or be slack in recognizing such unspeakable charity. For, as St Augustine saith, *There is no greater enticement unto love than to prevent the lover, and too hard is that heart, that if it would not request love, is not content at the least to requite it.*[12] And where was ever any that either sought so much or bought so dear the love of any creature as Christ did ours? What hath a man more than riches, honour and life? And all this did Christ spend in wooing our souls. As for his riches, he was born and died naked. Concerning his honour, he was sorted and executed with thieves. Touching his life, he was bereaved of it by a most vile and despiteful death.

Let us but consider the last tragical pageant of his Passion, wherein he won us and lost himself; and mark the excessive love shewn therein, which if any other than God had uttered, it would have been deemed a senseless dotage. Let us view him with the eyes of our heart, and we shall discover, saith St Bernard,[13] a most lamentable sight. We shall see his head full of thorns, his ears full of blasphemies, his eyes full of tears, his mouth full of gall, his body full of wounds, his heart full of sorrow, and yet in all these torments doth he cry to man, saith the same Saint, *More am I pained with the wounds of thy sin than with the wounds of my own body:*[14] more sorrowing at man's ingratitude than at his own affliction.

Where the Prince, saith Cassiodorus,[15] mourneth in such great agony, who would not weep when he weepeth, and sigh when he lamenteth? When instead of his royal crown, he is covered with dust, and his head is hoary with ashes, not with age. O work without example, grace without merit, charity without measure! What would he have done, if we had been his friends, that was content to do so much for us, being his enemies? What will he do, when he knoweth we love him, that did all this, when he knew we did hate him?

O Christian, saith St Augustine, *love the love of him that for the love of thy love descended into the womb of a Virgin*, and afterwards ascended to the ignominy of the cross, *that there he might couple his love and thy love together.*[16]* What Christian heart can think it much to suffer, being moved with this example? Yea, who would not glory with St Paul in his infirmities, and take greatest comfort in his desolations, seeing the most loving and faithful Spouse of our soul hath thus sweetened all our pains with the excess of his unspeakable

---

* R. S. by inserting the phrase *and afterwards ascended to the ignominy of the cross* has changed Augustine's meaning.

charity, and given us such a precedent in suffering that whatsoever we suffer for him must needs seem little?

The love of a mortal friend not only moves us but en-
forces us to love him again, and his perils for us make us
eager of perils for him, because thereby both our love to him
is best witnessed and his love to us most confirmed. And
shall not this love of an immortal well-wisher, who tendereth us more than we ourselves, and in all respects better deserveth to have his love countervailed: shall it not, I say, be
able to inflame us with desire to suffer for him and to testify
our affection in the midst of our torments if need so require?

We see a dog that is void of reason, in gratitude for having
received a bone or a crust of bread, ready to run upon the
sword in his master's defence only by an instinct of nature.
We think it the duty of our servant, if we give him but forty
shillings a year, to hazard himself in our perils and to fight in
our quarrels; and we condemn him as an ungrateful mis-
creant, if he stand not between us and our enemies, as a
buckler of our blows, though the danger be never so apparent. And shall a Christian heart be either more unnatural
than a beast or less thankful than a hired servant? Shall a
crust of bread prevail more with a brute thing, or a little
money with a hireling, than the food of angels wherewith
Christ hath fed us, than his precious blood wherewith he
hath bought us, than eternal felicity wherewith he will reward us? Yes, and shall men be so ready to serve the devil
that we see thousands every day careless to cast away both
body and soul in following his train; and shall we, to serve
our omnipotent and loving Lord, refuse to venture our
goods or bodies with so inestimable benefit and advantage of
our souls?

St Cyprian saith: *When Christ in the day of judgment shall show himself and lay open to the world the benefits which he hath bestowed, the rewards which he hath promised and the torments and pains which he hath suffered for man, then shall the devil, on the other side, most grievously charge us, and say unto God: "Lo, how much more right I have in man than thou. I never loved him, and yet he served me. I never did him good turn, and yet he obeyed me. Without wooing or wages I easily won him. What I suggested, he performed. Whatsoever I proffered, he embraced. No perils could stop, when I allured. No fear or love of thee could move him to abandon and forsake me. For obtaining a vain pleasure, he hath yielded to most servile drudgery. To please an appetite, he hath contemned all God's and man's punishments, and hath been ready to venture liberty, living, credit, yea, life and limb for achieving a delight that I cast in his fantasy; and yet he undoubtedly realized that instead of thy love, I bore him implacable malice, instead of thy suffering torments for him, I desired to be his eternal tormentor; and whereas thou didst promise eternal felicity, I could neither afford him nor wish him anything but endless damnation. Yet this could not, though foreseen and thought of, withdraw him from me but still he was ready to be drawn with my lure; and so soon as I set him any service to do, he forthwith put it in execution.*

On the other side, what hast thou prevailed with the miseries of thy poor nativity, with the grief and shame of thy painful circumcision, with thy three and thirty years' pilgrimage bestowed in his service? Hath thy fasting or praying, thy whipping or crowning, thy bloody death or passion, been able to countervail my suggestions? Despite all this hath not my motions been sooner obeyed than thy precepts and my will preferred before thy commandments? If therefore I have ruled him, reason it is that I should reward him; and if with me he contemned thy mercy, with me also let him feel thy severity."[17] In this manner shall the devil accuse us, and happy is he that in this life hath so testified his love by his patience in God's cause and willing sufferance of adversity that he may either prevent the accusation or be provided of a sufficient answer.

Considering therefore how glorious, how decent, yea and necessary it is for a Christian to take up his cross with Christ and tread the path of tribulation which he hath plained unto us by his own example, let us not be dismayed with these cross adventures that befall us. Let not the cruelty of our enemies, the sharpness of our miseries, the continuance of our afflictions, daunt our courage in God's cause. We are not better than our Master who suffered far more, nor wiser than God himself who judged and embraced the distresses of this world as fit for us passengers. Finally we are Christians, whose Captain is a Crucifix, whose armour patience, whose battle persecution, whose victory death, whose triumph martyrdom.

THE FOURTH CHAPTER

The fourth cause of Comfort in Tribulation is that Tribulation best agreeth with the estate and condition of our life

BUT even if this example of Christ and the title of a Christian were not such forcible motives to suffer adversity as they are, yet, considering where we are, what state we stand in, what dangers hang over us, and our ordinary miseries and wants, we shall find that our whole life is so necessarily joined with sorrows that it might rather seem madness to live in pleasure than odious to live in pain.

Consider, O man, saith St Bernard, whence thou comest, and blush whither thou goest and fear where thou livest, and lament. We are begotten in uncleanness, nourished in darkness, brought forth with throbs and throes. Our infancy is but a sickness, our life misery, our death horror. If we have anything that delights us, it is in such hazard that our fear of losing it is greater than our joy in the use of it. When we have something that annoyeth us, our aggravation at it increases, with the uncertainty that evil or worse may straightway follow on it.

Where can we cast our eyes without finding cause of complaint and heaviness? If we look up towards heaven, from thence we are banished. If we look towards earth, we are there imprisoned. On the right hand we have the saints whose steps we have not followed; on the left hand the wicked whose course we have pursued. Before us we have our death ready to devour us; behind us our wicked life ready to accuse us; above us God's justice ready to condemn us; under us hell fire ready to swallow us into endless and everlasting torments.

And therefore St Damascene[1] most fitly compareth us to a man pursued by an enraged unicorn who fell into a well while he was swiftly flying from it, and in falling got hold of a little tree, and settled his feet on a weak stay, and thus thought himself very secure. But looking a little better about him, he saw two mice, one white and another black, that were continually gnawing away the root of the tree on to which he held. Underneath him a terrible dragon with open jaws was ready to devour him. At the stay of his feet he found four adders that issued out of the wall. And after all this, lifting up his eye, he espied upon one of the boughs of the tree a little honey. Therefore, unmindful of all his dangers, not remembering that above the unicorn waited to spoil him and that beneath the fiery dragon watched to swallow him, that the tree was quickly to be gnawn away and the stay of his feet was slippery and not to be trusted: not remembering, I say, all these perils, he only thought how he might come by that little honey. The unicorn is death; the pit is the world; the tree, the measure and time of our life; the white and black mice, the day and night; the stop borne up by four adders, our body framed of four brittle and contrary elements; the dragon, the devil; the honey, worldly pleasure. Who therefore in so many dangers, would not think it a madness rather to be eager of vain delight than fearful and sad with consideration of so manifold perils?

O blindness of worldlings, *that love vanity and seek after lies* (Ps. 4. 3), *that rejoice when they have done evil and triumph in the baddest things, that have no fear of God before them* (Prov. 2. 14 and 18)! *A nation without counsel or prudence. O that they would be wise, understand and provide for the last thing* (Deut. 32. 28), lest it fare with them as Job saith, *They hold the drum and cithern,* and rejoice at the sound of the organ: they pass their days in pleasure and in a moment they descend into hell* (Job 21. 12, 13).

Far otherwise ought we to do that foresee these inconveniences, and rather with sorrowful hearts cry, *Woe unto me that my inhabitance has been prolonged* (Ps. 119. 5). For *upon the floods of Babylon*, what cause have we but laying aside our mirth and music *to sit and weep* (Ps. 136. 1), remembering our absence out of our heavenly Sion? In the vassalage and servility of Egypt, where we are so daily oppressed with incessant afflictions *and filthy works, of clay and brick* (Ex. 1. 14), that is of flesh and blood, what can we do, but with the Israelites, *lamenting our intolerable drudgery, cry out unto God* (Ex. 2. 23)?

Who is there that, considering himself a wandering stranger in this far and foreign country, and a drudge in the miry farm of this world, enforced to feed the swine (his earthly appetites and senses) and driven to so extreme exigencies as not to be suffered *to fill his belly of the husks that the swine did eat* (Lk. 15. 18): who, I say, considering this, would not, with the prodigal son, bitterly mourn, remembering the abundance and plenty of his father's house whereof he is deprived, and the most wretched plight into which he has fallen, through sin. *We are here in a barren, pathless, and waterless soil* (Ps. 62. 2), *in an obscure land, covered with the fog and shadow of death* (Job 10. 22). We are here in a place of

* *cithern*: a sort of guitar, strung with wire and played with a plectrum.

exile, in a hospital of Lazars, in a channel of ordure, in a dungeon of misery, in a sepulchre of dead carcasses, finally, in a vale of tears. Who could live in such places without sorrow? And who would not say with the wise man, *I accounted laughing, error; and to joy I said, why art thou in vain deceived* (Eccl. 2. 2)? *For laughing shall be mingled with sorrow, and the ending of our mirth shall be prevented with mourning* (Prov. 14. 13). *Happy is he that sitteth solitary*, and in the contemplation of these miseries *lifteth himself above himself. Happy is he that carrieth the yoke from his very youth* (Lam. 3. 27, 28). *Blessed are they that mourn and understand how much better it is to go to the house of lamentation than to the house of banqueting* (Eccl. 7. 3).

What comfort can a man reap in a place that is governed by the prince of darkness, peopled with God's and our enemies, where vice is advanced, virtue scorned, the bad rewarded and the good oppressed? What quiet or contentment of mind can be enjoyed where the pains be infinite, common and intolerable, the pleasures few, rare and damnable; where friendship breedeth danger to the soul, enmity vexation to the body; where want is miserable, plenty full of peril, and a man assaulted with implacable adversaries on every side?

My flesh, saith St Bernard, *is of earth, and therefore ministereth earthly and voluptuous thoughts, the world vain and curious, the devil evil and malicious ones. These three enemies assault and persecute me, sometimes openly, sometimes covertly, but always maliciously. The devil trusteth much upon the help of the flesh, because a household enemy is apter to hurt. The flesh also hath entered league with him and conspired to my subversion, being born and nourished in sin, defiled from her beginning, but much more cor-*

rupted by evil custom. For this it is that she coveteth so eagerly against the spirit, that she murmureth so daily, impatient of discipline, that she suggesteth wickedness, disobeyeth reason and is not restrained with fear. The crooked serpent, enemy of mankind, joined his force to her, he helpeth her, he useth her, and he hath no other desire, no other business, no other study but to cast away our souls. This is he that always endeavoureth mischief, that speaketh subtly, prompteth cunningly and deceiveth guilefully. He in-sinuateth evil motions, he inflameth venomous cogitations, he stir-reth broils, he fostereth hatreds, he moveth to gluttony, he pro-cureth lust, he incenseth the desires of the flesh. He prepareth occasions of sin and ceaseth not with a thousand hurtful trains to assay men's hearts. He beateth us with our own staff, he bindeth us with our own girdle, labouring that our flesh, which was given us as a help, might be rather cause of our fall and ruin. A grievous combat and great danger it is to wrestle against our domestical foe, especially we being strangers, and she a citizen. For she dwelleth here in her own country, whereas we are but pilgrims and exiled persons. Great is also the hazard in sustaining the often continual encounters against the devil's deceitful guile, whom not only his subtle nature but also the long practice and exercise of his malice hath made crafty.[2]

By these words of St Bernard we understand how little cause we have for joy in this life, in which we have to struggle hourly with so mighty, perverse and malicious enemies, who can never be so overcome or so thoroughly vanquished but that after a little respite they turn to bid us new battle, and with such variety and change of forcible temptations that they put us in continual danger and anguish of mind. This doth St Cyprian well express: *Man's mind, besieged on every side, environed with the vexation of the devil, is scarce able to prevent all temptations, yea scarce to resist them. If covetousness be subdued, up riseth lust; if lust be suppressed, there succeeded ambition; if ambition be condemned, anger incenseth. Pride puffeth us, drunkenness inviteth, envy breaketh peace, jealousy sundereth friendship. Thou shalt be constrained to speak what God's precept forbiddeth and to swear that which is unlawful. So many persecutions daily doth our mind suffer, with so many perils is our breast assaulted, and can it delight us to make long abode amongst these swords of the devil?*[3]

Moreover, if we consider our body: what it is, how brittle, how frail, how subject to corruption, how full of horrible diseases, stuffed with loathsome excrements, miserable in life and abominable after death, how can we take pleasure in a fountain of so much pain or not find it tedious to serve and to feed so noisome a thing?

But of all other miseries that deserve to be lamented there is one that passeth all the rest, and is of itself able, though there were none but it, to cross all possible comforts and to make him that seemeth merriest spend day and night in weeping and complaint. We have but one poor and silly soul, our only treasure and jewel, in whose custody consisteth our welfare, with whose loss ensueth all our discomfort. A soul of noble substance, of exceeding beauty, inspired by God the Father, redeemed by the Son, sanctified by the Holy Ghost, and endued with the image of the whole Trinity. A soul created to live with angels, to enjoy the love and company of an eternal Spouse, to be a citizen of heaven, to inherit a kingdom and triumph in royal dignity. This soul, I say, is not only exiled from her native country and in most lamentable sort debarred from her kingdom like a captive fettered in a most filthy dungeon, like a forlorn and left widow deprived of her spouse's fellowship, but is so perilously beset with the fore-recited enemies that it standeth in continual hazard to increase her present misery with an eternal loss, and in lieu of all her honours, endowments and dignities for which she was created, reap everlasting horror and punishment.

O fearful and uncomfortable case that is without cure! O hard and heavy danger that receiveth no security, whose easiest and only remedy is the severing of soul and body asunder! Thrice happy are the martyrs, whose bloody agonies purchase assurance of happiness and acquit them from all peril of ensuing torments. And thrice unhappy is our estate, whose hope of felicity hangeth on so fickle and slippery terms. St Augustine saith, *It is a slippery hope that amongst so many nourishments of sin looketh to be saved; uncertain is the victory when it is fought for amongst the enemies' weapons, and impossible, in a manner, is the delivery from burning where we are compassed in with flames.*[4] St Bernard well noteth, so long as in any creature there is power to sin, it is secure in no place, *neither in heaven nor in paradise, much less in the world: for in heaven fell the angel, even in God's presence: in paradise fell Adam from the place of pleasure: in the world fell Judas from the school of our Saviour.*[5]

Neither is it certain that, as St Augustine noteth, *he which of worse could become better, may not also of better become worse.*[6] For if St Paul said, *My conscience accuseth me of nothing, and yet in this I am not justified* (1 Cor. 4); if Job said, *I feared all my works, and though I be washed with the waters of snow and my hands shine as though they were most pure, yet wilt thou find me stained with uncleanness* (Job 9. 28); if David cried, *Enter not into judgment with thy servant for not any living creature shall be justified in*

54

thy sight (Ps. 142. 2); and the wise man, *No man knoweth whether he is worthy of love or hatred* (Eccl. 9. 1); *and who can say, clean is my heart and pure am I from sin* (Prov. 20. 9)? If these men, I say, stood in such fear of themselves, how much more ought we *in trembling and fear to work our salvation* (Phil. 2. 12), *and not to be without fear even of our released sin* (Ecclus 5. 5)? But rather *labour in our sorrow* (Ps. 6. 7), and *wash our bed with tears, and make them our bread, day and night, so long as it is daily said unto us: Where is your God?* (Ps. 41. 4) and till such time as *our soul is delivered, like a sparrow out of the fowler's snare* (Ps. 123. 7).

We read that the strumpet who came for judgment to Solomon, when she heard him call for a sword and command that her little child should be parted into two pieces, she presently fell into so vehement a passion of sorrow that *her bowels were moved for pity of her son* (3 Kgs 3. 26). We read that Agar (Gen. 21. 9) was driven out of Abraham's house and enforced to wander in the wilderness with her tender suckling. She saw that the infant was ready to die for want of water, and not finding the wherewithal to refresh it nor having the heart to see her little innocent give up the ghost, she withdrew herself afar off from it. Then, with pitiful moan and lamentation, she lifted up her voice to heaven, feeding her pensive and timorous thoughts with the doleful remembrance and continual fear of her child's departure.

We see what cold and trembling agonies surprise the poor wretch that pleadeth at the bar, while the jury deliberateth upon his final sentence. We see how doubtfully the sick patient hangeth in suspense between hope and fear, while the physicians are in consultation whether his disease be mortal.

Finally, if a young spouse, tenderly affected, and deeply enamoured of her new husband, see him assaulted by fierce and cruel enemies or enforced to wage in a hot and dangerous battle, what a multitude of frightful passions oppress her? How variably is she tossed up and down with cross and fearful surmises? Of every gun that is discharged, she feareth that the bullet hath hit his body ere the noise came to her ears. At every word that is reported of any that are slain, fear maketh her think that her best beloved is one. Every rumour costeth her a tear, every suspicion a pang, and till she see the battle ended and her husband safely returned, she hangeth between life and death, drawing every thing to sorrowful constructions and utterly refusing all kind of comfort.

O how hard and tough hearted are we towards our own souls, when seeing them in all the rehearsed dangers, we feel not in ourselves any motion of the like affections? The sword of God's justice hangeth over our souls, ready for our sins to divide us from eternal bliss. Uncertain it is, whether God will give not only a part, but the whole to the foul fiend that hath so often, through our iniquities, stolen us from our mother's side into his envious hands. Shall not we be moved with pity and grief? We are from paradise exiled with Agar into this barren desert, and cannot certainly assure ourselves that we have so much as one drop of grace to slake and mitigate the thirsting passions, which without it undoubtedly work the death of our souls and our final damnation. Can we, seeing not our child, but the chief portion of ourselves in such a taking, with dry eyes and unnatural hearts behold it without sorrow?

Are not we to stand at the bar in the day of judgment,

where the devils, our consciences and all creatures shall give most straight information against us? The twelve Apostles as our inquest, and Christ as our judge, whom we have daily offended, shall pass their verdict in most rigorous sort upon us, and that about our eternal death and salvation. And can we, until we hear what will become of us, do otherwise but live in continual fear and perplexity? Is not our soul in this body, as a Lazar in deathbed, uncertain of life so long as it coucheth therein, yea, in apparent danger of an endless death? Shall not we, till we hear the judgment of our heavenly Physician, who can quickly search and enter into our diseases, tremble, quake and fear a hard resolution?

Finally, is not our most beautiful and noble soul, is it not, I say, in the throng and press of most powerful, subtle, and barbarous enemies, having continual war, not only against *flesh and blood, but also against the princes and powers, against the rulers of the world of this darkness* (Eph. 6. 1 2)? Is it not also set in the reach of many occasions, allurements and provocations unto sin? And can we, seeing this, do any thing but mourn and live in continual anguish and pensiveness, until we see the battle ended and our soul safely delivered out of danger? O senseless and benumbed hearts of ours that at the consideration of so heavy and lamentable points cannot find scope and field of sorrow! Let us at the least be sorry for our want of sorrow, and bewail our scarcity of tears, least we fall into a careless security, and by not sorrowing as we should, stop considering the great causes we have for sorrow. For, as St Gregory noteth, *Oftentimes that which we know not through our sloth, we learn by tears, and an afflicted mind more certainly findeth a committed fault, and the guilt which in security it remembered not, being troubled it espieth*.[7]

Seeing that on every side we have such urgent occasions to mourn and pass the days of this our painful pilgrimage in grief and heaviness, we must content ourselves in tribulation rather than in repose, seeing by the first we are but invited to weeping and sorrow, which is the thing that we should profess, and by the last to comfort and solace, which the eminent dangers we stand in with reason will not comport. This both Christ and his saints hath so well understood that Christ, though it had been as easy for him to have been born an emperor and have had all the pleasures that heaven and earth could yield, would not in this vale of tears give so preposterous an example of mirth, but as one that knew whither he came, he entered into the world weeping, and in time of his abode with us lived with tears and torments.

What his saints have done, let all antiquity testify: how like men that had no feeling of worldly comfort they roved in deserts, lodged in desolate holes and caves, were clothed with hair and sackcloth, fed very little and grossly, chastised their bodies often and severely, endeavouring to keep themselves always in remembrance that they were mourners; and therefore, choosing place, habit, diet and exercise fittest for that doleful profession. The saints knew that heaven only was *a land of the living* (Ps. 51. 7; 141. 6), and that in this world we sit *in darkness and the shadow of death* (Lk. 1. 79), and therefore they wisely judged that *unfitting it is to have mirth and music in time of sorrow* (Ecclus 22. 6). No doubt they saw the tree of this life laden with some alluring and delicious fruits, but seeing that it grew in such a place that if they climbed it they were in manifest danger of falling into the bottomless pit of hell, they left it a prey for the ravening fowls of this world, contenting themselves with the bitter fruits of adversity. They knew that only on their arrival in heaven *they should reap in joy bearing their handfuls* (Ps. 125. 5). Therefore, in the world *they went weeping, sowing their seeds in sorrow* (Ps. 125. 6). They knew that they who would keep the feast in heaven, must first keep the vigil and the fast here. For otherwise he that will feast here in jocundity and disport, after this life, *shall be led to the grave, and in the heap of the dead shall keep a perpetual vigil in hell* (Job 21. 32).

The saints observed, as St Basil saith,[8] that the huge and noble cities, furnished with glory of munition, with authority of great personages, and all abundance both at home and abroad, in the end did show only their ruins as signs of their ancient nobility. The ship also that hath often escaped many shipwrecks, and a thousand times crossed the sea to the great advantage of the shipmen, in the end jostled with a blast, is shattered in pieces. Mighty armies that have often conquered in war have afterwards been made a miserable and bloody spectacle to their enemies. All nations and islands advanced to great power and sway have decayed in time, or changed their liberty with bondage. Finally, what havoc, loss, ruin or misery can be reckoned, whereof this wretched world hath not showed some example, yea, and that in the life of the godly.

Since all things here bend to decay and are tainted with death's consumption, the saints, like dying and passing persons, lived in mourning and a continual farewell, awaiting always their departure from these earthly solaces. They had little regard for the things that they were to leave, having their hearts settled upon the felicity that they tended unto. And, as men who desire to see the stars at noonday go down

F   59

into a deep and dark well so that they may the easier descry them, so they, desiring to have the eyes of their heart perpetually fixed upon the stars of heaven, that is the glory of the saints, descended into that profound, obscure and base kind of life, sequestering themselves from the light and pleasure of these inferior comforts. Yea, and they delighted in griefs so that they could the better appreciate their future happiness.

Consider how low Job went, when he cried, *I said unto corruption, thou art my father, and to the worms, you are my mother and sister* (Job. 17. 14). Consider how low St Paul went, when he said, *We are hungry, we thirst, and we are naked and beaten with buffets; yea, and what is more, we are made the refuse of this world, and dross of all, even until now* (1 Cor. 4. 11). How far went David when he said, *I am a worm and no man, the stale of men and the cast away of the people* (Ps. 21. 7)? They were not ignorant *that every valley shall be filled and every mountain and hill humbled* (Lk. 3. 5). They knew that the waters of grace *springing into life everlasting* (Jn 4. 14) rest not on the high and steep hills, but in the bottoms and low valleys, according to that, *Who letteth out his fountains in the valleys, and his waters shall pass in the midst between hills* (Ps. 103. 10).

They well understood, how convenient a thing it is, and conformable to the state of this life *to sit down in the last place* (Lk. 14. 10), as Christ counselled. For, as St Augustine saith, *Aloft is our country, but low is our way: who therefore seeketh the country, why shunneth he the way?*[9] O how much are the worldlings deceived, that walk *in great things and marvels above themselves* (Ps. 130. 1), that rejoice in the time of weeping, and make their place of imprisonment a palace of pleasure, that think these examples of the saints are follies and their ends dishonourable, that think they can go to heaven by the wide way which only leadeth to perdition. Well may we say to these, with St Augustine, *Whither you go? You perish and you perceive it not. That is not the way to the place you go unto, and to which you desire to arrive. Your meaning is to be happy, but those journeys which you run are miserable and lead to more misery; seek not so great a good by evil: if you mean to achieve it, hither must you come, and this way must you go.*[10]

The path to heaven is narrow, rough and full of wearisome and tiring ascents and cannot it be trodden without great toil. And therefore wrong is the way, gross the error, and assured the ruin of those who, after the steps and testimonies of so many thousand saints, will not learn where to settle their footing. It were enough to have the example of Christ only, who, as St Augustine noteth, crieth always unto us : *Which way wilt thou go? I am the way. Whither wilt thou go? I am the truth. Where wilt thou stay? I am the life.* And if this way lead us through austere and painful passages, if this truth teach us the trace of humility, if this life be not achieved without a doleful and dying pilgrimage, then *Woe be unto you that laugh for you shall weep* (Lk. 6. 25), *and happy are they that mourn for they shall be comforted* (Mt. 5. 4). For, as St Gregory saith, *He that is honoured in his journey, shall be condemned at his journey's end; and he cometh as it were by pleasant meadows to his prison, that by the prosperity of this world runneth to his ruin.*[11]

For in truth, the contentments of this life have true misery, feigned felicity, assured sorrow, doubtful delights, rough storms, timorous rest, solace full of sadness, and hope full of hazard. They are like fair weather in winter, nothing

61

durable; like a calm in the sea, always uncertain; like the steadiness of the moon, that is ever changing. They resemble the cockatrice's egg, fair without, and foul within; Nabuchodonosor's image that had the face and head of gold but earthen and brittle feet: or the sweet river that runneth into the salt sea; *Her filth is in her feet* (Lam. 1. 9), and *the last of her pleasures are as bitter wormwood* (Prov. 5. 4).

Seeing therefore that all our troubles, penalties, restraints and afflictions be but means to remind us of our place, state, dangers and profession, and but seeds of comfort and eternal glory, howsoever they seem here covered and corrupted in earth, let us solace ourselves in hope of our joyful harvest. We are but pilgrims, *and have no city of abode but seek a future place of rest* (Heb. 13. 14).

If the way had been beset with pleasures, with true delights, with unfading and odoriferous flowers, we would easily have slacked in our journey towards heaven, being drawn and withheld with the pleasant view and desire of these allurements. And therefore God hath made our thoroughfare tedious, uncomfortable and distressful so that we hasten towards our repose, and swiftly run over the cares of this life, imitating the dogs of Egypt, that of the river Nile drank running, lest if they stayed to take their full draught at once, they should be espied and stung by venomous serpents. Whereupon St Peter warneth us *like strangers and pilgrims to abstain from fleshly desires, which fight against the spirit* (1 Pet. 2. 11), remembering that this world is a deluge of miseries, and heaven only, our ark of security; out of which, though the unclean crow can find footing upon carrion and dead carcasses, and little care to return, yet the clean and chaste dove, abhorring such a loathsome abode, cannot find any rest without the ark, but with the wings of a penitent heart and longing desire, fluttereth still at the window, until it please our Noah to put out his merciful hand and receive it into the ark of his heavenly felicity.

FOURTH CAUSE OF COMFORT

THE FIFTH CHAPTER

The fifth cause of Comfort in Tribulation is that we suffer little of our deserts

B UT even suppose that the pleasures of this world and
the place and state of our life were such that they invited us to comfort and joy rather than to sorrow and
patient sufferance, yet if we consider what our life hath been,
what our sins are, what punishments thereby we have deserved, we are bound to think that God has dealt most
mildly with us, and be joyful for the small troubles which
have been allotted us where we might have been dealt most
intolerable chastisements.

What hath our whole life been but a continual defiance
and battle with God? Our senses, so many swords to fight
against him; our words, blows; and our works, wounds.
What have our eyes and ears been but open gates for the
devil to send loads of sin into our minds? What hath our
scent, taste and feeling been but tinder and fuel to feed and
nourish the fire of our concupiscence?

Our body, which ought to have been a temple of the
Holy Ghost, a chaste and clean harbour of an unspotted soul,
a bed of honour and a garden of delight for him that said, *My
delight is to be with the children of men* (Prov. 8 . 3 1) : what hath it
been but a haunt of devils, a stew of an adultress and a filthy
sepulchre of a corrupted soul as full of carrion and venom as
any poisoned carcass? What hath it been but a forge of
Satan, where, in the fire of our passions, kindled with his

wicked instincts, he hath enflamed our soul and made it so pliable to his purposes that he hath wrought it to most ugly and detestable shapes upon the anvil of every pleasure and sensual delight? As for the soul, which was betrothed and espoused to Christ in baptism, which was beautified with grace, fed with the repast of angels, and a treasury for all God's riches, which was a receipt* of the Blessed Trinity and ordained to the fellowship of angels in eternal bliss, what hath it been but a most riotous, disloyal and ungrateful losell?† Our understanding like a most lewd privado‡ hath been used to present unto the will incentives and instruments of sin. Our will hath been a most lewd and common courtezan, coveting and lusting after every offer that she liked. Our memory hath been a register and record of wicked and abominable sights, sayings and deeds for our sinful thoughts and fantasies to feed upon.

Finally, what parcel of our body, what power of our soul, whereof God hath given us the use, have we not abused to his dishonour? Warring against him with his own weapons, we have employed our life, motion and being to the continual incensing of him, *in whom we live, move and are* (Ac. 17. 28).

Seeing therefore that we have not only been sinful but even a lump and mass of sin, what think you was due unto us if God had dealt with us according to his justice? Let us call to mind how odious a thing sin is to God and then may we the better perceive how mercifully we are dealt withal, having our heinous faults chastised here rather than in hell; and how much we deserve of all our heavy scourges.

* *receipt*: receptacle. † *losell*: scoundrel.
‡ *privado* (Spanish): an intriguer.

65

Of God it is said: *Thou hast hated nothing of all that which thou hast made* (Wis. 11. 25). Only that nothing of which (as St Augustine expoundeth it) the Gospel speaketh, *without him was made nothing* (Jn 1. 3), that is sin: this nothing, I say, is the cause that to some things he beareth an implacable hatred. The devil in his nature is more amiable than man, being of nobler substance, of higher excellency, and endowed with higher prerogatives than we: yet who knoweth not how much God doth hate him?

We know what tender affection God hath always showed to mankind, for whose sake he hath made this world and enriched and garnished it with such glorious ornaments, besides other infinite tokens of a most tender love hourly showed unto us. And yet it is said, *Thou hast hated all that work iniquity* (Ps. 5. 6), and in the book of Wisdom, *Hateful is to God the impious and his impiety* (14. 9).

If therefore God so deeply detests both the wicked man and the devil himself for no other cause but only for their sin, how abominable must we think sin is? When we make a comparison of a thing that is evil in the highest degree, we can find nothing worse than the devil to liken it unto; and when we have named him, we think that we have reckoned the last and greatest evil that can be imagined. For which cause the devil was called *Malum*, the evil itself, by Tertullian[1] and the ancient Fathers, who could find no other name sufficient to express his naughtiness. And bad, odious and detestable though he is, sin which is the only cause of his odiousness is more odious and detestable. For if he were rid of sin, he would be a more glorious and lovely creature than any mortal man.[2] Since this most monstrous and abominable sin is in us, as well as in the devil, we should think ourselves

66

happy that we are not chastised as he is rather than murmur that we are afflicted as now we be; especially considering that as St Anselm well noteth, sin in us is more punishable than in the devil himself. For his sin was but one; ours infinite. He sinned before the punishment of sin was known; we, after notice and experience thereof. *He sinned, created in innocency; we restored to the same. He persisted in malice, being of God rejected; but we, being of God recalled. He was hardened against one that punished him; we against one that allured and tendered us. He against one that sought not him; we against one that died for us.* And lo, he also saith, *I find in myself a more horrible horror than in him, whose very image I abhorred.* [3]

Moreover, as sin is a strange and most dreadful darkness that no light can illuminate, and an extreme cold that no heat can abate, so must it be a most odious thing that an infinite love hateth, and the baddest thing that can be that an infinite goodness detesteth, and a most vile and execrable thing that Omnipotency cannot do. For if there were in it any spark or iota of goodness, God could not otherwise do but in some respect love it, approve it and be author of it.

And since we have suffered this ugly and filthy deformity to stick and fester in us so long, and consequently have been most abominable and loathsome in God's eyes, what rubbing, what rough entreaty or hard usage can we think too much to scour out so cankered a corruption? For, as St Bernard saith, *He that perfectly feeleth the burden of sin and the hurt of the soul either shall feel little or nothing at all the punishment of his body, nor esteem it much, whereby he knoweth his former offences to be cancelled and his future sins to be prevented.* [4]

The consideration of that which our sins have deserved is a most forcible motive to digest with patience any misery soever, though otherwise very tedious. Let us call to mind how God might justly have dealt with us, what he might have laid upon us, and still not have exceeded the bounds of his justice. Instead he hath shown himself full of infinite mercy. It is a general axiom and an approved verity, ratified by the common consent of all Fathers and Divines, that as God rewardeth above the deserts of our merits, and in his eternal recompense far exceedeth the value of our good works, so, on the other side, doth he chastise far underneath the rate of our misdeeds; and, his infinite justice considered, his greatest punishment amounteth not to the exceeding heinousness of the least mortal sin. For the injury offered to so infinite a Majesty by one so far inferior and so highly beholden unto him in such an opprobious and despiteful manner that it, in as far as is possible, robbeth God of his Godhead and payeth homage to the devil: this injury, I say, is so great that though God should double and treble all punishments of sin and lay them on one sinner's back for one only mortal offence, yet might he justly double them anew and as often as he thought good without doing any injustice to the offender, yea, and punishing him far less than his deserts were.

Let us now, therefore, consider what rigorous punishments God hath used upon sinners. First, if we count the temporal miseries common to all men which God hath caused in the world for the sin of Adam they will seem so many as might suffice, yea, and exceed the just measure of the desert of that sin. For if man had persevered in the state of innocency our bodies would not have been subject to any diseases nor our minds subject to any sorrow or disordered passions. The earth would have been a place of pleasure, the air temperate and all creatures obedient to man. Finally, all things would have been to our contentment and nothing to our annoyance.

If therefore we consider now the miseries of our bodies, such as hunger, thirst, nakedness, deformity, sickness, and mortality, or the troubles of our mind, such as fantasies, fears, perplexities, anguishes and divers imperfections, or the general scourges of plagues, war, a thousand hazards and calamities, and finally all the other encumbrances that in any way are incident to this life, they are so many in number, so grievous in quality and so ordinary in the experience of all that whosoever well weigheth them might think them sufficient scourges not only of one but of all the sins of mankind.

Do but cast your eyes into one hospital of lazars.* See the cankers, fistulas, ulcers and rottings, the wolls, sores and festered carbuncles. Weigh the miseries of the frenzy, palsy, lethargy, falling sickness and lunacy. Consider the diseases of the eyes, ears, mouth, throat and every parcel of man's body. On the other side consider the infirmities of the mind: the furious rages, envies, rancours and corrosives; the implacable sorrows and desperate passions; the continual hell, torments, remorse of conscience and infinite other spritish† fits and agonies. Consider the displeasure of superiors, the malice and enmity of our equals, the contempt, ignominy and reproach we receive from our inferiors, the fraud and treachery of all sorts and degrees. Go forward to the other ordinary molestations through loss of goods, limbs, liberty, friends, wife or children; through

* *lazar*: a person afflicted with leprosy or some loathsome disease.
† *spritish*; impish, malicious, mischievous.

dangers of fire, water, sword, beasts and infinite others of like quality. Remembering that all these things and the loss of the commodities and pleasures contrary to them befell unto man by reason of one only sin, and that in show but a light sin, let us not think it much if we, whose offences are most grievous and very many, suffer a few of these scourges, and those such as compared with divers others before recited have, in respect of them, scarce any colour or shadow of misery.

What sin have we committed that may not be deemed as exorbitant* as the eating of an apple? And how many have we done that seem far more detestable? Why then should we not expect the whole heap of afflictions to light upon us, or at the least the most noisome and grievous of them? Since God of his mercy has not permitted such punishments but laid a soft and easy hand upon us, we have more cause of thanksgiving than of any just complaint.

But passing to other particular scourges that God hath sent in this life for the divers sins and offences of men, we shall find them so many, so terrible and so intolerable that, without the experience of them, the thought of them would affright a right courageous and stout heart. In the Scriptures, what strange punishments we read of, such as the deluge of Noah (Gen. 7), the pouring down fire and brimstone upon Sodom and Gomorrha (Gen. 19), the opening of the earth to swallow in Dathan and Abyron (Num. 16), and a devouring fire to consume their confederates (Ps. 105)! How wonderful were the plagues of Egypt (Ex. 7–14): the turning of the waters into blood, giving more punishing remedies to their thirst than the punishment itself; the horror of

* *exorbitant*: criminal.

crawling frogs, leaving no place nor person unannoyed; the fiery stinging gnats, encumbering the air like clouds both within and without the houses; the most bitter and viperous flies that, not contented to sting without, gnawed with extreme torment a passage into the very entrails, leaving no part of the sinner unrevenged! How wonderful was the sudden death of the cattle of all the Egyptians; the sores and blistering biles and botches; the wonderful hail mingled with fire that killed man and beast wheresoever it fell; the clouds of locusts that covered all the earth like sand, devouring the very roots of the herbs and plants that the hail had spared; the fearful and palpable darkness; the killing of all the first-begotten, both of man and beast; and finally, the drowning of Pharaoh and his innumerable army in the Red Sea! I omit the slaughter and mortality of men: of the Bethsamites for curiously beholding the ark (1 Kgs 6), of the Philistines for robbing it from God's people (1 Kgs 5), of the Israelites for David's numbering of them (2 Kgs 24); the devouring of the disobedient prophet by a lion (3 Kgs 13), of the children that scoffed at Eliseus by wild bears (4 Kgs 2), of Achab's soldiers by fire from heaven (4 Kgs 1); the turning of Lot's wife into an image of salt (Gen. 19).

Finally, leaving the Scriptures I will come to the strange revenges of God mentioned by other authors. First, what intolerable usage hath there been of divers people by the rage and fury of barbarous tyrants? What spoil of their goods, shedding of their blood, oppressing of innocents, persecutions of the godly, deflowering of virgins, abusing of matrons, compulsion unto wickedness and terrifying from all virtue hath there been? What inconveniences and miseries have ensued by war; and what alteration of estates, subversion of kingdoms, slaughtering of men, destroying of cities and confusion of all order?

To take one example, what a tragical and strange vengeance did God show upon the Jews at the last destruction of Jerusalem for their horrible sin in murdering Christ?[5] I omit their rifling and spoil by divers Roman magistrates, their servitude under strangers, the surprising of other cities of Jewry and the driving all the inhabitants into that one City of Jerusalem. The mere taking of Jerusalem was the occasion of such miseries, that if they were not recorded by such authentic writers it would be almost incredible that so many, and so strange calamities could befall in so short a space.

First, the famine was so great that not only were members of the same family at weapons with each other for a bit of meat, but the soldiers ranged about the city like hungry wolves and if in any place they felt but the scent of victuals, rushed in with drawn swords and were ready to rip open the bellies and bowels of their own citizens to fetch out the meat which they had eaten. They then fed upon that loathsome stuff so brutishly gotten and imbrued in the blood of the first eater, as upon a dainty and delicate dish. The children were in defiance against their own parents; brothers and sisters were mortal enemies; father and mother at deadly feud with their own offspring, all ready to murder one another for every bit that any of them put into their mouth, so far did the extremity of hunger abolish all feeling of natural affection. Yea, and what is more, men were enforced to chew beasts' dung and, after they had eaten up the flesh, to take their repast upon the most filthy excrements. Others fishing and raking in the sinks and channels, gathered from thence food, which to them in those times seemed not unpleasant, though it was in fact most detestable and beastly. Some fed upon the leather of their bucklers and shoes; others on trampled and broken hay. Finally, men who had been used to all variety of viands and delicious fare were now driven to so base and abominable diet that brute beasts themselves would by nature abhor it. I leave it to your consideration what mortality and strange diseases this famine was likely to breed.

But besides this there were at the same time such civil mutinies, such domestical uproars amongst themselves that even Titus, their mortal enemy who lay in sight about their city, hearing of their mutual slaughters, was deeply moved with compassion for all his implacable enmity, saying that they needed no foreign enemies to work their confusion, so bloody were the tragedies they raised amongst themselves.

Neither was this the greatest of their miseries, for afterwards, besides the unmerciful havoc that the Romans made of the Jews when the city was taken, there was found another thing that bred occasion of a greater and most cruel massacre. For the Jews, unwilling to enrich their enemies with their treasure and thinking to save somewhat from the general spoil, swallowed into their bodies as much gold, pearl and precious stones as nature would bear. When the Romans afterwards found this out by their excrements, they left rifling their houses and in a most barbarous way began to ransack their bodies and bowels. So that whereas they thought their bodies were their surest coffers, they found by a rueful experience their own folly. For, when they might with their treasure have redeemed their lives, they so

73

hoarded it up that they could neither use it to their own profit, nor could the enemy take it from them without spilling their lives.

Finally, besides the battering down of the walls, the defacing of the city, the burning of the temple, there were, as Josephus reporteth, partly by famine, partly by sword, eleven hundred thousand Jews put to death. Four score and ten thousand others were the relics and only remnant of that nation who were scattered and most miserably dispersed into divers parts of the world. So ended in this most shameful and opprobrious way the glory of the Temple after eleven hundred years of standing, and this most famous, strong and glorious nation after the honour of so many ages.

Much like unto this was the destruction of Carthage, which after seven hundred years of glory and majesty was in the end overthrown. The walls were turned into dust and the city burnt continually for the space of seventeen days together. Not only were its buildings and treasures consumed into ashes, but it was also a funeral pile to the Queen and her two sons and divers other desperate multitudes, who rather chose to be the fuel of their country's fire than captives of their foreign enemies. Of which Orosius saith: *In the end the wretched citizens everywhere threw themselves with a final desperation into the fire and the whole city became a funeral pyre. Now it is left small in situation and bare of walls; and part of the misery, to hear what it hath been before.* [6]

It were an infinite task to exemplify the desolations, ruins and calamities that by war have fallen upon all nations and provinces. Every history and chronicle of former times and even the very experience of our days giveth so large proof and notice of this that none can be ignorant how terrible a scourge it is, having in it so small resemblance of the eternal horror of hell. And thus it appeareth how man's offence by man hath been revenged.

Let us now see how the whole world hath conspired to the just punishment of God's enemies. And first, to begin with the earth, what a terrible instrument of God's justice hath this element been? All Achaia was so strangely shaken with an earthquake that two cities, Bura and Helice, were swallowed up.[7] Another earthquake also happened in Trajan's time which overthrew four cities in Asia, two in Greece and three others in Galatia.[8] About the same time was a great part of Antioch in like manner overthrown. In the ninth year of Titus and Vespasian three cities of Cyprus were by the like accident destroyed.[9] I omit the earthquakes of Constantinople, Rhodes and Caria,[10] though all were memorable for terrible effects. I will not speak of the earthquake that happened in Rome,[11] out of which vamped so intolerable a stench that the very birds that flew over it fell down dead; and which could only be closed up by the devouring of a man who voluntarily leaped into it.[12] I omit divers other wonderful calamities[13] which God hath permitted to make us understand that we ought not to marvel so much at our present afflictions as to muse on God's mercy. For we are attainted with the like crimes and yet are not swallowed up quick with our families, houses, children and goods, as the sinners of former ages were.

Neither have fewer vexations happened by means of water. There was Noah's flood (Gen. 7) which left in the world no more than eight persons alive, destroying cities, towns, men and beasts. Since that time there have also happened other inundations, though not so general as that, yet

doubtless such as testified sufficiently God's deep and immortal hatred against sin. Of Ogigius' flood, we read that it
wasted almost all Achaia.[14] Deucalion's deluge consumed
the greatest part of Thessalia.[15] And Diodorus[16] writeth of
an island in Egypt, called Pharos, that was altogether covered and drowned by a strange eruption of waters. I will
not reckon the overflowing of rivers, yea of little brooks, that
by continual rain and snow swelled so high that they have
drowned many cities, destroyed many towns, spoiled corn
and cattle and left behind them most rueful monuments of
God's deserved indignation.[17]

How often also and how daily we see that by divers alter-
nations the air hath been a means to chastise men's iniquities. What wreck and havoc hath been made by storms and
tempests? What terrible and frightful casualties by thunder?
What strange mortality by pestiferous vapours and exhala-
tions, corrupting and infecting the air and breeding infinite
diseases in men's bodies? Eusebius writeth that Ethiopia
was so pestered with the plague and infectious diseases that
it was almost brought to utter desolation. Rome, in L.
Genucius' and Q. Servilius' Consulship, was consumed for
two whole years with so general a pestilence by an infectious wind, that all the inhabitants were either dead or by
extreme leanness left in as good as deadly terms.[18]

Yea, and in L. Cecilius Metellus' and Q. Fabius Maximus
Severinus' time,[19] the infection and mortality were so great
that first there were not enough to bury the dead, and in the
end there were none at all. The great houses were void of
living and full of dead bodies, furnished with ample patri-
monies but without any to enjoy them. Yea, the misery
grew to so lamentable an issue that not only could a man not

live in the city but not so much as approach unto it, so intolerable was the stench of the dead carcasses rotting in their houses and in their own beds.

Neither was that wonderful punishment of God showed in M. Plautius Hipaeas' and M. Flaccus' days, of less terror. Throughout all Africa there swarmed innumerable multitudes of locusts which devoured not only the corn, fruits, herbs, leaves and twigs, but even the bark of trees and dry wood. And then the locusts were lifted from the earth by a sudden tempest and gathered into globes, they were carried in the air a long time, and in the end drowned in the African sea. Afterwards, the sea washed them up in huge heaps upon the shores, rotting and putrefying where they breathed out such a noisome and pernicious savour that, together with the beasts and birds dying and corrupting in the fields, they greatly increased the former annoyance. There died eight hundred thousand men in Numidia when Micipsa reigned, and two hundred thousand more about the sea coast, towards Carthage and Utica; and in Utica itself, thirty thousand soldiers. There death was so sudden that there were carried out fifteen hundred of the younger sort in one day and by one gate alone of this one city. And the multitude of vermin was unendurable when alive, and even less tolerable when it was dead. For in dying they destroyed all things that could have been consumed if they had lived longer. Most detestable infections were conceived, increased and fostered in men's bodies by breathing and drawing in the corrupted air. Now we see how severe God's justice hath been in times past, and how merciful he hath been to us to have spared us from the same rigorous punishments, since our sins have been so grievous that they deserved not only this our present and, in comparison, very small adversity but the most bitter portion of the forenamed vengeance.

Now if we consider what desolate effects fire hath wrought, not only in hell and purgatory where the torment thereof is unspeakable, but in this very life, we shall find them no less fearful arguments of God's justice than have been touched heretofore. I omit the ordinary casualties whereby by God's permission many towns and cities have been utterly consumed. I omit also the burning of Constantinople in Arcadius' time by fire descended from the element,[20] the overthrow of a great part of Rome's walls by lightning,[21] the burning of many parts of the same city by sudden fire, which no man knoweth from whence it issued.[22] I omit the strange judgments of God upon divers tyrants, persecutors and wicked persons by thunder-flashes. I will only set down some other extraordinary and notorious declarations of God's severity by fire of the most terrible sort. In a place of Italy, called Ager Calenus,[23] there burst out with a sudden breach and opening of the earth a most horrible flame, which burnt continually for three days and three nights, turning many acres of ground and all that was in them into ashes, not sparing so much as the very roots of the trees. How often hath Mount Aetna in Sicily belched out huge flakes and globes of fire, throwing them very far on every side to the great ruin and consumption of cattle, corn, towns and villages. It has also burst out with whole floods of fire which turned all things into ashes and smoke, and made a most lamentable waste and spoil to the utter undoing of the inhabitants, to say nothing of the inconvenience which they breed by the filthy savour and enflaming of the air. The city Catana and the adjoining places had this scourge so grievously and so often that all its houses were covered and oppressed with heaps of burning ashes. The Romans agreed to release them ten years' tribute so that they could repair the inestimable damages of one such eruption. But the most notorious of all was the eruption of the island of Lipari, of which Julius Obsequens and Orosius[24] write, where, as though hell's mouth had been opened, not only the earth, but even the sea itself boiled with such excessive heat that even the very rocks were burned and dissolved, the pitch of the ships melted and the boards scorched and the fishes turned up their bellies suddenly in the same waters and seas wherein they were bred. The men also who could not fly very far from that place were stifled and their bowels burnt within them, so miraculously was the air enflamed.

To pass from heat to cold we read that four thousand soldiers, who at the siege of Asculum fled from Pompeius, were frozen so stiff upon the top of a mountain, that standing there in the snow with their eyes open, and their teeth bare, no man could otherwise perceive that they were dead, except by their stillness.

It were too long to rehearse the invasions of wild beasts, though as Diodorus writeth,[25] divers cities of Libya were disinhabited by the continual incursions of lions. And Livy reporteth of a serpent of huge size which devoured a great multitude, bore down and crushed a number, and, with his poisoned breath, wrought the bane of divers others, although in the end it was overcome and destroyed by Regulus' army and engines after the loss of many soldiers.* This prodigious and fearful example ought to put us in mind of

* The book of Livy about this incident has not survived. R. S. must be using a different source, probably Orosius.

God's singular mercy towards us. Although he neither lacks the like abundance of fire, cold, wild beasts and horrible monsters, nor we the like abomination of sins, as worthy to be chastised in the same manner, yet he is contented notwithstanding to abate our deserved hire,* and with a fatherly pity to give us a warning not to offend hereafter rather than a scourge for our former trespasses.

I will not enlarge on how the heavens by concourse of planets and divers pernicious influences have caused no small misery. Amongst others let that only accident suffice of the extraordinary broiling and parching of the sun through the whole world, mentioned by Plato:[26] upon this occasion the vain poets, not acknowledging it as a work of God's omnipotent hand, framed the ridiculous fable of Phaeton. I will not also stay to show how the angels, both good and bad, have been executioners of God's indignation; of these let the Scriptures suffice. Of the good, it saith, *The praises of God in their mouths, and two-edged swords in their hands, to do vengeance upon nations and correction among the people* (Ps. 149.6,7). We have many examples of their actions in this behalf. For who killed with the plague threescore and ten thousand for David's numbering of the people (1 Kgs 24)? Who in one night slew a hundred, fourscore and five thousand Assyrians (4 Kgs 19)? Who whipped Heliodorus for robbing the temple (2 Mac. 3)? Who struck into Herod that horrible disease whereby he was eaten with vermin (Ac. 12)? Finally, who poured those scourges on the world whereof St John speaketh in the Apocalypse but the *Angel of our Lord*? There are many divers examples in the Scriptures of the bad angels: those that tormented Saul (1 Kgs 16);

* not to exact full payment for our sins.

afflicted Job (Job 1); choked the seven husbands of Sarah (Tob. 6). There are some called *stormy winds* (Ps. 148. 8), and the *principalities and powers of the present darkness* (Eph. 6. 12), who, like roaring lions, go about seeking whom they may devour (1 Pet. 5. 8), and are called sometimes dragons, sometimes lions, otherwhiles serpents, adders and basilisks (Ps. 90. 13) for the divers mischiefs that they work on us. Besides these, I say, the daily experience of possessed person, of sorceries, witchcrafts and enchantments, wrought by their means, gives us sufficient intelligence of their manifold scourges, which if God had permitted them to have practised upon us according to our deserts and their malice, we would have thought our present distresses favourable and gentle corrections in comparison to their unmerciful and hellish usage. But thus we see how truly it is said in the Book of Wisdom: *His anger shall take harness and arm all creatures to the revenge of his enemies. He shall put on justice for his breastplate and shall take for his helmet certain judgment. He shall take equity as an impregnable buckler. He shall sharpen his dreadful wrath into a spear, and the world shall fight with him against the senseless persons. His throwing of thunderbolts shall go directly, and shall be driven, as it were, from a well-bended bow and shall hit at a certain place. From his stony anger shall fall hail showers, the waters of the sea shall be enraged against them, and the floods shall roughly concur. Against them shall the spirit of might stand, and like a whirlwind shall divide them, and shall bring all the land of their iniquity to a desert, and shall overthrow the seats of the mighty* (5. 18–24).

Now, let us consider these penalties and heavy scourges, and remember that they were not mere casualties but permitted and procured by the omnipotent hand of God, sovereign moderator of all creatures and umpire of man's transgressions. Let us consider also on the other side that the least mortal sin that we have committed deserveth not one but all the said punishments, yea, and a thousand times more. Let us not think it much therefore that a least part of so huge a heap of miseries is fallen to our lot. Let us rather rest astonished and marvel at the secret judgments and mercies of God. For while he is still of like justice, ability and power, and his creatures as much at his commandment, rule and obedience, and our sins as many, as horrible and as worthy of revenge, nevertheless, the same things that were scourges and most cruel tortures to our forefathers are helps and comforts unto us.

When two guilty wretches are convened before the same judge for crimes of like tenor and quality, if the one be condemned to endure the extremity of the law, hath not the other great cause to tremble and quake, yea, and undoubtedly to look for the same judgment? But now, if contrary to his deserts, the judge mitigate his sentence, and, in lieu of a rigorous chastisement, appoint one far more easy than that which was alloted to his fellow, hath he not great cause to be grateful to the judge for the benefit of his delivery rather than in any way to murmur or repine at his verdict?

How then can we, having so many examples of persons condemned for the sins whereof we are also guilty, do anything but highly praise the mildness of our heavenly Judge, who, having so hardly used others, hath mercifully spared us and relented the heavy hand of his justice to lay so easy a burden upon us? Yea, when we either look up to heaven or down to earth, or on the air, fire or water about us, remembering how terrible they have been against others, we can only muse how fortunate we are that they have been withheld from wreaking upon us the like indignation.

But to pass from preambles to the thing indeed, from shadows to the truth, from gentle warnings to the penalty itself, I will leave the revenge of sin showed in this life, and come to that which is prepared in the next, for all the forementioned miseries are but very small resemblances and forerunning signs of the torments of hell. This we may gather from Christ's own words, who, reckoning all those calamities, said: *Nation shall rise against nation, and kingdom against kingdom, and there shall be great earthquakes in places and great pestilences and famines and terror from heaven; and there shall be signs in the sun, moon and stars, and upon earth distress of nations for the confusion of the sound of the sea and waves, men withering for fear and expectation of what shall come upon the whole world, for the powers of heaven shall be moved* (Mt. 24; Lk. 21). Having, I say, reckoned all these, he addeth: *These are but a beginning of the griefs* (Mk 13. 8; Mt. 24. 8): as if to say these wonders and strange events are but prognostications of things to come, as a smoke in respect of a terrible ensuing fire, or a mustering of soldiers before the sad battle. What therefore will the pains be that these beginnings portend, and how rigorous a sentence that hath so fearful remonstrance before the judgment?

But, lest I be too tedious, I will not stand to make a full declaration of the torments of the next world but only briefly touch so much thereof as may be enough for us to guess at the rest. First, not only the terror and pain of the aforesaid afflictions, but all other painful and unpleasant things that are scattered and dispersed in divers places and creatures throughout this world shall be there united and joined to the revenge of sin. And in such a way that, whereas here divers of them are sufficient alone to work our temporal death, and he that hath endured one is past fear of sustaining any other, there every sinner shall sustain them all in far more cruel manner than any of them can here punish, and besides them also infinite other pangs, proper and peculiar to hell. So that whatsoever there is in the whole world, or ever hath been or shall be, that can pain sight, hearing, scent, taste or feeling; what disease or vexation soever can here torment the heart, the head, joints, bones, sinews, veins or any parcel or member of our body; whatsoever can most or least trouble or annoy our will, memory or understanding or any power of our mind: all these and a thousand times more shall jointly at one instant, and that for ever, most unmercifully torment each sinner in every part of his body and soul.

And to descend to some particulars: first, if we consider the place, the very names thereof may give us to understand how miserable a thing it is to be thrust into hell. It is called *a bottomless depth*, *or pit*, *a profound lake of the wrath of God* (Apoc. 20. 1; 21. 8); *outward darkness* (Mt. 8. 12); *a pond burning with fire and brimstone* (Apoc. 21. 8); *a well of perdition* (Ps. 54. 24); *a huge chaos of confusion* (Lk. 16. 26); *a prison* (Apoc. 20. 7); *a furnace of fire* (Mt. 13. 42); and is by Job thus described: *an obscure land covered with the fog of death; a land of misery and darkness, where the shadow of death, and no order but everlasting horror inhabiteth* (Job 10. 21–22). Neither, as St Cyril noteth,[27] can any deliver him thence by flight nor provide any escape because he is fast shut up.

The prison wall is insuperable, the gaol full of darkness, the fetters insoluble and the chains cannot be unfastened by force. Finally, whatsoever can make any place odious and detestable shall be all there united to store that room with furniture fittest for sinners' deserts.

Neither shall the comforts of the company any whit relieve the discomfort of the place. For first they shall have the devil and his angels (Mt. 25. 41) in most horrible and frightful shapes. How fearful these are may be gathered by the words and description set down in Job. *Who*, saith God, *shall open the gate of his countenance? Throughout the compass of his teeth appeareth fear. His body is like founded shields, compacted together with scales pressing one another. . . His sneezing is like the blazing of fire and his eyes like the eyelids of the morning. Out of his mouth come lamps like flaming torches of fire. Out of his nostrils issueth smoke as out of a kindled boiling pot. His breath maketh the coals burn and flame goeth out of his mouth. . . His heart shall be hardened like a stone and pressed hard together like the hammerer's anvil* (Job. 41. 5–15). In hell, saith Cassianus, dwell the hideous fiends whose arms are like dragons' heads, whose eyes shoot out fiery darts, whose teeth stick out like elephants' tusks and sting in their torment like scorpions' tails, and whose sight striketh terror, dolour and death into the beholders.[28]

From this world hell shall have, as St John noteth, the *timorous, incredulous, accursed, murderers, fornicators, witches, idolaters and liars* (Apoc. 21. 8); to whom St Paul addeth, *adulterers, effeminate sodomites, thieves, covetous persons, drunkards, railers and extortioners* (1 Cor. 6. 10), the very riffraff and dregs of mankind. Neither is here an end of their number. The Prophet Isaias telleth us of more: *There*, saith he, *shall the beasts rest and their houses shall be filled with dragons. There shall ostriches dwell and the apes shall leap. There shall the screech owls give an echo in the houses and the sirens in the temples of their pleasure* (Is. 13. 21–22).

O unhappy place and company! what torments in this life come near to any of these miseries? And yet how often, alas, have we deserved them both and a great deal more! Perchance thou thinkest there is either some pleasant sight, some comfortable talk or music, some sweet odours, delicious junkets or other pleasures of the body that abate the horror of the place and company. Alas, what can they in hell see but devils in hideous and monstrous forms, most fearful and threatening shapes, barbarous and spritish cruelty, unmerciful rending, worrying, slaughtering, scourging and torturing, the torments of others, and especially their fellows in sin; above them, an implacable Judge; underneath them, an unquenchable fire; about them, indefatigable tormentors; on each side, desperate and miserable company; everywhere, inevitable and endless torments. Finally, as Isidore saith, *The fire of hell hath light to damnation that the wicked may see whereof to be sorry; but it hath no light to their consolation that they may see whereof to be solaced.*[29]

There shall be confusion of most frightful noises. For their music there shall be the horrible terror of thunder, winds, storms and tempests; the horrible roaring of the devils, the sparkling of the flames, the cursing and blasphemies of the wicked, the weeping and gnashing of teeth; continual screeching, howling, sighing and sobbing; continual hissing, barking, grumbling and bellowing with all other odious and fearful noises: woe, yea and alas, woe shall everlastingly fill their ears; and this shall be their harmony to recompense the disordered abuse of their hearing in this life.

Neither shall their scent be free from most noisome

savours. For besides the stench of the fire and brimstone, besides all the filth and corruption of this world, that in the latter day shall (as some hold) be voided into hell, the channel and sink of all uncleanness, the very bodies of the damned shall be more unsavoury than any carrion or dead carcass. And they will be so pestered and crammed together that they shall lie sprawling upon one another like heaps of frogs or toads, mingled with serpents, basilisks and other most ugly and unclean worms and vermin. We may easily guess what their torments shall be in that behalf.

Now for their taste, what comfort can it yield when there be these rehearsed annoyances; yea, what discomfort shall it adjoin to the former miseries? And of this is said, in Job, *His bread in his belly shall be turned into the gall of cockatrices:* * *he shall vomit out the riches which he hath devoured and God shall pull them out of his belly; he shall suck the head of a cockatrice and the tongue of the vipers shall kill him* (Job 20. 14–16).

Their mouths shall continually be stuffed and forced full of abominable poison, and filth most bitter, sour, salt and loathsome. The roof of their mouths, lips, tongue and gums shall be perpetually tormented with gnawing venomous worms whose taste shall be as painful as their tearing. Finally, what an unresty bed and intolerable torment shall be felt in every part of their whole body, now broiling in fire, mangled by worms and tearing fiends, whipped and harried by the devil and perpetually tumbled in fire and brimstone, amid that mass of carcasses and monsters?

And we should remember that this very body of ours, which we now bear about us and whose present misery we so much lament and think so grievous, deserved all these

---

* *cockatrice*: see note, p. 20.

unspeakable pains, yea, and more miserable torments of mind, since the time we committed the first mortal sin in all our life until this instant and for evermore. For our imagination should have been in continual frights and fears of the present errors and pains; our understanding vexed with a desperate and obstinate conceit of God's implacable justice, of the eternity of these pains and of the loss of everlasting felicity; the memory also pestered with remembrance of the joys past and sorrows present, comparing every sense's pleasure with the incumbent pain, and the opportunity that was once offered to avoid those punishments, from which there neither is now, nor ever will be, any spark of hope of release.

For, as St Gregory saith, the damned suffer an end without end, a death without death, a decay without decay, because their death ever liveth, their end always beginneth and their decay never ceaseth.[30] But they are always healed to be new wounded, always repaired to be new devoured. They are ever dying and never dead, a perpetual prey never consumed, eternally broiling and never burnt up. Now therefore, if there be any man so innocent that he may say, *My conscience accuseth me of nothing* (1 Cor. 4. 4) and is so assured of his integrity that he may vaunt, *In my whole life my heart hath not reprehended me* (Job 27. 6), such a one might marvel with some ground why he should be so afflicted, though if he weigh how St Paul, who said the first, and Job, who uttered the last words, were turmoiled, he might think himself as well worthy of their troubles as either of them. But if like most of us, he is one who has been fleshed and nusled* in sin from childhood, he hath rather cause to mar-

* *nusled*: variation of *nuzzled* and *nurtured*.

vel why he is not in hell, than why he is in prison; why he is not rather condemned to the eternal loss of heavenly treasure than to the temporal loss of a few worldly goods; finally, why he is not adjudged to a death that would be an unhappy beginning to a more unhappy endless progress, than to a death, that ending all misery, beginneth an endless felicity?

THE SIXTH CHAPTER
The sixth cause of Comfort in Tribulation is that the cause we suffer for is the true Catholic Faith

Bᴜᴛ now to come to the principal drift of this my discourse, namely, to comfort you in your tribulation. What more forcible thing can I set before your eyes than the cause of your persecution, the honour of your present estate and the future reward of your patient and constant sufferance? First, the cause which you defend is the only true and Catholic religion. That which impugneth you is erroneous and blasphemous heresy. Our weapons in this action are prayer, fasting, exhortation and good example.

We defend that Church which is avouched by all antiquity, confirmed by the blood of infinite martyrs, gainsaid by the heretics of all ages, and most undoubtedly approved by all testimonies. We defend that Church of Rome, to which, as St Cyprian saith, *misbelief can have no access;*[1] whose faith, St Jerome affirmeth, can *suffer no forgery and, guarded as it is by St Paul's authority, cannot be changed, even though an angel teach otherwise than hath been preached.*[2] We defend that Church of Rome, which, as Cyril saith, *remaineth unspotted from all seducing and heretical circumvention;*[3] of which Theodoret writeth, *It hath always been clear from stench of heresy.*[4] We defend that Church of which Rufinus noteth, *In the Church of the city of Rome no heresy hath taken its beginning; ancient custom is there duly observed.*[5] Also Gregory Nazianzen observeth that *in old Rome the true faith hath been kept even from the times of our forefathers, and hath always been retained, as is fit for a city that ruleth the whole world to have evermore a sound Faith of God.* [6]

We defend not a Church singled from others, not the dismembered Church of Arius, Berengarius, Luther or Calvin. These Churches take their several names from their founders so that they are known, as Lactantius and St Jerome note, [7] to be no longer members of Christ but the Synagogue of Antichrist.

But we defend the Catholic whose name, as St Augustine is witness, [8] no heretic dareth for shame claim as proper to his own sect, since in all ages and by all persons it hath been ever the known style of men of our profession. We defend a Church founded by Christ, enlarged by his apostles, impugned by none but infidels and condemned heretics. Its doctrine can be derived from no late author, is never touched with variableness, change or contrariety in essential points of belief. This Illyricus, our professed enemy, hath sufficiently shown in his *Centuries*, where from age to age he setteth down the sayings of the Fathers that manifestly approve our faith, howbeit maliciously he termeth them, *naevos Patrum*, the wens or warts of the Fathers: and yet for his doctrine he cannot find in all antiquity so many sound and unblemished places as he findeth for the confirmation of ours.

And therefore, well saith Vincentius Lyrinensis that our religion imitateth the course of our bodies. For though there be great difference between the flower of childhood and the ripeness of old age, yet it is the same man that was then young and is now old: and though the parts of children's bodies be neither so big nor strong as they be in full growth,

H

yet are they the very same, equal in number and like in proportion: and if any have altered in shape, unagreeable to the former, or be increased or diminished in number, the whole body either waxeth monstrous or weak or altogether dieth. So ought it to be in Christian doctrine, that though by years the same be strengthened, by time enlarged, and advanced by age, yet always it remains unaltered and uncorrupted.

And though the wheat kernel sown by our forefathers hath sprung to a more ample form by the husbandman's diligence and hath more distinction of parts and is become an ear of corn, yet hath the substance of wheat been retained, and no cockle reaped where the wheat was sown.

But now touching the sects that impugn us, as with all other heresies we can show their late beginning, their new doctrine, either unheard of before or condemned in other heresies, the general opposition against them by Councils, Universities and Catholic Doctors, their variety and sudden change in doctrine and the division of their disciples, as the world knoweth of Luther and Calvin and all histories do report of others. Tertullian, Optatus, Melivitanus and St Augustine,[9] with other Fathers, set down these notes to detect heresies: the demanding of the beginning of their belief, the cause of their long lurking and the origin of their cathedral seat.

We defend that Church, which, not withstanding the rage of the Jews in her infancy, the barbarous tyranny of pagan Emperors in her childhood, the outrageous persecutions of heretics in her ripe age, notwithstanding all other brunts and encounters of Satan, has remained impregnable. Yea, the more it hath been lopped and pruned, the more hath it shot out and flourished; the more it hath been suppressed, the better hath it prospered; and like the Ark of Noah was rather alofted and advanced to the view of all nations when the swelling of the waters drowned all other sects.

For, as St Leo noteth,[10] the Church is not diminished with persecutions but increased; and our Lord's field is always best furnished with most abundance of corn when the kernels that are single in their sowing are multiplied in their growth. This surely could never be unless it were miraculously maintained by God. For, as Gamaliel said, *If it were the counsel or work of men, it would have been dissolved* (Ac. 5. 38), but because it is the Church of God, *the gates of hell have not been able to prevail against it* (Mt. 16. 18), being *the firmament and pillar of truth*, as St Paul calleth it (1 Tim. 3. 15). St Chrysostom also saith about these same words of St Matthew, that only God was able to ensure that a Church founded upon one fisherman and a base person should not fall although shaken with such boisterous tempests.

For though the Catholics have been temporally* so weak, their numbers small compared with their enemies, the princes who have impugned them most mightily and their decrees, menacings and torments to suppress them unbearable, yet, because they were built upon a sure rock, not all this blustering of winds nor eruption of waters have had power to overflow or to bear them down, but that in the end they have had, and always shall have, the upper hand of God's enemies.

Neither can any say that it is not our Church, but theirs, that was thus persecuted. For there hath always been tyrannical persecution most violently bent against the See of

* *temporally*: in temporal things.

Rome and against the Pope and his followers, insomuch that, of the Popes themselves, there have been above thirty martyrs. Besides, if we read all antiquity, we shall not find one that hath suffered for any part of our adversaries' religion, but only such as are by all ancient authors registered for damnable heretics. Whereas we can allege divers that have died and been persecuted for points of our belief, who have been honoured since their deaths and acknowledged for saints by all Christendom, until Luther's time.

For how many virgins have been cruelly put to death for not breaking their vow of virginity? If they had only consented to marriage they might have easily escaped, as, for instance, St Agnes, so highly praised by St Ambrose,[11] and divers others. How many have been banished and put to death by the Arian Emperors for cleaving unto the Pope and the faith of Rome? Did not St Alban die for receiving a clergyman, and St Thomas of Canterbury for defending the liberty of the Church against usurped authority? Were not divers put to death in Copronymus' time for defending images? Finally, how many monks, hermits and religious men, whom our adversaries disclaim for their religion, how many, I say, have been martyred for their faith, as Palladius and St Damascene write?[12]

Neither do I reckon these in particular to the exclusion of all the other martyrs, for doubtless in all persecutions none died martyrs but of our faith, as is apparent by their histories. But I cite these particulars to show that those who have suffered for these self-same points for the which we are now chiefly persecuted have generally been accounted martyrs in former ages. So that it sufficiently appeareth that all the general persecutions have been raised against our Church, and that, notwithstanding all their cruelty, it yet endureth, and shall to the world's end.

On the other side, although there hath been two hundred arch-heretics, broachers of new sects, since Christ's time, and though they have for a season flourished and prevailed, having Emperors, Bishops and Potentates to defend them, infinite books and writings to divulge their doctrines, and all temporal aids to set them forward, yet we see that their memory is quite abolished, their names commonly unknown, their books perished and no more mention of them than the condemnation and disproof of their errors recorded by Catholic writers. The same, doubtless, will be the end of Luther's novelties, which being but parcels of their corruptions revived and raked out of oblivion, as heretofore they vanished with their prime devisers, so will they now with their late revivers. And we see this almost even already verified, since among so many of Luther's progeny there are found scarce any (and, peradventure, none at all) that dare avouch or take upon him the patronage of all his articles. Yea, and his scholars are already so strangely sundered into most contrarious and divers sects that it is a most manifest token and proof that God is not the author of their opinions, seeing he is only the God of peace and not of dissension. For Lindanus long since, in his dialogue named *Dubitantius*, reckoneth up threescore and eighteen divers sects sprung all since Luther's first preaching, and added to those that are of later growth they are now well near a hundred, all different from each other in essential points of faith as Prateolus sheweth in most of them.

This doubtless is the providence of Almighty God as it hath been in all other heresies of former days, that the in-

constancy, variety and sudden change, the dissension of doctrine and division of scholars, both from their masters and
amongst themselves should be a manifest argument that
their assertions proceeded from the spirit of error, were
maintained with the spirit of pride and obstinacy, and should
be quickly ended by the spirit of discord and contradiction.
This doth Irenaeus observe of Simon Magus and of Valentinus,[13] St Augustine of the Donatists and Manichees,[14]
Epiphanius of the Marcionites and Montanists,[15] Rufinus[16]
and Hilarius[17] of the Arians, and Evagrius of the Euty-
chians,[18] who were scarce so soon sprung as they were
spread into must contrarious branches, or, as St Augustine
speaketh, *into very small mammocks.**

Once they swerve from the compass of the Catholic
Church's censure by allowing and interpreting the Scripture in the sense that their single spirit suggesteth, as they
be of divers fantasies and humours, they fall into divers and
sundry persuasions; and then not yielding to any umpireship but their own, they are past all means and possibility of
agreement. Origen[19] finds a parallel in that act of Samson,
when he bound three hundred foxes by the tails and tied fire
in the midst and sent them to burn his enemies' corn. So,
saith he, must the true Catholic doctor take the repugnant
opinions and contradictions of heretics, and by conferring
them together deduce thereby a conclusion against them,
which may serve as fire to burn up their own fruits.

And indeed there is nothing of more force to shew their
madness than this presumption upon their self-arbitrement
which is the cause of all their discord. For, as St Chrysostom
noteth,[20] just as he would judge a man mad who, seeing the

* *mammock*: scrap or shred.

smith take a red-hot iron with his tongs, would adventure to take the same in his bare fingers, so may we deem the philosophers mad who went about to compass our faith in their bare reason, and the heretics of our time who adventure upon the credit of their single spirits to decide all controversies and interpret God's word, which the cunningest smiths of all antiquity never durst handle but by the tongues of the Catholic Church's censure.

As a man taking the King's image set forth by a rare workman with exquisite cunning and with most choice precious stones should change it from man's shape to the likeness of a fox or dog, using still the same metal and the same precious jewels, though rudely and grossly disposed, and should then vaunt that this were the King's true portraiture, so artificially wrought by the first worker and thus delude the ignorant with the beauty and glistening of the precious stones: so do the heretics, saith Irenaeus,[21] who change the faith of God's Church into the fables of their own fantasy and seek to set forth their follies with the authority of God's word, wrested by their perverse spirits against its true meaning in order more easily to blind the simple.

The pirates used in the dark night to set lights in the shallow places and hidden rocks so that the ships thinking to find some sure haven, should direct their course by these lights, and thus be guilefully drawn to their own ruin. So the devil, saith Origen,[22] setting the light of the Scripture and counterfeit piety upon the rocks of heresy, allures under the colour of truth the simple passengers of this life to their own perdition.

Therefore we are warned not to believe every spirit. The better to avoid the variance, presumption and malicious fraud of heretics we always stand by the verdict of the Church and her chief Pastor, to whom God hath promised the infallible assistance of his spirit. We have ever defended with one accord one only faith, agreeable to itself in all times, places and persons, which is the self-same for which we now suffer persecution. Wherefore we call all ancient writers to witness, who, by their books and many by their blood, have laboured before us in the same quarrel and confirmed the same faith, though assaulted by other kind of enemies.

But if comparison with saints be not presumption, this, for our great comfort, may we say: that though the cause of religion were always honourable, yet it is in us more worthily defended than of any martyrs of former ages. For they defended either against epicures and heathens, or against the Jews and rabbis, or against some one heretic and his offspring. But we are now in a battle not only against men of our times, who are epicures in conditions, Jews in malice, and heretics in proud and obstinate spirit, but against the whole rabble and generation of all heretics that since Christ's time have been in league with Satan, the father of lying, and his whole army; who, albeit they be fast chained in hell and there reap the fruit of their blasphemies, yet have these companions of theirs borrowed all their weapons and revived some of all their heresies. So that in combating them we challenge all the old heretics into the field. We must in one age sustain a multitude of enemies, jointly assaulting us, every one of whom hath, in times past, made work enough for divers doctors in several ages, according as they did rise one after another.

Against Simon Magus, Cerdon, and Florinus we must defend that God is not author of sin. We must defend that the whole Church cannot err against Nestorius, that traditions are to be observed against Cerdon, Arius, Eunomius, Aerius, Nestorius and almost all heretics; that faith alone sufficeth not, against Aetius, Eunomius and Simon; against the same together with Valentinus that good works are necessary; that man hath free will against Simon, Valentinus and Manichaeus; that the Fathers' writings are of great authority against Paulus Samosetanus, Aetius and Eunomius; that sins are not alike and that virginity is to be preferred before matrimony against Jovinian; that Baptism is necessary to salvation against Manichaeus, Eutyches and Philoponus. We must defend the Sacrament of the Altar against the Donatists and the Arians who trod it under their feet and gave it to their dogs; and against Berengarius and the Iconomachies who made it but a figure of Christ's Body. The Sacrifice of the Mass we must defend against Manichaeus; the Priest's ornaments against Pelagius; purgatory against the Armenians; relics, chastity of priests, voluntary poverty and prayer for the dead against Vigilantius and Aerius; the vow of obedience against the Lampetians, churches and altars against the Eustachians and Eutyches. We must defend Confirmation against Novatian, Confession against Montanus, Matrimony against the Apostolici, the Sacrament of Holy Orders and the Priesthood against the Pepuzites who gave it to women, Lent and other appointed fasts against the Gnostics, Eustachians, Arians and Jovinians. All these men are condemned and registered in the catalogue of heretics by St Augustine, Epiphanius, Irenaeus, Tertullian and all antiquity. Finally, we must defend in a manner all Catholic truths against all heretical innovations.

I am ashamed to say that we are forced to defend that Christ is come against the Jews; that he is of the same substance with his Father and *homoousios* against the Arians: yea, and that there is any Christ, or God at all, against the Politikes and Atheists.

Yet undoubtedly if ever there were any need, even when Epicurus' sect most flourished, to prove a God, a hell or a heaven, then surely there is now, when heresy is grown so ripe and the infinite sects and divisions so spread, beside new daily uprisings, that the variety of religions hath abolished almost all religion. It is indeed true that this uncertainty among so many beliefs hath made the greatest part of our country believe none at all. Yea, and we see the lives, consciences and dispositions of men in this behalf to be at such a pass that should the Prince but command them to adore Mahomet or renew the memory of the old gods and goddesses, such as Jupiter, Juno, Venus with the rest of that crew, there would be thousands as ready to embrace them and seem as zealous in their service as now they be in a belief of—they cannot tell what themselves. And this in truth is the end and last step that heresy bringeth men unto.

Seeing therefore that Peter's ship now saileth not against the wind of one evil spirit nor against the stream of all heresy, it is no less necessary than glorious for us to employ our last endeavours in its defence. We should think our limbs happily lost, our blood blessedly bestowed and our lives most honourably spent in this so noble and important a business. And although it may seem much for men of one age to fight with the enemies of so many, for Catholics of one belief to engage against hosts and armies of all sundry sects, yet this comfort we have to encourage us: first that as there are some medicines of such quality that they are not only profitable for this or that disease but have a general and common force against all, so, the Catholic Faith, saith Hilarius,[23] hath so universal a remedy not only against every heresy but against them all, that it can be neither hindered by the strangeness of the disease, nor overcome by the number, nor deceived by the variety. But the infallible assistance of God's spirit serveth as an electuary against all heretical pestilences.

Secondly, we fight against such as derive their pedigree from the offals and condemned castaways of God's Church, whose weapons and wards* have been severally blunted and broken by the champions of former times, so that they are less able to offend us or defend their unhappy posterity. Whereas we, on the other side, are counter-guarded with the assistance of aids so invincible that as yet they have never been discomfited; so there is no possibility that they should be hereafter.

What an assured defence of our cause have we in the continual and never interrupted descent and succession of Bishops in the See of Rome? From St Peter's time until this day we are able to give a certain account of them, and to shew of every one the same belief which they have delivered unto us from hand to hand without change or alteration: as Cardinal Bellarmine† learnedly sheweth in the fourth book of his first Tome and third Controversy against the impious obloquies of heretics of our time. This, saith Irenaeus,[24]

* *ward*: an appliance for guarding, e.g. part of the hilt of a sword which protects the hand: notches and projections in locks designed to prevent opening by a wrong key.

† R. S. attended Cardinal Bellarmine's lectures on Controversy in the Roman College.

confoundeth all heretics, who were always themselves the first and oftentimes the last pretended Bishops of their belief: neither lawfully descended from any apostle, nor orderly installed in their cathedral seats, but intruded by themselves without any usual creation. This same point St Jerome, St Epiphanius and St Augustine[25] oppose against sectaries as an unconquerable engine, as indeed it is. After the decay of all other patriarchal and apostolical Sees, such as Antioch, Alexandria and Jerusalem; after so many alterations and violent changes of the temporal state of Rome, from Emperors to Kings of the Goths, from them to Exarchs of the Greeks, and another while to Consuls, and of these some by right, some reigning by usurped authority; likewise after so many massacres, sackings and overthrows of the city itself, this succession hath never failed, this authority never decayed but hath always continued and persevered as it shall do to the end of the world.

Secondly, what an assured proof of our religion against all the adversaries' cavils hath the Church of Rome in the innumerable miracles worked through divers famous and holy men, adherents and defenders of the same, whereby God hath averred the truth thereof? For the devil may work some feigned wonders above man's reach, which are in the compass of natural causes. By inveigling and deceiving our sense or imagination he may make something appear a miracle which in fact is none. Yet things which surpass the ability of any creature and are only in the power of Almighty God, neither the devil, nor any other, can do by natural means, but only as the instrument and agent of God, as, for instance, to give sight to the blind, to restore a limb to the maimed, to raise the dead, and such like, which men of our belief in all ages since Christ have done. For, to omit Christ and his apostles, to omit also others of the Primitive Church, many whom our adversaries cannot deny to have been of our Church have wrought very extraordinary miracles.

First, there are the miracles of Gregory Thaumaturgus, about which St Basil, St Jerome, and St Gregory Nazianzen write;[26] then the strange cures and raising of the dead by St Anthony, St Hilarion, St Martin and St Nicholas, about which St Athanasius, St Jerome, Sulpicius and others write. Yet it is well known that St Anthony and St Hilarion were professed hermits and monks, and consequently enemies to those that condemn and reprove monastical life. After them we have those about which St Gregory speaketh in his *Dialogues*,[27] of which many were done by monks and other religious persons.

And to come to our native examples, how many miracles wrought St Augustine and his company in reclaiming our country, as St Bede and St Gregory report[28]—to omit those of St Cuthbert, St John, St Oswald, St Dunstan and divers others registered by the same St Bede[29] and our own chronicles? It were a folly to call in question the religion of these men, seeing that by the testimony of all writers it is as apparent that they were addicted to the Catholic Roman Church, as that there were any such men at all.

Now, if we come to later times, let St Malachias, so highly commended in St Bernard's works,[30] let St Bernard's own life written by Godfrey, a man of the same time, let St Francis' miracles registered by St Bonaventure, St Dominic's, St Thomas of Aquin's, St Bonaventure's own be testimonies whose faith is the truest, seeing that all these were themselves monks and friars and first founders of divers religious orders, professors of perpetual poverty, chastity and obedience, and vowed persons. All which points are condemned by our adversaries and maintained by us.

Finally, to come to saints yet fresh in memory, what miraculous things have been wrought by St Bernardine and St Catherine of whom St Antoninus writeth; by St Antoninus himself of whom Surius writeth; and in our days, since Luther rose up, by the Reverend Father Francis Xavier, of the Society of Jesus, in the Indies, whose wonderful miracles are not only certain by most diligent inquiry and security made for the true knowledge of them by the King of Portugal, but the miraculous conversion from infidelity to the Roman Faith of so many thousands, yea, and so many kingdoms, yieldeth an undoubted assurance of them. Since these holy men are manifestly known by our adversaries' own confession and by their lives and writings, as men of our religion, seeing also their miracles were such as giving light to the blind, limbs to those that want them and reviving the dead, which the Fathers admit to be above all power of conjuring, sorcery or enchantments; seeing, finally, these miracles have been wrought, either for testimony of their virtue, which cannot be true virtue without true faith, or for proof of their religion, which all authors assure us was the same as ours, what greater certificate can we have of the goodness of our quarrel, since we are sure that God, the only author of these supernatural effects, cannot witness any kind of untruth?

To doubt whether these miracles be true, or truly reported, being written by so grave and authentical authors, is nothing else but to condemn all histories, books and registers of antiquity, and only to allow that, whereof our own sight and sense ascertain us, which is extreme folly. More-over, if we consider both the sincerity and sanctity of our faith, and the professors thereof, and the absurdity and cor-ruption of our adversaries' belief and behaviour, we shall soon know by the fruits, in whose garden the best tree groweth. For, as concerning our faith, its principles, rules and grounds are such that though they be above reason, yet are they not against it; neither yield they scope to such as live according to their prescript of licentiousness or riot, but keep them in awe and compass of their duty towards God and man.

On the other hand, the very articles of our adversaries' religion are of such tenor that they cannot in reason and piety be held for religious truths; nor being believed can they restrain men's consciences to the limits of virtue, but rather open them a wide gate to a desperate and dissolute life. For he that affirmeth all the actions of man (even the very best) to be damnable sins (as Calvin and his followers avouch) and therewith that all sins are of equal deformity and heinousness touching death and damnation, what heart or encouragement can he have to follow virtue, or what bridle can hold him from plunging himself in the puddle of all vice since the one is as great an offence and as punishable before God as the other. And this faith which sayeth that the merit of a good action is not imputed to the doer, holdeth also of any wicked work whatsoever. Again, a Calvinist who believeth the commandments of God to be impossible for man to keep, and withal, that howsoever he break them, it neither can nor ought to make him doubt of his election, which dependeth only upon God's predestination, why should he not think it folly to endeavour to observe God's law, being an impossibility? Yea, and upon certainty of his salvation, why should he not become careless to break any commandment and take what course most pleaseth his sensual appetite? Further, he that maketh God the author of sin and the enforcer of man to wicked and impious acts as well as the director to any virtue, and withal knoweth that if he be damned, it shall be for no other sin than such as by God himself he was constrained to commit, must needs think his case most miserable in being so disabled from avoiding such an offence, and God a most rigorous and unjust judge that condemneth a man for that fault which he forced him unto. The effect of this and such like principles well appeareth in the unchristian and irreligious behaviour of sundry estates, and especially of the Protestant ministers, teachers and defenders of the same, who are known, in most places, to be so loose and lewd and so far disordered that their own sheep do greatly mislike their ungodly behaviour.

But now, on the other side, for proof of the sincerity of our religion, I appeal only to the common experience of Catholics' lives, both in this and former ages. Let all histories witness their sincere dealing, plain words, simple attire, frugal tables, unfeigned promises, assured love and amity and most entire and friendly conversation one with another. Let us consider their large hospitality in housekeeping, their liberality towards the poor and their readiness to all merciful and charitable acts. Let us remember their assiduity and continual exercise of prayer, their straight observation of long fasts, their austerity and rigour in other chastisements of their bodies, and we shall find what different manners and fruits proceed from our belief and from the doctrine of the new doctors.

Yea, and the chiefest things laid to our charge by infidels and heretics are that we keep men too much in awe, that we restrain them too much from carnal liberty, that we have too much of the Cross of Christ, *a scandal to the Jews and folly to the Gentiles* (1 Cor. 1. 23). So doth Pliny[31] report of us, in his Epistle to the Trojans, that we detest all vices and live most holily, and that we have only two faults: the one is that we are too ready to spend our lives in God's cause, the other that we rise too early before day to sing praises unto Christ. These faults our Gospellers take most notice of before all others. So for the most part (excepting those lies that the heretics father upon us) the greatest complaints they have against us are for prescribing fasts, forbidding flesh on certain days, condemning marriage of priests, monks and other vowed persons; for prescribing confession, satisfaction and penance in this life for men's sins; for avouching prayer, fasting, alms and other good works as necessary to salvation; for requiring an exact obedience of the temporal to the spiritual, and of all to Christ's Vicar here on earth; for condemning the arrogancy of their self-governing spirits, refusing all other judgment besides their own in matter of controversy and in understanding the Scriptures and such like points that may in any way bridle them from following the full liberty of their carnal appetites.

Yet for all they thus disallow our doctrine, the truth itself enforceth them sometimes (as of old it did the very devils) to speak most reverently of our religion and professors. Luther, in his book against the Anabaptists, confesseth that in Popedom there is most of Christian goodness, yea all Christian goodness, and admits that he and his received it from thence. He grants that we have the true Scriptures,

Baptism, the Sacrament of the Altar, the true keys of jurisdiction, the true office of preaching, the true catechism, our Lord's Prayer, the Ten Commandments and the Articles of Faith; in the end, he concludeth with these words: *I avouch moreover, that in Popedom there is true Christianity, yea the very kernel of Christianity*. So that this kernel being but one, according to that saying, *there is but one faith and one baptism* (Eph. 4. 5), either he must be of our religion, or else, since by his own confession we have the true kernel, he hath nothing but the husk and shell for him and his disciples.

Now, concerning the professors of our faith, St Athanasius, St Jerome and Sulpicius write that the infidels themselves bear very great reverence and did much honour to St Anthony, St Hilarion and St Martin. Totila, an Arian Prince, honoured highly St Benedict. Calvin called St Bernard a godly writer. Luther, Melanchthon and the Augsburg Confession call Bernard, Dominic and Francis saints. All these men being (as is before said) monks, friars and religious persons, are undoubtedly known to have been far from the Protestants' or Puritans' religion. And though the heretics said nothing, yet doth all antiquity cry, and infinite miracles yield, certain warrant of the holiness and virtue of the Catholic Fathers.

But we need not to range far for examples of good life. For (God be thanked) even our adversaries themselves are so fully persuaded of our good behaviour that if a man in company be modest and grave in countenance, words or demeanour, if he use no swearing, foul or unseemly speech, if he refuse to join in lewd company and dishonest actions, he is straight suspected for a Papist. And, on the other side, if a man be ruffianly, quarrellous, foul-spoken and lewdly conditioned, he is never mistrusted for a Papist but taken for a very sound and undoubted Protestant.

Let also the records of assizes and sessions be searched and let it be but shewn how many hundred Protestants are yearly executed for felonies, murders, rapes, extortions, forgeries and such like crimes, and how few recusants have been ever, in so many years, attached justly with such like offences. Let but the neighbours of Catholic and Protestant gentlemen be witness who live best and are readiest in all good deeds and works of charity.

Let the jailers and keepers of prisons report what difference they find in the lives of Catholic and Protestant prisoners. And if all these say, as the truth is, that we go beyond the other in Christian duty, then may we, by their own testimonies, avouch the tree of our religion to be good, seeing that, as Christ saith, *An evil tree cannot bring forth good fruit* (Mt. 7. 18). Whereby we may also infer that the religion of our adversaries is evil, since the fruits thereof are so extremely bad, as daily experience sheweth, that even among heathens and infidels there is found more truth, honesty and conscience than is now in the Protestant multitude, so well have they profited in the licentious principles of their religion.

We must remember that the apostles were not without cause called *salt of the earth* (Lk. 5. 13), and *Light of the world* (Lk. 5. 14), because their doctrine should have effects agreeable to the properties of these things. For as the salt preserveth flesh from vermin, stench and corruption, and the light is a means to discern the good from the bad, the miry from the clean way, our friend from our foe: so doth the true faith give remedies against all stench and corruption of vice, and showeth the path of virtue and truth from the dirty way of sin and error.

THE SEVENTH CHAPTER

The seventh cause of Comfort in Tribulation is that the state of the persecuted in a good cause is honourable

Now, concerning your state, how can it be anything but honourable when your cause is so good? For the cause honoureth the combat and assureth you of the final victory. Your counterpeers* are mighty, their force very great, their vantage not unknown, their malice experienced, their torments to flesh and blood intolerable. But your Captain hath always conquered, your cause hath been always in the end advanced, your predecessors never lost the field. Why then should you have less hope of the victory? Christianity is a warfare, and Christians spiritual soldiers; their conflicts continual, though their enemies be divers.

In the beginning our faith was planted in the poverty, infamy, persecution and death of Christ. In its progress it was watered and dunged with the blood and slaughtered limbs of God's saints. It cannot come to the full growth unless it be fostered with the continual showers of martyrs' wounds.

You are the choice captains whom God hath allotted to be chief actors in the conquest. Your veins are conduits out of which he meaneth to derive the streams that shall water

* This word, apparently coined by R. S., presumably means equally matched opponents.

his Church. He hath placed you as the fairest and surest stones in the forefront of his building to delight his friends and confound his enemies with the beauty and grace of your virtuous life and patient constancy.

Now is the time come for the light of the world to blaze out beams of innocency, for the salt of the earth to season the weak souls bending to corruption, yea, and for the good shepherd to spend his life for the defence of his silly flock. *The lopping time is come* (Cant. 2. 12): the branches and boughs of full growth are lopped so that the tree of the Church may sprout out more abundantly with young twigs.

Now is that time come of which Christ forewarned us: *It shall come to pass that he that killeth you shall think he doth God a good piece of service* (Jn 16. 2). And as St Cyprian saith, *Lo, the things that were said are now done: and now since that which was foretold is fulfilled, that which was promised will be also performed, our Lord himself assuring it, and saying: When you see all these things to come to pass, then know you that the kingdom of heaven is near at hand* (Lk. 21. 31).[1] When we see the flower, we hope for the fruit and take it as a presage of a calm, temperate and pleasant season. Our flowers that foreshow the happy calm of our felicity grow out of these thorns, and of these briars must we reap our fruit. If the stalk wound, the flower healeth: if the reaping be troublesome, the fruit is the more delightsome.

Let no man deny the sea to be deep, saith St Ambrose, because the shores be shallow, nor heaven to be clear because it is sometimes cloudy, nor the earth to be fertile because it is somewhere unfruitful, nor the crop of corn to be good because it is mixed with barren oats. So think not the harvest of a good conscience lost though it be interrupted with some sorrowful and bitter flowers.

The ignorant, perhaps, will condemn us, that think it no folly to make account of the gall of Tobias' fish (Tob. 6). Let them muse at our madness that most willingly feed on Samson's honeycomb, when it is taken out of the lion's mouth (Jg. 14. 8). Let us not regard their phrenetical laughters and raving scoffs: *a sensual man understandeth not the things appertaining to God* (1 Cor. 2. 14). We know that the flower of Jesse gave his most pleasant scent, and came to his full growth upon the Cross. We know that the fruit of life was not gathered without thorns. We know, finally, that gall was chosen in extremity by the most experienced and perfect taster, and the honeycomb not eaten till after his resurrection, when it was in a manner fetched out of the lion's mouth, whom he had, by his death, victoriously foiled. Our choice agreeth with our Captain's examples, and both the time and our cause moveth us thereunto.

We are offered two keys, the one of gold set with diamonds, rubies and pearls, curiously wrought, and hanged in a chain of a great price; the other of old rusty iron, unhandsome and shapeless to behold and tied in a rotten cord. Yet we know that the rusty key openeth the door to infinite treasure, the other to a sink of corruption and a dungeon of despair. Which of these two keys were in reason to be desired? This rusty key is trouble and affliction; the key of gold is worldly prosperity. The first openeth heaven's gates, for *by many tribulations must we enter into the kingdom of God* (Ac. 14. 22). The other openeth hell's doors: *for gold and silver have destroyed many* (Ecclus 8. 3).

We must now remember the last will, that, as St Ambrose saith, Christ made upon the Cross: *The author of life hanging upon the Cross made his will, allotting to every one works of piety: to his Apostles, persecution; to the Jews, his body; to his Father, his soul; to the Virgin, a Paranymph,* to the sinner, hell; to the thief, Paradise; to the repentant Christians, he commended the cross.*[2] Whereupon St Maximus well saith, *that all the life of a Christian, that will live agreeable to the Gospel, is a perpetual cross and martyrdom.*[3]

We must now acknowledge our profession and not be ashamed of our inheritance, which Christ allotted unto us. We must say, with St Paul: *The world is crucified unto me, and I to the world* (Gal. 6. 14). To put themselves in mind of this, the old Christians, in Tertullian's time, were wont to pray with their arms stretched out, as men already crucified in mind, and ready in God's cause to be crucified also in body. Whereupon Tertullian, speaking of this gesture in prayer, saith: *While we are thus praying with our arms spread abroad, let the hooks dig us, the gibbets hang us, the fires consume us, the swords cut our throats, the beasts fly upon us. The very behaviour of a Christian in prayer sheweth him ready for all kind of torments.*[4]

A wise shipmaster, when he setteth forth from the shore and goeth to sea, laying aside the remembrance of wife, children, house and family, employeth his body and mind only to the due performance of his office, in avoiding the dangers and directing his ship to a gainful haven. You are now launched out of the port of worldly prosperity into the sea of temporal discomfort in God's cause. Therefore it behoveth you to unencumber yourselves of all earthly cares.

---

* *Paranymph*: friend of the bridegroom, who accompanied him when he went to fetch home the bride: hence best man. R. S. is referring here to St John (cf. Jn 19. 27: *Behold thy mother...*).

You must display the sail of your soul upon the mast of Christ's Cross, betake you to the tackling of virtue, keep your hand upon the stern of good order and discipline, and being parted from earth, lift up your eyes towards heaven. You must direct your course by the motion of the stars and planets, that is, by the example of former saints, so that having Christ for your pilot, the inspirations of the Holy Ghost for your gale, you may go through the storms of persecution, overcome the surges of worldly pleasure, pass the shelves of alluring occasions, avoid the shipwreck of deadly offence, and finally, safely arrive to the port of life and perfect repose.

Now is the time whereof the spouse, in person of the Church, said, *Arise, North, and come, South wind, blow through my garden, and let the spice thereof flow down* (Cant. 4. 16). These winds now blow, and it is now time that the spice fall, and the virtues and constant examples of saints, that lay hidden and covered among the leaves, be with this persecution shaken from them and laid open for every one to gather. We must now ascend *to the mount of myrrh*, which is in taste bitter, and *the hill of frankincense* (Cant. 4. 6), that giveth no sweet savour, except when it is resolved by fire.

Our heavenly smith hath now brought us into the forge of trial and kindled the coals of persecution to prove whether we be pure gold and fit to be laid up in his treasury. Now, while this wind is stirring, cometh the winnower with his fan to see who is blown away like light chaff and who resisteth the blasts like massy wheat. That which liveth hidden in the young blade of corn is displayed in the ripe ear. That which is concealed in the flower is uttered in the fruit. Many believers are deemed equal, whom trial proveth of unequal faith. The persecutor's tribunal sheweth what was covered in the bud, agreeably to that saying, *By their fruit you shall know them* (Mt. 7. 20). Many flowers promise a multitude of fruit, but when they are once put to the proof by storms of wind very few persevere to the full growth. So many seem faithful in the calm of the Church, but when the blasts of adversity bluster against them few are found in the fruit of martyrdom. The cunning of the pilot is not known till the tempest riseth, nor the captain's courage till the war beginneth, nor the Catholic's constancy till the persecutor rageth.

Persecution, as Tertullian noteth, is *the shovel which purgeth out our Lord's floor, that is the Church, fanning the confused heap of the faithful, and severing the corn of the martyrs from the chaff of deniers.*[5] This is the ladder of Jacob's dream (Gen. 28), which showed to some the way into heaven and to others the descent into hell. This is the water of contradiction by which God's servants are proved, as is written: *Thou has taken trial by temptation, and judged us at the waters of contradiction* (Deut. 33. 8). This is the water at which our heavenly Gedeon testeth who are fit soldiers to assist him against the Madianites. He severeth such as fell on their knees for greediness and thirst of worldly vanities from those that drank from their hands only as much as their necessity required. Of whom God saith: *In those three hundred men that have licked the waters* [from their hands], *will I deliver you* (Jg. 7. 7).

St Chrysostom[6] reporteth, that many times the shepherds of Cappadocia lie three days together covered with snow, for the care they have of their flocks. And they of Libya are contented to wander for whole months after their flocks in deserts full of cruel wild beasts, preferring the care of their cattle before their own dangers. How much more are the Pastors, yea all the Catholics of this time, bound to endure the pinching and freezing cold of what adversity soever, yea and the hazards of cruel persecutors, who like wild beasts have turned this vineyard of our country into a barren desert rather than allow (so much as in us lieth) Christ's flock either to be scandalized by our example or destitute of our necessary endeavours?

For if in a serious and earnest battle, upon which the state of the commonwealth depended, the King himself were in complete harness, and in person ready with his weapons to fight for his kingdom, if, then, any of his nobles came into the field with a fan of feathers instead of a buckler, and a posy of flowers instead of a sword, and in every way more like a carpet knight* than a man of arms, the King could not but take it in very evil part. So surely must Christ, if in this spiritual war against his Church, for which he fought in person and received so many wounds, we should look on, more like worldly wantons than true soldiers, and not be as ready as our King and Captain to venture our lives in the same quarrel.

Now therefore is the time for us to prove ourselves. Now must it be known whether we be *vessels of honour*, or *reproach* (2 Tim. 2. 20, 21); whether we be signed with the name of the Lamb, or touched with *the mark of the beast* Antichrist (Apoc. 14. 9); whether we be of the wheat or of the cockle; and finally, whether we belong to the flock of Christ or the herd of Belial.

---

* *carpet knight*: a contemptuous term for a stay-at-home soldier.

THE EIGHTH CHAPTER

The eighth cause of Comfort in Tribulation is the honour of imprisonment for the Catholic Faith

AND a thousand times happy are you, whose prisons are proofs and whose chains are pledges of your future immortality. And a thousand times happy (I say) are you whose estate is both glorious here and a sure way to the unspeakable glory of the world to come. For, as St Cyprian saith, *By the long tract of time you diminish not your glory but increase it; so many are your praises as days; so many increases of merits as courses of months.*[1]

Of you there is no doubt, whether you be for the barn or for the fire (Mt. 13. 30*): *Your prison lodging is your barn,*[2] for you being laid up there are like clean wheat and precious corn. For though the prisons be in themselves folds of Satan to harbour his lewd flock, yet when the cause ennobleth the name of a prisoner, the prisoner abolisheth the dishonour of the place. What thing of old was there more odious than the Cross? What place more abhorred than Mount Calvary? What rooms more reproachful than the grates and dungeons of the saints? Yet now, what thing more honourable than the holy Cross? What place more reverenced than the aforesaid Mount? What sanctuaries more desired than the dungeons of the saints? So doth God deprive the devil of his usual haunts, and frameth mansions of great merit and

---

* *Gather ye first the darnel, and bind it in bundles to burn; but the wheat gather ye into my barn.*

ports of salvation for his own servants from kennels ordained for the couching of his hell-hounds.

A reproachful thing it is to be chained in sin, gyved in wickedness, and shut up in the deadly prison of mortal offence. It is a miserable thing to be enthralled in the vassalage of the devil, in servile subjection to our lawless appetites and in slavish bondage of worldly vanities. But, *O feet happily chained, which are directed a safe way to Paradise! O feet for a time foreslowed with fetters and bolts, but shall hereafter with a glorious journey swiftly run into their country!*[3]

It is honourable in God's quarrel to be abridged of bodily liberty for maintaining the true liberty and freedom of our soul. Since birds are accustomed and naturally delighted with the full scope of the air, though they be never so well fed in the cage, they are always poring at every cranny to see whether they may escape. They understand not that in the cage they are safer from the kite, hawk and fowler than abroad; neither mark they the benefit of their assured repair from hard weather and worse food. But for a reasonable creature, and withal a Christian Catholic, it must be thought an imperfection to prefer a dangerous liberty to the benefit of his prison in so good a cause, especially considering how many perils of our souls are cut off thereby, and how highly our spiritual welfare is advanced. In this let us not be like the senseless birds but rather imitate them in another property, which is that in the cage they not only sing their natural note both sweeter and oftener than abroad but learn also divers other songs more pleasant and delightsome. And so we both keep, and oftener practise, our wonted devotions, and besides, learn new exercises of virtue, both for our own comfort and example of others.

And when might you so freely range among the choirs of angels as when you are sequestered from the distractions of vain company? When could you take a fuller repast of the sweet fruits of prayer and contemplation than when the onions, garlic and flesh-pots of Egypt are furthest out of scent and sight? Your eyes are not too much troubled with impious and wicked sights; your ears are not annoyed with bloody outcries and heinous blasphemies; you are quit from many scandals, and severed from occasion of divers temptations. Finally, if you do not think of prison as a prison you shall find it a retiring place fittest to serve God. If it restrain you of temporal comforts, your booty is gainful, for by loss of transitory rewards you deserve eternal. If your body be chastised, your soul is cherished, and the pining of the one is the pampering of the other. You forsake a paradise of poisoning delights for a place that yieldeth cause of grounded and true solaces. Yea, and as Tertullian noteth, if you weigh from whence you came, and where you are, you shall find that you are rather delivered out of prison than committed into it.

Greater darkness hath the world which inveigleth and blindeth not only the eyes but the hearts of men. Heavier chains and shackles doth the world lay on us which do fetter and entangle our very souls. Far worse ordure and stench doth the world breathe out—I mean ribaldry, carnality and all kind of brutish behaviour. Finally, more prisoners and guilty persons hath the world, not to be judged by the umpireship of any earthly magistrate, but by the censure and verdict of Almighty God. Happy therefore are you, if you can reckon yourselves translated out of prison into a place of preservation, which, if it be cumbered with darkness, yourselves are lamps to light it; if it charge you with gyves, yet are you loose and unbound towards God; if you be pestered with unsavoury smell, you are frankincense and savour of sweetness; if it affright you with expectation of judges, yourselves hereafter *shall judge nations and rule over people* (Wis. 3. 8). *O blessed prison*, saith St Cyprian, *which your presence hath honoured! O blessed prison that sendeth the men of God to heaven. O darkness brighter than the sun itself and more clear than the light of this world,* [4] where the temples of God are now placed and your members sanctified with your divine confessions of faith! Let them who have fastened their affection upon worldly vanities complain of the difficulties of the prison. A Christian Catholic, even out of prison, hath renounced the world in his baptism, and it little importeth in what place he be in the world for he has by promise and profession vowed never to be of it. Let them complain of the prison that know not the glory and sovereign prerogative of that place. But it is a great shame for a Catholic who hath Christ for his author, the apostles for his witness, all former saints for testimony, not to think worthily and reverently of the honour of suffering in God's quarrel.

When one that knoweth not the virtue of herbs walketh in the fields or hills, he treadeth under foot without any regard whatsoever groweth in his way, making no more account of one herb than of another. But if he come into a physician's house, and seeth there besides wholesome herbs many strong and unsavoury weeds, he thinketh that there must be some secret virtue in them to cure diseases. And if he see the experience of their operation, he taketh much more account of them; and whereas before he trampled with contempt upon them, he now would be as careful to gather them. Even so, one that knoweth not the virtue and honour of the cross, chains and prisons of Christ, despiseth and abhorreth them as contemptible and dishonourable things. But if he comes into this school of our heavenly physician (I mean the Scriptures), and sees there these things honoured and views the strange operation of them, not only in Christ himself, but in St Paul, St John Baptist and others, how can he choose but hold them in great esteem, and be ready, if occasion serve, to try their force on himself, although the ignorant may judge them as unprofitable weeds and badges of disgrace?

What places are of more price than kings' palaces, yea, what place so glorious as heaven? And yet St Chrysostom saith that kings' courts, and heaven itself, yieldeth to the glory of the prison which harboureth Christ's prisoner.[5] For as the prince's presence honoureth the basest cottage and maketh it more esteemed and resorted unto than the most stately buildings, so the presence of God's prisoner in the most infamous dungeon maketh it a court and resort of angels, and a paradise where God himself delighteth to walk and take pleasure in the constancy of his afflicted servants. For such is the honour that chains give a captive in God's quarrels that his room, whatsoever it be, is honourable, and his fetters adorn him more richly than any princely or imperial robes. St John Baptist was more honoured when he had achieved that title *John in chains* (Mt. 11. 2), than Mardochaeus with Assuerus' royal garments (Est. 6), more glorious than Solomon in his costly habit (3 Kgs 10), and more adorned than Herod when in his gorgeous attire he usurped the part of God (Ac. 12).

Yea, think not only what pomp emperors or worldly

potentates have shown in gold, jewels or any ornaments of highest price, but also what they might have shown had they been able to execute all their desires. Yet it can still be said with St Chrysostom : *I am ashamed to compare riches or the pureness of gold with such chains.* [6]

It was a great prerogative to be an apostle, a doctor or an evangelist. It was a singular favour to be rapt into paradise and to the third heaven and to hear secrets that it is not lawful for man to speak. It was a rare privilege to heal any disease, not only with the touch of hands, but with the touch of handkerchiefs and girdles. Yet, as St Chrysostom well understandeth, none of these rare privileges is so great as martyrdom. He saith, *Marvellous things were these, but not like to those others: they cast him into prison, whipped with many stripes.* [7] And this St Paul himself seemed to acknowledge in his letter to Philemon, where he omitteth his usual style of *Paul an Apostle* or *Servant of Jesus Christ* and beginneth his epistle with *Paul a prisoner of Jesus Christ.* In this he seemeth to follow the custom of great personages, who when they are enhanced from inferior dignities to more honourable titles, they always in their letters omit their other and set down their principal style, proper to their new achieved preferment.

But now to speak of the highest glory which men chiefly esteem. What place is there more acceptable than heaven? What seat more to be desired than the throne on God's right hand? What company is there comparable to the fellowship of angels? What dignity so great as that of the celestial spirits who have their room next unto God? And yet St Chrysostom thought St Paul's prison a worthier place; his clogs and chains, worthier seats; his fellow captives, more honourable company; and the state of Christ's prisoner, a more surpassing dignity. And if you ask the cause, he will answer that it is more glorious to a stout soldier, more pleasant to a true lover, to suffer for their Captain and labour in service of their love than to be honoured by him. *I account it more honourable*, saith he, *to be troubled for Christ, than to be honoured by Christ*. For if Christ, becoming man, stripped himself of his majesty, and thought it not so honourable to be in his glory as to hang upon the cross for us, how much more ought we to deem it a singular preferment to suffer for his sake? The apostles greatly rejoiced that they were vouchsafed this honour. *They went rejoicing from the presence of the council, because they were thought worthy to suffer reproach for the name of Jesus* (Ac. 5. 41). But we never read, that they so rejoiced at their power over devils, their gift of miracles, or other especial favours. This well declareth how they prized their persecution more than their authority. And therefore Christ said, *Blessed are you*, not for commanding devils, nor for raising the dead, or healing the lame, or working of infinite wonders, but: *You are blessed when men hate you and persecute you and speak all the evil they can against you for my sake* (Mt. 5. 11).

But if it were a blessedness to work wonders, then the chains of Christ also were able to make us blessed. What greater miracles than for chains that are fast bound to unloose (Ac. 16. 26); for those that have their hands manacled and their feet fettered to shake the foundations of the prison, to open locked and fast-barred doors without key or other material instrument; to unchain not only the fast-bound bodies but the enthralled and captive souls? What stranger thing than the same chain that bindeth the body in earth to bind the soul to God in heaven; to make a prison of miscreants a Church of Christians; and the nest of vipers a nursery of saints? What greater wonder than gaolers to desire to be unbound by their chained captives, and yield themselves voluntary prisoners to those whom they violently kept in durance?

And if these seem small matters, consider what reverence the very senseless and unreasonable creatures bear unto Christ's chains. The viper durst not sting the hand of St Paul bound by those chains (Ac. 28). Neither tempest, storm, sea nor shipwreck could drown those passengers whom these chains defended (Ac. 27). How did Felix tremble and quake at chained Paul's speeches (Ac. 24)? How much were others heartened and comforted by the force of his fetters (Ac. 27)? How many did he bring to Christ while he was bound for him, glorying that these converts seemed so much the fairer because they were bred in his captivity (Phil. 1)?

What prisoner for God's cause would not cry with David: *My bands fell off to my great glory* (Ps. 15. 6)? Who would not willingly hearken to those comfortable speeches that exhort us to embrace the chains of wisdom, that is to embrace the chains of Christ who is the wisdom of his Father? *Put thy feet into her* [*Wisdom's*] *fetters and thy neck into her chains; set under her thy shoulder and her fetters will be unto thee a fortress of strength, and foundations of virtue, and her chains a stole of glory. For the beauty of life is in her, and her gyves are bands of salvation* (Ecclus 6. 25, 26, 30, 31).

Where did Joseph begin to be a decipherer of dreams, a searcher of secret interpretations, but in prison (Gen. 40)? Where did Jeremiah prophesy most boldly and truly the overthrow of his enemies, but in prison (Jer. 33)? Where did Samson recover his strength and victoriously revenge himself upon the Philistines, killing more at his death than in his life, but *when he was brought forth of prison to play before them* (Jg. 16. 25)? Manasses, a most wicked idolator and an impious king, was never converted until he was a captive (2 Par. 33). Jonas came not to full knowledge of his fault, but when he was imprisoned in the whale's belly (Jon. 2). Joseph's brethren never entered into consideration of their offence in betraying him, but when they were kept in restraint (Gen. 44).

So we see how prison is a school of divine and hidden mysteries to God's friends, a fountain of revenge against his enemies, and a cell of repentance to careless offenders. O how true a saying is that: *In the bands of Adam will I draw them unto me, and in the chains of charity* (Os. 11. 4). How truly may they be called chains of charity and love that have not only force to appease the justice and stir up the mercy of God, but even have power to suppress and bridle the inflexible enmity that nature hath engrafted! Who could live untouched among hungry lions, but a Daniel who was God's prisoner (Dan. 6)? Who could walk in the midst of flames without burning, but such as were bound and should have been burned in God's quarrel (Dan. 3)?

These prisoners of God Basil compareth to a stone called Amianthon, which, by its nature, becometh in the fire as bright as a fire-coal but when it is taken out is clearer than before and cannot be in any way stained or defiled.[8] For their bodies were not only purged as gold but were more than gold, since they were not even solved and came purer out of the furnace than when they were cast in. These are they that are visited by angels, as St Peter was (Ac. 12); fed by prophets as Daniel was (Dan. 14); honoured by heavenly light and earthquakes, as St Paul and St Silas were (Ac. 16). Of these it is verified, that *from prison, gyves and chains, they come out to a kingdom* (Eccl. 4. 14), as did Joseph and Daniel. Joseph was made lord of all Egypt (Gen. 39), and Daniel was again made one of the three chiefs under Darius. Both were, from the thrall of the dungeon, advanced to the throne of princely dignity.

In these have all we afflicted Catholics our chief confidence, hoping that their chains will plead for us, their prisons protect us, and their prayers obtain us some end of our miseries. We doubt not, but *Our Lord hath looked from heaven into earth, that he might hear the groans of the chained in prison* (Ps. 101. 20). We assure ourselves, that *Our Lord hath heard the poor, and hath not neglected those chained for him* (Ps. 68. 34). And therefore we daily cry, *let the groans of thy prisoners enter into thy sight* (Ps. 78. 11).

Wherefore be not you dismayed, but rather take comfort in your present estate. If you be despised by the bad, you are honoured of the good. If you be disgraced of men, you may right well look for your praise from God. St John Baptist was always worthy of honour, for his rough habit, his hard diet, his innocent life, his high function and great prerogatives; yet so long as he was at liberty, and the people were admiring his life and reverencing his person, we hear no great mention of him made by Christ. But when as soon as he became *John in chains*, fallen into worldly disgrace though preferred to this Christian honour, the Captain straightway sounded the soldier's renown, and God himself rehearsed the catalogue of his divine praises (Mt. 11). These were so

127

great that they could never have been worthily enough rehearsed by man's tongue; yet they were never so worthy to be uttered by Christ's own mouth as when they had their chief complement and perfection, which was the honour of his chains.

Now let the captives of the world flatter themselves with the vain title of liberty. Let them triumph in their chains of gold, in their jewels of pearl and precious stone, in their gorgeous and stately robes. Let them boast of their freedom, when every thread and ornament about them is a manifest mark of their captivity; when, I say, their tongues are enthralled to potentates' ears, their actions and all their behaviour framed to the liking of great personages' eyes, their sense, bodies and minds servile to their own sensualities.

These captives of the world, St Chrysostom noteth, are like kings who are taken captive by a barbarous prince. The prince, for his own glory and for their greater ignominy, suffereth them to keep on their princely robes and to wear their crowns, and, in this attire, forceth them to most base and servile offices.[9] For so these men, though on the one side by their bravery they seem of great might and at large liberty, yet on the other, if you consider their most base and fitting slavish actions and their daily drudgery in sin, you cannot but realize that, enthralled in so heavy a bondage, they are the more miserable for their apparent glory.

Lightning often leaveth the velvet and costly scabbard whole, but consumeth the more worthy thing, which is the sword, which can easily be perceived by the lightness of the scabbard. In the same way the pernicious fire-flash of sin leaveth the body and goods sound and impaireth not the outward state, but killeth the soul and leaveth it dead, which can easily be perceived by the gaudy lightness of a man's outward behaviour.

Let us not yield to such folly but rather rejoice in our enclosure. Let us glory in our bands, remembering that the longer we wear them the more honour we shall purchase by them, and the better we like them the more benefit we shall reap of them. *The man that suffereth once*, saith St Cyprian, *hath but one victory, but he that always dwelling in pain, doth encounter with sorrow, and is still not conquered, is every day crowned.*[10]

And again, *Blessed are those amongst you*, saith the same saint, *who remain in prison, for by the lingering of your torments you will proceed to more ample titles of merit, and will have as many rewards in the heavenly payment as the days you have in present pains.* These are the true ornaments for Christians to boast of. This captivity is our principal freedom, and the prisons are ports where God harboureth us here, and from whence he conveyeth us unto the shore of eternal felicity. Of this saith St Cyprian: *They have put shackles upon your feet and have bound your happy members, the temples of God, with infamous chains, as though the spirit could be bound with the body, or your gold could be stained with the contagion of their iron.*[11]

But comfort yourselves and think this entreaty no hard usage; howbeit it proceedeth of a malicious hatred in them. For, *to men consecrated unto God, and professing their faith with religious virtue, these are not chains but ornaments: neither do they fetter Christian feet to their infamy, but honour them to their crown and glory.*[12] Of this did Solomon forewarn us, showing us the protection and care that God hath of those that suffer for him, and how glorious an estate they be in. *He descended with him into the pit and forsook him not in his chains, till he brought him a sceptre of a kingdom and power against those that did oppress him: and showed them liars that did defame him, and gave unto him an eternal glory* (Wis. 10. 13–14).

Remember, therefore, the goal, and you shall comfortably pass over the race. Regard not so much where you are as where you shall be. Think not so much of the comforts that you want as of the wager that you win. Grieve not at the company from which you are barred but rejoice in that for which you are prepared, and assure yourselves that how few soever you see, yet you to whom Christ and his angels have continual access are not alone. *He is not alone*, saith St Cyprian, *who hath Christ for his fellow; he is not alone, who keeping the temple of God undefiled, is never without God wheresoever he be*.[13]

Finally, let us consider that our life is but a warfare, and we are always in the field against our professed enemies, for in our baptism we bid them battle by defying and renouncing them. Since the times be such, that those who stick to the truth are in a manner designed to the slaughter house, we can truly say, *For thy sake we are mortified all the day, and are accounted as sheep for the butchery* (Ps. 43. 23).

Considering these things let us take our prison as a place of preparation and as a private school of exercise to train and instruct us for public, serious and most sharp affrays. For, as Tertullian saith, it is not for the advantage or behoof of a valiant soldier to come from disports to bloody strokes, or from the carpet to the camp; but it is necessary to be hardened first in rough entreaty of themselves, in hard usage and toilsome travails.[14] They should learn in peace to digest the disasters and incommodities of war, and by these forerunning labours inure their bodies to unease and foster the courage and prowess of their minds.

Happy therefore are you, what troubles soever you sustain for the exercise of your virtue and better enabling both of body and mind. Such was the preparation of the champions and soldiers of proof in former ages. They were restrained of liberty, withheld from chamber works, straitened in their diet from sweetmeats and pleasant drinks. The more they were laboured, the better they approved, and the more they were turmoiled in trouble, the more hope they had of victory. They knew that virtue and constancy gathereth force with hardness and rigour and doth languish and fall to ruin with softness and ease. This they did for a corruptible crown, which they were neither certain to attain nor sure to possess. We therefore, aiming at an incorruptible reward, let us reckon prison a place of trial, that we may be brought unto judgment well fortified against all encounters and be able to say unto the Judge that, *as much fear and terror as he brought, so much force and fortitude hath he found*.[15]

THE NINTH CHAPTER
The ninth cause of Comfort in Tribulation is that death itself is comfortable to the good

AND now to draw to the end of your conflict, for your final comfort I put you in mind of a most comfortable thing. If you be put to death in the cause of the Catholic faith, your death is martyrdom and your foil victory. And therefore, since we must die, let us, as St Cyprian saith, embrace this happy occasion, *to pass over our mortal end with the reward of immortality, neither let us fear to be killed, who by being killed are sure to be crowned*.[1] Death of itself is not so odious to the good because we have infinite motives to wish it rather than to eschew it, and to desire it rather than to fear it.

Sweet, saith St Chrysostom,[2] is the end to the labourers; willingly doth the traveller question about his inn; often thinketh the hireling when his year will come out; the husbandman always looketh for the time of his harvest; the merchant is still busy about his bills to know the day of payment; and the woman great with child is ever musing upon the time of her delivery. No less comfort it is to God's servants to think of their decease, seeing that there is their heart where they have hoarded their treasure. For, as St Bernard noteth, where the conscience is clear, *death is looked for without fear, yea, desired with delight and accepted with devotion*.[3]

To us it killeth our most dangerous and domestical

enemy. It breaketh the locks, unlooseth the chains and openeth the door to let us out of loathsome prison (Ps. 141. 8). It unloadeth us of a cumbersome burden which oppresseth our soul (Wis. 9. 15). Who would not willingly be out of the way of fortune and rid of the infinite hazards and perils of daily casualties? Who would not be glad to settle his soul in security out of this dangerous sea, wherein, as St Bernard saith, *the rareness of those that pass over safe and the multitude of others that perish in their passage sufficiently proveth the peril?* In the ocean sea, of four ships not one doth miscarry, but in the sea of this world, of many fours not one is saved.

This world is the kingdom of Satan; what servant of God can love to live in it? It is a place of banishment, and who is so unnatural as not willingly to forsake it? Can any choose always to hang in hazard rather than once to fall for his felicity? Can any desire to live in the gunshot of the devil's assaults rather than to enjoy the port of assured security?

We are promised that here we shall be persecuted, and hated by the world, that we shall weep and live in sorrow, that we shall be despised and put to shame, and have neither rest of body nor perfect contentment of mind. We are assured, on the other side, that in the next life our reward is great, our repose without trouble and our comfort without cross. Our tears shall be turned into triumph, our disgrace into glory, all our miseries into perfect felicity (Jn 16). Who therefore would not rejoice quickly to die: seeing that death is the passage from this world to the next, from all present aggrievances to all possible happiness?

Well may the brute beasts fear death, whose end of life is the conclusion of their being. Well may the epicure tremble who with his life looketh to lose his felicity. Well may the infidels, heretics or unrepentant sinners quake, whose death is the beginning of their damnation. Such as here have their heaven and who have made this prison their paradise, whose belly was their god and their appetites their guides, may with reason rue their death, seeing they have no portion in the land of the living. They have sown in sin and what can they look to reap but misery? Vanities were their traffic and grief will be their gain. Detestable was their life, and damnable will be their decease. Of such it is verified: *O death, how bitter is thy remembrance to a man that has planted his peace and contentment in his worldly substance* (Ecclus. 41. 1)!

For indeed, most miserable is the sinner's decease. *But precious is the death of saints in the sight of our Lord* (Ps. 115. 15). Here they have their pain and in heaven they look for their payment. Here they have sown in tears and there they shall reap in joy (Ps. 125. 5). Their judge is he for whom they have suffered, and therefore doubtless will be merciful. Their accusers are made dumb by their former repentance and therefore cannot be prejudicial. Their conscience is cleared by humble confession and therefore cannot be fearful. Hope is their staff to keep them from sliding. Righteousness is their safe-conduct to warrant them from arrest. Grace is their guide to keep them from erring. Their wounds and sufferings in God's cause are wards to assure them of comfortable entertainment. Their frays and wrestlings against their own passions are badges of perfection and will find free access. Finally, the hell that they have passed here will ensure for them a crown in heaven.

They are goodly fruit, more fit for the golden plate and king's table than to hang longer on a rotten bough. They are pleasant and sweet roses more worthy to be honoured in the prince's hand than left upon a thorny stalk. Yea, they are glorious rubies, rather to be set in the crown of glory than here to be trodden under foot by dirty swine. What can they see in this world to detain them?

They run, saith St Chrysostom,[4] for a great wager and not *quasi in incertum*. They regard not whether the way be green and pleasant or rough and miry. They weigh not who seeth them, nor what they say of them. Though they be reviled, they stay not to answer. Though they be stricken, they stand not to revenge. Though their house burn, their wife complain, their children cry, they turn not back to bemoan them. Their mind is wholly on the wager; if they run not, they win not, and therefore their only joy is to come soonest to their goal.

If they look upon the world, they see it like a sea where many trusting to the waves are drowned, others are beaten with the billows against the stony rocks, divers labour to attain divers shores, some by help of a weak plank, some by some fragment of the broken ship. They see many forced to help themselves with only their hands, and many others, overcome with the surges, to have yielded up the ghost and left a multitude of dead carcasses to the water's rage. They see that they themselves are also tired with the smallest storms, and that their hold is very fickle. Therefore, what greater comfort can befall them than to be quickly landed in a safe port? There, beholding the perils they have escaped, they can rejoice the more at their attained security.

David, describing this tedious voyage or navigation of God's servants through this stormy sea, showeth how eager and desirous they were to be delivered out of the same

(Ps. 106*). *They*, saith he, *descend into the sea* of this life, *in the ships* of their mortal bodies, *doing their work in many waters* of worldly afflictions. True it is that *they see* the merciful *works of our Lord* in cherishing them, *and his marvels in* confirming them: but all this they see *in the depth* of their distresses. *He spoke and the spirit of tempest rose up* in their persecutors, *and the waves* of adversity *were raised high* against them. *They mount as high as heaven and fall as low as hell*, and amaze them so for the time that *their life pineth away in miseries*. For *they are tossed and made to stagger like a drunken man* with the continual variety of new surges and griefs, *and all their wisdom* in patiently suffering and firmly hoping for God's help is swallowed up, and seemingly unprofitable against their enemies' rage. And therefore, *they cried unto our Lord, when they were distressed* in this dangerous manner, and desired to have a short cut to their voyage's end. They esteemed it a singular benefit that *he led them* by death *out of their distresses, and altered their storm into a calm wind, and guided them to the haven that they wished for*, that is, the haven of security, in which most of them desired to be.

If we consider the poor, their life is led in such agony, pain and neediness that every one must loathe it. If we behold the rich and mighty, their felicity is folly and their joy is vanity. If we look on potentates who seem the very flower of mankind, we find oftentimes that they are poor in their riches, abject in their honours and discontented in their delights. Their bodies are sacks of dung; their souls, sinks of sin; miserable their birth, wicked their life and damnable their end.

Look, says St Augustine, *into the graves, survey all the em-*

* The words in italics in the remainder of this paragraph are taken from this Psalm.

perors, dukes, states and worthies of former ages, and see who was master, who man; who rich, or who poor. Discern, if thou canst, the captive from the king, the strong from the weak, the fair from the deformed.[5] These words import that, if after life there is no more difference of persons than there is in the ashes of velvet and coarse canvas or of divers woods burnt up in one fire, it surely is folly to care for these bodies or to desire their long continuance. For in the end they must be resolved into earth and dust and cannot live here without a multitude of cumbers as we find almost in every other thing. And therefore after having perused all the miseries of our life, we may think it a great benefit of God that whereas there is but one way to come into this world, yet there are very many to go out of the same.

What can there be in life, either durable or very delightsome, when life itself is so frail and fickle a thing? Our life, saith the Scriptures, is like *the print of a cloud in the air*, like *a mist dissolved by the sun* (Wis. 2. 3), like *the passing of a shadow*, like *a flower that soon fadeth* (Ps. 102. 15), like *a dry leaf carried with every wind* (Job. 13. 25), like *a vapour that soon vanisheth out of sight* (Jas 4. 14). St Chrysostom calleth it one time a heavy sleep, fed with false and imaginary dreams;[6] another time he calleth it a comedy[7] (although in our days it is rather a tragedy of transitory shows and disguised persons). Sometimes he calleth it a bird's nest made of straw and dung that the winter soon dissolved.[8] St Gregory Nazianzen likeneth it to the child's game of building houses of sand on the shore where every wave washeth them away;[9] yea, and as Pindar saith, it is no more but the dream of a shadow. It passeth away like one that *rideth in post*; like a ship in the sea that leaveth no print of the passage; like a bird in the air of whose way there remaineth no remembrance;

like an arrow that flieth to the mark, whose track the air suddenly closeth up (Wis. 5. 12). Whatsoever we do, whether we sit, stand, sleep or wake, our ship, saith St Basil, always saileth towards our last home, and the stern of our life keepeth on an inflexible course.[10]

Every day we die, and hourly lose some part of our life; even when we grow, we decrease. We have lost our infancy, our childhood, our youth and all till this present day. What time soever passeth, perisheth. And this very day death secretly by minutes purloineth from us. This St Gregory well expresseth, saying: *Our living is a passing from life: for our life with her increase diminisheth, and by that always impaireth, whereby it seemeth to profit.*[11] Future things, saith Innocent, are always beginning, present things always ending and things past are quite dead and done.[12] For while we live, we die, and when we leave living, then we leave dying. Better therefore it is to die to life than to live to death, because our mortal life is nothing but a living death, and life continually flieth from us and cannot be withheld and death hourly cometh upon us and cannot be withstood. No armour resisteth, no threatening prevaileth, no entreaty profiteth against death's assault. If our life be spared despite all other peries and chances, yet time and age in the end will consume it.

We see the flood that riseth in the top of a mountain fall and roll down with a continual noise; it gusheth out with a hollow and hoarse sound, then it runneth roaring down other craggy and rough cliffs; it is continually crushed and broken with divers encounters till at the foot of the hill it entereth into the sea. And so fareth it with man's life, he cometh into the world with pain, beginneth his course with pitiful cries and is continually molested with divers vexations; he never ceaseth running down till in the end he fall into the sea of death. Neither is our last hour the beginning of our death but the conclusion; for then is come what hath been long in the coming, and fully finished what was still in the ending. Why therefore should we be unwilling to lose that which cannot be kept? Better it is, since death is debt and nature's necessary wreck, to follow St Chrysostom's counsel: *Let us make voluntarily that which must needs be necessary, and let us offer to God for a present that which of due and debt we are bound to render.*[13]

What marvel if, when the wind bloweth, the leaf fall; if, when the day appeareth, the night end? Our life, saith the same Saint, was a shadow, and it passed; it was a smoke, and it vanished; it was a bubble, and it was dissolved; it was a spider's web, and it was shaken asunder.[14] No wise man lamenteth that he lived not a year sooner than he was born, so why should he lament that within a year or less he shall live no longer? For he loseth nothing that he then had, and he shall be to the world but as he then was. God made Adam's garment of dead beasts' skins (Gen. 3. 21), to put him in mind that he was condemned to die and to make the remembrance of death so familiar to him that the loss of life might not affright him since he would always carry the livery of death upon him.

And as Daniel, by spreading ashes in the Temple, discovered the treachery and falsehood of the priests of Babylon (Dan. 14*), so we, by pondering our thoughts and

---

* Daniel, in order to prove that the God Bel did not eat the food laid out for him, scattered ashes, which showed the footprints of Bel's priests who came by night to eat the food.

memory with the dust of our grave, and by frequent repetition of our decease, shall soon realize that the vanity of this life, the trains of the devil and our secret temptations are such that we would rather wish to cut them off by losing life than to continue them by avoiding death.

If anything makes death tedious, it is the want of consideration of it. The old men have it right before them, the young men hard behind them, all men daily over them, and yet we forget it. Familiarity with lions taketh away the fear of them. Experience of tempests giveth heart and courage to endure them. And in war, the soldier, seeing so many hourly bereaved of life, setteth little or nothing by it. If therefore we wish to be out of all fear of death, let us continually remember it. If we make our horse used to the race before we run for the wager, if we acquaint ourselves with the weapons before we fight for the victory, much more should we take heed that we come not unprovided to this last combat.

The good pilot when he guideth his ship sitteth at the stern; and so the provident Christian, to direct his life, must always sit at the end of the same; the mindfulness of death being his stern, he may fear it the less and provide for it the better. This is the door whereby we must go out of bondage. As the prisoner that waiteth for his delivery taketh greatest comfort in sitting upon the threshold so that when the door is opened he may the sooner get out, so ought we always to have our mind fixed upon the last step of our life, over which we are sure that we must pass, though how or when, we know not. For this cause that holy man, John the Almoner, Patriarch of Alexandria, commanded that his tomb, which was being built, should be left imperfect, and that his servants should put him in mind every day to finish the same, so that, having his eye always fixed upon this door of death, he might the better prepare for the passage through it.

After the fire of virtue has been raked up, the memory of death is the ashes which continue the better and are the fitter to enkindle the courage of our mind so that when death cometh indeed and these ashes are unraked, we may rather rejoice that our flame hath found a vent to mount to her natural sphere, where it will shine to our glory, than have sorrow that it parteth out of the chimney of our flesh, where it was in danger to be quenched with our iniquity.

It was not without cause that God likened death to a thief. For the thief, when he findeth the man of the house watching and upon his guard, saluteth him in courteous sort and acteth the part of a friend; but if he find him asleep, he cruelly murdereth him and robbeth his treasury. So death is very comfortable to those that are prepared for it, and only terrible to those that sleep in sin and are careless of their end.

To these belongeth that saying: *The death of the sinner is worst* (Ps. 33. 22*). It is evil because it severeth from the world; worse, because it severeth from the body; and worst of all, because it severeth from God; for they make the world their paradise, their body their god and God their enemy. To such death is hateful, for they are tormented with the pangs of the dying flesh, amazed with the fits and corrosives of the mind, frighted with the terror of the future and grieved with remorse of the past. They are stung with the gnawing of a guilty conscience, discomforted with

---

* *Mors peccatorum pessima*. R. S. has translated *pessima* as worst, but also takes the sense *evil* in his commentary.

the rigour of a severe judge and annoyed with the thought of their loathsome sepulchre. And thus, though death of itself be not bitter, yet is it bitter to the wicked.

Yet, as St Ambrose noteth, even to them is life more bitter than death. For more grievous is the living to sin than the dying in sin. For the wicked man, while he liveth, increaseth his offence, and when he dieth offendeth no more. Therefore by his life he augmenteth his torments, and by his death he abridgeth them. It is the fear of death that is terrible, and it is not indeed so grievous to die as to live in perpetual fear and expectation of death. *For he that feareth God shall make a good end, and in the day of his decease he shall be blessed* (Ecclus. 1. 13). *And happy are the dead henceforth that die in our Lord. They shall rest from their labours*, saith the spirit, *for their works do follow them* (Apoc. 14. 13). The noonday light shall rise unto them at the evening of their life, and when they think themselves quite consumed, they shall rise as bright as a day-star (Job 11. 17).

As St Augustine saith, because they desire to be loosed and to be with Christ they endure to live with patience and are ready to die with joy. They fear not death because they feared God in life; they fear not death because they rather feared life; and an evil death is but the effect of an evil life. Their life was a study how to die well and they knew that since death passed through the veins of life, it lost the bitterness of death and took the taste and sweetness of life. Neither are they amazed with the foregoing gripes* and extremities, because they take them as the throbs of childbirth by which our soul is born out of this loathsome body and brought forth to an eternal felicity. They fear not the

* *gripes*: spasms, pangs.

devils whom they have stoutly resisted. They have confidence in God whose wrath they have appeased with repentance. The horror of the grave doth nothing move them because they do but sow therein a carnal and corruptible body to reap the same in the resurrection incorruptible and spiritual. This made Simeon so joyfully sing: *Now thou dost release thy servant, O Lord, according to thy word in peace* (Lk. 2. 29). This made St Hilarion so confidently say unto his soul: *Depart, why fearest thou? Depart, O my soul, why doubtest thou? Almost threescore and ten years hast thou served Christ, and fearest thou death?*[15] This made St Ambrose on his death-bed give this answer to those that wished him longer life: *I have not so lived that I am ashamed to live amongst you, neither fear I to die because we have a good Lord.*[16] This made a bishop, St Augustine's familiar friend, say, when his flock seemed unwilling to see him die, *If I should never die, well; but if ever, why not now?*[17] These saints knew that death is but God's officer to summon before him whom he meaneth to call. They thought it an unchristian part to gainsay in deeds that which they prayed every day in words. For every day the Christian saith, *thy will be done*, and how preposterous a thing is it, saith St Cyprian, when God's will is that we depart, not willingly to obey him?[18] If we repine and grudge against his pleasure, do we not follow the guise of stubborn and evil-deserving servants who cannot without sorrow and grief be brought before their master? Do we not go enforced by mere necessity rather than with any remonstrance of good will or duty? And can we, for shame, desire a man to be honoured with eternal rewards when he can hardly be entreated to come and receive them, or to enjoy for ever the glory of God's presence when he shunneth the door whereby we must enter into it? Well might those words be repeated to us, which in St Cyprian's time were said in a visit to one that lay a-dying: *You are unwilling to suffer in the world, loath to depart out of the world, what should I do unto you?*[19] A worthy rebuke to those that are loath to die.

The chased hart, to avoid the greedy hounds, flieth oftentimes to the hunter's protection, and though pursued by him, yet by nature hath trust in his mercy. One enemy sometimes findeth favour at another enemy's hand, where he least looked for it. Why then should a dutiful child fear to go to his heavenly Father, a penitent soul to his sweet Saviour, an obedient member to be joined with his head? If he came into this world to redeem us, why should we doubt that at our death he will receive us; especially if we die for him as he died for us? He that accepteth his enemies, will he reject his friends? And he that bought us so dear, will he refuse his penny-worth? If he affect our company so much in earth, that he said: *my delight is to be with the children of men* (Prov. 8. 31), hath he now so forgotten his old love as not to admit us to his company in heaven? He came hither to buy us an inheritance, and he went from hence to prepare it for us, and when we are to enter into possession will he exclude us? Who can imagine that he who is contented here to be our food and to abase his majesty to enter into our soul, dwelling in this cottage of clay and unpleasant dungeon, that he, I say, will not in our chiefest need be our friend and advance our departing soul to the comfort of his presence? Can he that hath been our guide and guardian all the way forsake and shake us off in the end of our journey? No, no, *the eyes of our Lord are upon those that fear him . . . that he may deliver their souls from death* (Ps. 32. 18–19).

Let us remember his love in adopting, his truth in promising, his power in performing, and our fear of death will be soon altered into desire of the same. He came to open heaven's gate, and what meant he but that we should enter in? He came to earth to invite us unto him, and why departed he from earth but to have us follow him? Finally, he abandoneth none, but is abandoned by them: he is easily found where he hath been carefully sought. He is most ready to crown the victorious conqueror. All which considered, we may well say, with St Ambrose, *that death to the good is a quiet haven, and to the bad may be counted a shipwreck.*[20]

THE TENTH CHAPTER

The tenth cause of Comfort in Tribulation is that
the violent death and foregoing torments are
tolerable in a good cause

NEITHER let the violence of death nor the multitude
of torments affright us. We have but one life, and
but one can we lose: Goliath (1 Kgs 17) was as
much hurt by David's little stone as Samson (Jg. 16) by the
weight of a whole house. And Heli (1 Kgs 4) had as much
harm by falling backwards in his chair as Jezabel (4 Kgs 9) by
being thrown down from a high window. And all they that
stoned St Stephen (Ac. 7) to death took no more from him
than an ordinary sickness did from Lazarus (Jn 11) and doth
daily from us all.

One death is no more death than another, and the easiest
as well as the hardest taketh our life from us. A glorious
martyr of our days,* executed for the Catholic Faith in
Wales, well understood this point. When the sentence of
his condemnation was read—that he should be drawn upon
a hurdle to the place of execution, then hanged till he was
half dead, afterwards unbowelled, his head cut off, his body
quartered, his quarters boiled, and set up in such and such
places—he turned unto the people, and with a smiling
countenance, said: *And all this is but one death.*

Yet if the foregoing torments daunt our constancy, let us

* Blessed Richard Gwyn, one of the forty martyrs whose cause for
canonization has been resumed, was martyred at Wrexham on 15 October
1584.

consider what we are, what we avoid, what we look for, and whom we serve. We are Christians, and ought to have more valour than heathens. By short punishments we avoid eternal and more grievous afflictions; with small conflicts we purchase unspeakable glory; we suffer for a God that hath suffered more for us. Let us but consider what men have suffered for false gods, for the devil and for vainglory, and we shall think our torments the more tolerable. Tertullian[1] writeth of a courtesan called Leœna, who tired of her tormentors, in the end spat her tongue in the tyrant's face that she might also spit out her voice and so be unable to betray her accomplices, though violence should chance to make her willing.

It was the fashion amongst the Lacedemonians for choice young gentlemen to offer themselves to be whipped before the altars of their false gods, while their own parents exhorted them to constancy, thinking so much honour gained to their houses as they shed blood; yea, and accounting it greater glory that their life should yield and depart from their body rather than their body yield or depart from the lashes.* The history of Mutius Scaevola† is known, whose constancy Seneca commended saying: Contemptuous both of his enemy and of flames, he watched his hand melting in his enemies' fire until, against his will, an order was given that the fire should be taken from him. I reckon this a much greater thing because it is rarer to conquer an enemy with a maimed than with an armed hand.

* R. S. here refers to the custom of scourging youths before the altar of Artemis Orthia.

† Caius Mutius Scaevola, a noble Roman, who, having failed to kill Lars Porsena, was reputed to have held his right hand in a fire to show his indifference to flames.

It was an ordinary pastime amongst the Romans for men to shew sport in wrestling and to strive with lions and other wild beasts for a vain proof and boast of their valour. They esteemed the print of brutish tusks glorious ornaments, the ravages of bloody claws badges of honour, and their comeliness increased with the number of scars. St Cyprian,[2] speaking of them, saith: *What meaneth that, I pray thee, what thinkest thou of it, that they [the Romans], whom no man condemned, cast themselves to wild beasts, and they persons of ripe age, of comely feature, gorgeously attired, who living adorned themselves for a voluntary funeral, and gloried (poor wretches) in their own miseries?*

But why need I reckon profane examples, though indeed they ought to move us so much the more, in that these men suffered more for a puff of vainglory than we do for eternal felicity? We want not glorious examples of our own saints in our own cause. And because the particulars are infinite, I will set down only some general speeches of their torments. Cyprian, speaking to a persecutor, saith: *The innocent, just and dearest unto God, thou thrustest out of their houses, thou spoilest of their patrimony, thou loadest with chains, thou lockest in prisons, thou devourest with wild beasts, swords and fire. Thou usest long torments in dismembering their bodies, thou multipliest variety of punishments in tearing out their bowels. Neither is thy barbarousness content with usual torturings; thy witty cruelty deviseth new pains.*[3] And in another place, speaking of the martyrs, he saith: *The tormented stood stronger than the tormentors, and the beaten and torn members overcame the beating and tearing hooks. The cruel and often double scourging could not conquer their unconquerable faith, though they were brought to such a pass that the tormentor had no whole nor sound parcel of*

limbs, but only gory wounds whereupon to continue his cruelty.[4]
Arnobius speaking to the persecutors saith: *You with your
flames, banishments, torments and beasts, wherewith you rend and
rack our bodies, do not bereave us of our lives, but only rid us of
a weak and sorry skin.*[5] *You put us*, saith Tertullian, *upon gallows and stakes, you tear our sides with forks. We are beheaded,
thrown to the wild beasts, and condemned to toil in the metal
mines.*[6]

Not inferior to these were the torments of the fathers
of the Old Testament, of which St Paul speaketh, saying:
*Others were racked, not accepting release that they might find a
better resurrection. And others had trial of mockeries and stripes:
moreover also of bonds and prisons. They were stoned, they were
hewed, they were tempted, they died in the slaughter of the sword,
they went about in sheepskins, in goatskins, needy, in distress,
afflicted, of whom the world was not worthy, wandering in deserts,
in mountains, in dens and caves of the earth* (Heb. 11).
And of these torments of martyrs, all historiographers do
make so often and such large mention that there can hardly
be devised any kind of cruelty that they reckon not amongst
the passions of God's saints. Nor are there fewer who have,
besides torments, endured most valiantly the last brunt of
death, thinking themselves most happy when they had
obtained any means to depart this life.

Lucretia sheathed her knife in her own bowels to make
her chastity renowned. Empedocles threw himself into
Aetna's flames to make his memory eternal. Peregrinus
burnt himself on a pile of wood, thinking thereby to live for
ever in men's remembrance. Ashdrubal's wife, at the surprising of Carthage, rather chose to burn out her eyes and
yield her body to her country's flames than to behold her

husband's misery and become herself her enemies' prey. Regulus, a captain of the Romans, rather than ransom his own life with the death of many, was content to be rolled in a hogshead sticked full of sharp nails. And Cleopatra suffered herself to be bitten and stung with most venomous vipers rather than be carried as captive in triumph.

Did not Saul and his esquire run upon their own swords to avoid the Philistines' rage (1 Kgs 31)? Did not Judas hang himself in desperation, to hasten his journey towards his deserved punishments (Mt. 27)? And yet all these with their death began their hell. They did for a vain humour what we are forced unto for God's cause. And, as Tertullian well noteth, *Not without cause hath our Lord permitted these examples in the world, but for our present exhortation and future confusion, if we be afraid to bear in truth for our salvation what others have desired for a vanity to their perdition.* [7]

Now, if I were to recite the glorious examples of those that have constantly died in a good cause, the number is so great, their courage so glorious, that it would require a whole treatise by itself. Consider the example of Abel who was cruelly murdered, Jeremy who was stoned, Isaias who was sawn asunder, and Zachary who was slain between the temple and the altar. Consider the courage of the Holy Innocents who have in their childish bodies shewn hoary and constant minds, and in that weakness of years been superiors to all tyrants' torments. Consider the tender and soft virgins, who being timorous by kind, and frail by sex, have nevertheless in God's quarrel altered their female relenting hearts into unfearful and hardy valour, and been better able to endure any outrage than their enemies to practise upon them. Consider the whole multitude and glorious host of martyrs, whose torments have been exquisite, bloody and with all kind of extremity, and yet their minds undaunted and strong, and their agonies always ended with triumph and victory.

And if all these examples be not forceable enough to make us unafraid of death, let us consider how many ways we may suffer casual mischances and sudden deaths without merit. *Those things*, saith Tertullian, *may benefit us, if they be constantly endured, which, whether we will or no, are incident unto us.*[8] How many unawares have been burnt up in their own houses, how many slaughtered by beasts in the fields, how many by the same devoured in cities? How many consumed in common pestilences, murdered by thieves, slain by their enemies? And even in our days how many see we not only desperately to venture in war, to run upon the swords, to contemn perils, to be lavish of their lives, but divers also forced against their wills to enter the same dangers, and to cast themselves away, and that oftentimes in unjust quarrels to the damnation of their souls? Finally, who is he that, maugre whatsoever he can do, may not suffer by misfortune that which he feareth to suffer in God's cause? Why therefore should we fear that which cannot be avoided?

The very necessity of death should make us not unwilling to die, when experience sheweth us mortal. Live well and die well, we may: but live long and not die, we cannot. We should not think our life shortened when it is well ended. He dieth old enough that dieth good; and life is better well lost than evil kept. We but go the way by the which all the world before us hath gone, and all that come after us shall follow; and at the same instant with us, thousands from all parts of the world shall bear us company. If we be taken away in the flower of our age, how could it be better bestowed than on him that gave it? And all our loss therein is concluded in this, that being passengers upon this worldly sea, we had a stronger gale to waft us sooner over to our desired port. If we die in this cause, our pitcher is broken over the fountain where the water is not lost but only returned thither from whence it was first taken. We are not in prison for theft or murder; when we are called out to die, we look beyond our present death. Our body is our hold, our death our delivery; when the jailor calleth, we have a clear conscience and fear not his threatening. If he menace death, he promiseth life, and his killing is our reviving.

It is a shame for a Christian to fear a blast of man's mouth, when he hath such invincible shores to support him, such as no man nor devil is able to overthrow. *Fearest thou man, O Christian*, saith Tertullian, *that art to be feared of the angels, for the very angels shalt thou judge; thou who art feared by the devils, for over the devils hast thou received authority; thou who art to be feared of the whole world, for in thee is the world to be judged?*[9] How often, for a point of honour, have we been ready to challenge our counterpeers into the field? How often have we, for our pleasure, used desperate and breakneck games, thinking it glory to contemn death for a bravery, and a stain on our courage to shew any cowardice in mortal hazards? Now therefore may Tertullian's words be well objected unto us: *Why grudgeth man to suffer for his remedy that which he grudgeth not to suffer upon a vanity? Displeaseth it him to be killed for his salvation, whom it displeased not to be killed for his perdition? And will he who gaped so wide to let in the poison be loath to receive the medicine?*[10]

Now ought we to renew that wonted courage, and be as careless of our lives when they are to be well spent, as we were when we should have spilt them for a vanity. When the devil led us in his service, he could, with a vain hope of praise, wean us from love of our lives. Shall we then think that God dealeth hardly, when, with so glorious rewards, he enticeth us from the same? Is death pleasant when the devil commandeth it, and is it uncomfortable when it is at God's appointment? For this very end hath God ordained martyrdom: that by whom man was wilfully foiled, him he should manfully foil again.[11]

In sin and heresy we were venturous and bold, or rather presumptuous and rash. When we were unarmed, naked, and without force, no terror could amaze or cool our audacity. Now that we are reclaimed to virtue and true religion, harnessed with God's grace, guarded under his banner, protected by his angels, and fortified by the prayers, sacraments and good works of the Church shall we be more fearful than we were without all these succours? We are allotted to a glorious combat, in which the comfort alone of our honourable lookers-on in heaven were enough to hearten us against all affronts. St Cyprian saith, *When we skirmish or fight in the quarrel of our faith, God beholdeth us, his angels behold us, and Christ looketh on. What a glorious dignity is it, how great a felicity to fight with God as ruler, and to be crowned by Christ as judge of the combat!*[12]

Let us therefore with our whole might arm ourselves, and prepare ourselves for this conflict. Let us put on the *breast-plate of justice* (Eph. 6. 14), so that our breast may be guarded against our enemies' darts. Let our feet be shod so that when we begin to walk upon the basilisk and adder, and to tread under foot the lion and the dragon, we be not by them stung and supplanted (Ps. 90. 13). Let us carry the shield of faith to repair us from our enemy's shot. Let us hide our head in the helmet of salvation, that our ears yield not to bloody menacings, our eyes detest heretical books and services, our forehead always keep the sign of the Cross, and our tongue be always ready to profess our faith. Let us arm our hand with the sword of God's spirit so that it refuses to subscribe to any unlawful action and defends only the true Catholic faith. Being thus armed with a pure mind and uncorrupted faith and sincerity of life, *let God's camp march to the battle that is bidden us: let them that persevere be armed lest they lose the benefit of their late standing: let the yielders be armed that they may recover the loss of their former falling: let honour to the constant, and remorse to the lapsed, be a spur to the skirmish.*[13]

It hath always been accounted, saith Tertullian,[14] a most worthy experience of combaters to put in trial the strength and agility of their bodies, and measure it by the multitude of commenders, having their reward for their goal, the assembly for their judge and the common verdict for their pleasure. The naked limbs bear away many wounds, the buffets make them stagger, the spurrings jostle them, the plummet staves rend them, the whips tear them, yet no man condemneth the captain of the conflict for exposing his champions to such violence. Complaints of injuries have no place in the field but every one marketh what reward is appointed for those galls, wounds and prints of the stripes, as the crowns, glory, stipend, public privileges, portraitures and graven images and such like monuments, wherewith the world doth (as it may) eternalize them with a certain perpetuity, and procure them a continual resurrection in their posterity's remembrance. *The champion himself complaineth not. He would not be deemed to feel any pain, because the crown covereth his wounds, the wager shroudeth his blood. Greater is his victory than his injury. Whom on the one hand you think sore, on the other you see not sorry.*[15]

How much more than the champion in his fight ought we to glory in our martyrdoms! Not only should we not condemn, but highly praise our heavenly Captain for exposing us to these bloody frays. The husbandman scattereth his corn in the earth, yea, he burieth it and covereth it in the furrows. He rejoiceth when the showers come to root it, the frost to nip it, the snow to lie over it. And yet he hath in that seed all his hope of gain. The rain moveth him not, when he thinketh on the harvest, nor the corrupting of the kernel, when he thinketh on the ripe ear of corn. Let us not therefore condemn our Husbandman for delighting in our passions. For well knoweth he that, *unless the kernel of wheat fall upon the ground and die, itself only remaineth* (Jn 12. 24). And therefore suffereth he these persecutions, because thereby, *he will multiply your seed, and augment the increases of the fruits of your justice* (2 Cor. 9. 10). Wherefore herein, *God's liberality appeareth more than his rigour. For whom he had drawn out of the devil's throat by faith, he would have to trample down by virtue, lest he should only have fled, not foiled his enemy. It pleased him, whom he called to salvation to invite unto glory, that we might not only rejoice as delivered, but also triumph as crowned.*[16]

If therefore, as St Chrysostom saith,[17] the storms and rage of the sea seem tolerable enough to the mariner, the winter and foul weather to the husbandman, the murders and wounds to the soldiers, the cruel blows and stripes to the combatant, all in the hope of a temporal and transitory reward, much more should all worldly miseries seem tolerable to us, in hope of heaven. Other kings and potentates never conquer without killing, never triumph without cruelty, never enjoy the pleasures of this life without the miseries of many men's deaths. But the soldiers of Christ are most honourable, not when they live in daintiness, pomp and majesty, not when they murder impiously, cruelly and brutishly: but when they suffer humbly, stoutly and patiently in his quarrel.

Let our adversaries therefore load us with the infamous titles of traitors and rebels, as the Arians did in the persecutions of the Vandals, and as the Ethnics were wont to call Christians *Sarmentitios* and *Semiassios*, because they were tied to halfpenny stakes and burnt with shrubs. So let them draw us upon hurdles, hang us, unbowel us alive, mangle us, boil us and set our quarters upon their gates to be meat for the birds of the air, as they used to handle rebels. We will answer them, as the Christians of former persecutions have done: *Such is the manner of our victory, such our conquering garment, in such chariots do we triumph. What marvel therefore if our vanquished enemies dislike us?*[18]

Take comfort therefore in these words, and with joyful hearts cry: *For with me, to live is Christ and to die is gain* (Phil. 1. 21). You have heretofore lived to die, but then shall you die to live for ever. Here you so lived that you were continually dying, but then you shall once die, never to die more; or rather by abridging a lingering death, purchase an everlasting life. You shall leave a ruinous and base cottage and pass to a most glorious and blessed place, whose very pavement,

set with so many bright and glorious stars, may give you a
guess what rooms you are like to find above. It cannot grieve
you to depart with the prodigal son from this dirty village
and the company of swine to your father's house (Lk. 15).
You must needs willingly cast off your sack of dung to receive the first stole, when you are invited to the great supper. I hope you have neither oxen to try, nor farm to see,
nor new wife to withhold you from going (Lk. 14).

You have had toil enough in the servitude of Egypt. You
have wandered long enough in the desert in continual battle
with your and God's enemies. Now if you die, the time is
come to take repose and enjoy the felicity of the land of
promise. You have been on Mount Sinai with Moses, *when
thunderings began to be heard, lightnings to flash, and a thick
dark cloud to cover the Mount* (Ex. 19. 16).* Now are you
called unto Mount Thabor, where enjoying his glory, whose
terror you have already sustained, you may say with St
Peter: *It is good for us to be here* (Mt. 17. 4).† The harvest of
the Church, whereof the Spouse speaketh in the Canticles:
I have reaped my myrrh with my spices (Cant. 4. 14), is not yet
done. You are grown up in this field and are part of the crop
that must be reaped by martyrdom to be laid up in God's
barn. You are the myrrh to embalm not the dead bodies, but
the dead souls of heretics. You are spice to season by the example of your constancy the bitter griefs and passions of poor
Catholics.

Remember how often you have been with Christ at his
supper (Lk. 22), and reason now requireth you should fol-

---

* This occurred on Mount Sinai before God gave the ten commandments to Moses.

† This is a reference to the Transfiguration of Christ on Mount Thabor.

low him to Gethsemani, not to sleep with St Peter, but to sweat blood with Christ. Your life is a warfare; your weapons, patience; your Captain, Christ; your standard, the Cross. Now is the alarm sounded and the war proclaimed. Die you must to win the field. And you, who have professed to be Christ's champions, know that the captains-general of his army (I mean the apostles and all the most famous soldiers since their time) esteemed this the most sovereign victory —by yielding, to subdue; by dying, to revive; by shedding blood and losing life, to win the goal of eternal felicity. Elias must not think much to let fall the worthless mantle of his flesh, to be carried to Paradise in a fiery chariot (4 Kgs 2). Gideon may willingly break his earthen flagons, to shew the light that must put to flight his enemies (Jg. 7). Joseph must leave his cloak in the strumpet's hands rather than consent to her lewd enticements (Gen. 39). And the young man of Gethsemani rather ran away naked than, for saving his sindon, fall into the synagogue's captivity (Mk. 14).

When the beavers are hunted and see themselves straitened, they bite off their own stones, for which by kind they know themselves to be chiefly pursued, so that the hunter having his desire may cease to follow them any farther. Now, if nature hath taught these brute things so painful a means to save themselves from bodily danger, how much more ought reason and faith to teach us to forgo willingly not only liberty and living but even our very life, and purchase thereby the life of our souls, and deliver ourselves from eternal perdition?

You have every day in your prayers said, *Let thy Kingdom come:* now is the time come to obtain your petition. The kingdom of this world is in the waning, and the age thereof beginneth to threaten ruin. The forerunners of Antichrist are in the pride of their course, and therefore, St Cyprian saith: *We that see already great miseries, and foresee greater to be at hand, let us account it time happily gained, if we may quickly depart to prevent their coming.*[19] The winter is not so full of showers to water the earth, nor summer so hot to ripen the corn, nor the spring so temperate to prosper young growth, nor autumn so full of ripe fruit as heretofore it hath been. The hills, tired with digging, yield not such store of marble. The wearied mines yield not so great plenty of precious metal: the scant veins wax daily shorter. In the sea decayeth the mariner, in the tent the soldier, innocency in courts, justice in judgments, agreement in friendship, cunning in arts, and discipline in manners. The hot sun giveth not so clear a light; the moon declineth from her accustomed brightness; the fountains yield less abundance of waters; men are not of so perfect hearing, so swift running, so sharp sighted, so well formed, nor so big and strong limbed, as heretofore. We see grey heads in children, the hair falleth before it be full grown. Our time doth not end in old age, but with age it beginneth, and even in our very birth our nativity hasteneth to the end. Finally every thing is so impaired and so fast falleth away that happy he may seem that dieth quickly, lest he be oppressed with the ruins of the dying world.

Let them that esteem the world their friend, and are not only in the world but also of it, make account of this life. As for you, the world hateth you, and therefore how can you love it, being hated of it? We are here pilgrims and strangers, and how can we but willingly embrace the death that assigneth us to our last home, delivering us out of these

worldly snares, and restoreth us to Paradise and the Kingdom of Heaven? Our country is heaven; our parents, the
patriarchs. Why do we not hasten to come speedily to our
country and to salute these parents? There a great number of
our friends expecteth us, a huge multitude desireth our
coming, secure and certain of their own salvation, and only
careful of ours. What unspeakable comfort it is to come to
the sight and embracing of them? How great is the contentment of their abode, without fear of dying, and with
eternity of living?

There is the glorious choir of apostles; a number of rejoicing prophets; the innumerable multitude of martyrs,
crowned for the victory of their bloody frays and passions.
There are the troops of fair virgins, that with the virtue of
chastity have subdued the rebellions of flesh and blood.
There are the companies of all God's saints, who bathe in
eternal felicity, having happily passed over the dangerous
voyage through this wicked world. There is the centre of
our repose, the only seat of unfailing security. Who can be
so unnatural an enemy to himself, as to eschew death which
is the bridge to this unspeakable contentment?

Therefore there is little cause either to love life or fear
death, and great motives to lament that our inhabitance is
prolonged and our decease adjourned. Let not then their
threatenings appal us, for they can only kill the body, and
have nothing to do with the soul. Their greatest spite
worketh to our profit, for when they think that they have
given us and our cause the greatest wound, then have they
deepliest wounded themselves, and procured our highest
advancement. They unarm us of blunt and bending weapons,
they strip us of slight and paper harness, and against their

wills they arm us with more sharp and pricking swords, and with armour that yieldeth to no kind of violence. When they think to have rid us from encountering their wicked endeavours, they do but better our ability to resist and vanquish them, altering us from earthly soldiers to heavenly warriors, from timorous subjects to mighty sovereigns, from oppressed captives to glorious saints. They think that by killing Abel, Cain's sacrifice will be accepted, not remembering that Abel's blood cryeth out against them (Gen. 4). By pursuing Elias with many soldiers (4 Kgs 1), they think to have the upper hand, not remembering that the fire will fall from heaven in his defence. They think by stoning Stephen (Ac. 7) to have foiled their chief enemy, not considering that his principal persecutor (Paul) will succeed in his room, and be unto them a more victorious adversary. Let them still continue their rage, let them think themselves wise in this ignorant folly: but let us, though we lament at their offence, yet rejoice in our felicity.

THE ELEVENTH CHAPTER

The eleventh cause of Comfort in Tribulation is that Martyrdom is glorious in itself, most profitable to the Church, and honourable to the Martyrs

WHAT greater preeminence is there in God's Church than to be a martyr? What more renowned dignity than to die in the cause of the Catholic faith? And this crown our greatest enemies set upon our heads. Although none can sufficiently utter its glory except those who have experienced it, yet we can gather some of its greatness by conjecture. Martyrdom is the noblest act of fortitude, since death is the hardest thing for nature to overcome. It is also the greatest point of charity by God's own testimony, who said: *Greater love than this no man hath than that he lay down his life for his friends* (Jn 15. 13). It is the principal act of obedience commended so highly in Christ who *became obedient even unto death* (Phil. 2. 8). In St Augustine's verdict martyrdom is more honourable than virginity.[1] Finally, it is the very chiefest act of effect of all virtues. If therefore, as the divines say, that work or action which proceedeth from the greatest number of good causes concurring to the same is more perfect or meritorious, then must martyrdom be a most glorious thing, which requireth the concourse of all virtues, and that in the highest degree.

Martyrdom hath the privilege of the sacrament of baptism, and is compared therewith by St Augustine. *In martyr-*

dom, saith he, *all the mysteries of baptism are fulfilled. He that must be baptized confesseth his faith before the priest and answereth when he is demanded; this doth also the martyr; he acknowledgeth his faith and answereth the demand before the persecutor. The baptized is either sprinkled or dipped in water; but the martyr is either sprinkled with his blood or not dipped but burned in fire. The baptized by imposition of the bishop's hands receiveth the Holy Ghost; the martyr is made a tabernacle of the same spirit: it is not he that speaketh, but the spirit within him. The baptized receiveth the blessed sacrament in remembrance of the death of our Lord; the martyr suffereth death itself for our Lord. The baptized protesteth to renounce the vanities of the world, the martyr, besides this, renounceth his own life. To the baptized all his sins are forgiven; in the martyr all his sins are quite extinguished.*[2]

St Cyprian, alleging a reason why no crime nor past offence could prejudice a martyr, saith: *Therefore is martyrdom called a crown as well as a baptism, for that it baptizeth and crowneth together.*[3] Thus, as no offence committed before baptism can do the baptized any harm, so also doth martyrdom so cleanse the soul from all spot of former corruption that it giveth thereunto a most undefiled beauty.

Yes, and martyrdom hath this prerogative above baptism. For, though baptism perfectly cleanses the soul and releases not only the offence but also the temporal punishment due unto the same, yet the root of sin sticketh in the flesh and the party baptized retaineth in him the badge and cognizance, yea, the scars and tokens of a sinner. But martyrdom's virtue is such that it not only hath the same effect as baptism but forthwith purchaseth for the soul a perfect riddance from all concupiscence and inclination to sin, and maketh it not only without offence but unable to offend any more. It doth not only gather the fruits or lop the branches or fell the tree, but plucketh it up by the very roots, and disableth it from springing up again. With the brood it killeth the dam, it consumeth both the weed and the seed together, and cleanseth us both from the mire and from the stain or spot that remaineth after it. And therefore the Scripture saith of martyrs, *These are they that came out of a great tribulation, and have washed their stoles, and whited them in the blood of the Lamb* (Apoc. 7. 14).

Tertullian saith, *The filth is washed away by baptism, but the stains are cleared by martyrdom, for Isaiah promiseth that red and scarlet should become as white as snow or wool,*[4] as if to say, martyrdom is as much more forcible than baptism as is the water that taketh out dirt and stain together than that which washeth the dirt away but leaveth the stain behind; not that this stain importeth any sin, but the infirmity which original sin hath caused, and from which actual sin proceedeth. Baptism taketh away our fault, and martyrdom our frailty. Baptism giveth us the key, but martyrdom letteth us in. Baptism maketh us members of the militant, martyrdom of the triumphant, Church. Baptism giveth us force to walk to our journey's end and to fight for the victory, but martyrdom settleth us in repose and crowneth our conquest.

Baptism bringeth us forth as the mother doth the child, to whom she giveth most of those parts which are in men, but those that she giveth are so impotent and weak that, though they may be used in childish actions, yet they suffice not for the principal things that man needeth till by process of time they be further enabled. In the same way baptism giveth us grace whereby we may weakly turn the powers of our mind to God, and have an obscure and, in a manner, childish kind of knowledge and love of him; but the chief actions wherein our felicity consisteth ensue not straight upon our baptism, but with long toil we must labour for them before we can attain to so great ability. But martyrdom bringeth us forth as the lioness doth her whelp; who, breeding but one in all her life, beareth it six and twenty months in her belly, till it grow perfect in proportion, able and strong in all limbs, armed with all its claws, and even the cheek teeth full grown, so that it cometh forth fully made and free from the impotency of other broods, as Epiphanius writeth.[5] And this martyrdom doth with our soul, bringing it forth with such perfection that it is straight enabled to have the perfect sight and love of God (wherein consisteth our bliss and happiness), without any delay of further growth or sufficiency.

In the baptism of water, saith St Thomas, the passion of Christ worketh by a certain figurative representation; in the baptism of spirit, by desire and affection; in the baptism of blood, by perfect imitation. Likewise the power of the Holy Ghost worketh in the first by secret virtue, in the second by commotion of the mind, in the third, by fervour of perfect love. As imitation is so much better than figurative representation, so much doth the baptism of blood surpass those of water and spirit.

Baptism is the cloud by which Moses guided God's people, and shrouded them in the desert (Ex. 13); but martyrdom is the river Jordan, through which Joshua leadeth them into the land of promise (Jos. 2). Baptism clothes us, like Mardochai, in royal attire, yet leaves us subjects; but martyrdom, with the robes, investeth us also with royal dignity (Est. 6). No man is so foul a leper that this water of Jordan cannot cure him (4 Kgs 5). No man is so blind but that washing in this pool of Siloe cannot restore him to sight (Jn 9). No disease is so incurable that this pond of Probatica cannot perfectly heal (Jn 5).

Martyrdom accomplisheth the labours of the virtuous and godly, and satisfieth for the sins of the sinful and wicked, and is to the one a reward, and to the other a remedy. *We have seen*, saith St Cyprian, *many of noble faith, who aspired to this title of martyrdom so that their death might honour their serviceable devotion. We have seen others who have stood without fear, so that by redeeming their offences with their blood they might be reckoned to be washed in it, and, whereas they were accounted dead while they were alive, now live again though they be dead. For this death maketh life more perfect and recovereth the grace that was lost.* [6]

And if St Chrysostom, extolling baptism, saith that it not only maketh us free but also holy; not only holy but just; not only just but children; not only children but heirs; not only heirs with Christ but members of Christ; not only members but temples; not only temples but also instruments of the Holy Ghost; [7] then may I further enlarge myself in the praise of martyrdoms and say that martyrdom giveth a freedom void of all servitude, a holiness and justice without any fault or fear of loss. It so maketh us children, that we cannot become enemies. It maketh us heirs with Christ, not only of his grace but also of his glory. It maketh us members that cannot be cut off, temples that cannot be defiled, such instruments of the Holy Ghost as cannot be abused. Finally, it giveth us the crown, whereof baptism is the pledge; in all which points it is superior unto it.

To pray for the baptized is a benefit, *for no man knoweth*

what his end shall be (Eccl. 9. 12). But St Augustine termeth it an injury to pray for a martyr, seeing we ought rather to commend ourselves to his prayers: *It is an injury to pray for a martyr, to whose prayers we must be commended.*[8]

For these causes doth the Church call the dying days of a martyr his birthday. For though we be born again by baptism, yet are we not come to a full birth and perfect healing. For, as St Augustine saith, *The children of God, so long as they live a mortal life, struggle with death; and though it be truly said of them that as many as are led by the spirit of God are God's children:* yet so long as the body oppresseth the soul, oftentimes *like children of men, with carnal motions they fall into their own frailty and so perish.*[9]

Likewise St Augustine, writing on the words of St John, *He came not into judgment, but passed from death to life* (Jn 5. 24),* saith: *Lo, in this life there is yet no life, we pass from death to life, to avoid coming unto judgment.*[10] We therefore, saith Origen, do not celebrate the day of the saints' nativity, which is their entrance to all griefs and molestations, but the day of their death, which is a riddance of their sorrows and a farewell to the devil's assaults.[11] We celebrate the day of their death, because though they seem to die, yet indeed they die not.

As another Father saith, *When you hear named the birthday of the saints, understand that it is not the day which bred them of flesh into the earth, but that which brought them from the earth into heaven, from labour to rest, from temptations to quiet, from torments to delights, from worldly laughters to a crown of glory.*[12] For, as St Cyprian noteth, *We know they are not lost, but sent*

---

* *He that heareth my word . . . cometh not into judgment but is passed from death to life.*

to shew us the way, and gone from us to make way before us.[13]
Eusebius Emissenus saith : *We call their birthday the day when
their martyrdom and the glorious profession of faith begot them to
external life while it put them to a temporal death, and after a
short pain brought them forth to perpetual pleasure.*[14]

Those days are rightly called birthdays, on which those
born into this misery of man's frailty are suddenly born
again to glory, turning their end and death into a beginning
of an endless life. For if we call those birthdays on which in
sin and sorrow we are born to sorrow in this world, more
justly may these be called birthdays on which from corruptible light they come into the brightness of the next
world, and the sons of men ascend to the adoption of a
Heavenly Father.

These considerations are enough to encourage us to be
greedy of martyrdom, which is so glorious a thing, rather
than in any way slack in embracing it when it is offered.

But if we consider, moreover, how beneficial martyrdom
is to the Church, and how important a means to advance
God's glory, no true member of Christ, nor true child of the
Catholic Church, can be so unnatural as not to rejoice that
he hath so good an occasion to discharge his duty to them
both and in such an acceptable manner. *The martyrs*, saith St
Chrysostom, *uphold the Church like pillars, they defend it like
towers, they bear off the rage of water like rocks, keeping themselves in great tranquillity. Like lights they have dispersed the
darkness of impiety, and like oxen have drawn the sweet yoke of
Christ.*[15]

The more corn is watered with showers of rain, the more
plentiful harvest doth it yield. And the vine also, when it is
pruned, spreadeth out its branches in great pride and is

more loaden with fair clusters, for the injury it seemeth to suffer returneth to its greater increase. It is beneficial to the field to set on fire the stubble so that the ground may be more fertile and abundant. *So*, saith St Cyprian, *in martyrdom the foregoing fall is a preparation for greater fruit, and condemneth life to death that by death life may the better be preserved*.[16] And for this reason Theodoretus compareth the persecutors to men who try to extinguish flames with oil and thereby rather increase them; and to carpenters who, felling trees, cause many more to spring than they cut down.[17] For the more martyrs are slain, the more daily spring up in their place. *This*, saith St Hilarius, *is peculiar to God's Church: while it is persecuted, it flourisheth; while it is trodden down, it groweth up; while it is despised, it profiteth; while it is hurt, it overcometh; while it is contraried, it better understandeth; it is most constant when it seemeth to be conquered*.[18]

The force of the death and blood of martyrs is wonderful. Their glorious course is very fitly expressed in the silk-worm. Eating itself out of a very little seed, it groweth to be a small worm. Afterwards, when it has fed a certain time upon fresh and green leaves, it waxes to greater size and eateth itself again out of the other coat. Then it worketh itself into a case of silk, which when it hath once finished, casting the seed for many young to breed on, and leaving the silk for man's ornament, it dieth all white and winged, in shape of a flying thing. Even so the martyrs of the Catholic Church first break out of the dead seed of original sin by baptism. Then, feeding on the sacraments and leaves of God's word, they grow to more ripeness, and casting off the coat of worldly vanities, they clothe themselves with the silk of virtue and perfection of life. Persevering in this work to the end (even when the persecution is greatest) they finally, as need requireth, shed their blood as seed for new offspring to arise, and leave, moreover, the silk of their virtues as an ornament to the Church. Thus departing white with their good works and winged with innocency of hands and cleanness of heart, they presently fly to their heavenly repose, agreeable to David's saying: *Who shall ascend to the mount of God? The innocent of hands and clean of heart* (Ps. 23. 3).

Though the ripe fruit of the Church be gathered, yet their blood engendereth new supply, and it increaseth the more when the disincrease thereof is violently procured. It is like the bush that burned and was not consumed (Ex. 3). From its own ruins it riseth, and from its own ashes it reviveth, and increaseth by that which maketh the world decay.

The phoenix, as Epiphanius, St Clement and others report, when she is come to her full age, gathereth a pile of myrrh, frankincense and other spices in some high mount. When the spices are kindled by the heat of the sun, she suffereth herself to be burnt up, and of her ashes there first breedeth a little worm, which in the end becometh a phoenix again.[19] So the martyrs, when God's glory demands it, gather a pile of virtue and good works in the mount of the Catholic Church, and make that bundle of which the spouse speaketh: *My beloved is unto me a bundle of myrrh* (Cant. 1. 12), and exposing themselves thereupon to the scorching heat of persecution, they sacrifice themselves in the flame of patience and charity, so that by their death the posterity of the Church may be preserved.

For, as St Ambrose noteth, *the great goodness of our God, who is so plentiful of mercy and so cunning an artificer of our salvation, will have the merits of martyrs to be our patronage by setting*

before our eyes the high reward of virtue. While he commendeth
unto us the true faith in the hard conflict of martyrdom he maketh
the affliction of our forefathers an instruction for their posterity. O
how great is God's care over us! He examineth them to inform us,
he spoileth them to spare us, and turneth their passions to our
profit.[20]

For we find by experience that whosoever suffereth,
though he suffer for his offence, is pitied, and naturally
misery, though deserved, cannot but breed remorse and
tenderness in the beholders. But now what must these beholders feel when they see men of innocent behaviour,
of virtuous conversation, learned and grave persons, with
comfort offer themselves to extremity, rejoice when they
are tormented, smile when they are dismembered, and go
to death as they would to a banquet? They see men who
neither want dignities to withdraw them, nor friends nor
family to pull them back, nor powerful enemies to affright
them, but are ready to change their dignity with disgrace,
to forsake their friends, and give themselves into the hands
of their mortal foes, only for the defence of their conscience.
When they have beheld such things they must needs say, as
as they did in St Cyprian's time: *It is a thing worthy to be known,*
and a virtue that deserveth deep consideration, for which a man is
content to suffer death.[21]

The martyrs want no means to search out the truth, having both read and heard that which can be said on either side.
They want no wit and judgment to discern the good from
the bad, being persons known to be of deep insight and discretion. They can have no pleasure in pains, nor any temporal allurement, to move them to undertake so great
misery. Yea, they have many delights, honours and prefer-

ments to withdraw them from it, and with altering opinion, and speaking a word, might easily avoid it. Sure therefore it is that they find it necessary to do this and that their soul lieth upon it, or else flesh and blood could never digest so heavy calamities. And though others, more worldly wise, do the contrary, yet we may easily see that pleasure, profit and vanity withdraweth the most part of men from God, for *narrow is the way that leadeth to life, and but few they be that find it* (Mt. 7. 14).

Those that suffer have comfort in the knowledge that their death raiseth many from death, and their patience maketh every one inquisitive of their religion. *For every one*, saith Tertullian, *seeing such constancy, is cast in some scruple and waxeth inquisitive what quarrel we maintain, and when he knoweth the truth, he straight embraceth it*. And again: *Every most exquisite iniquity of yours against us is a greater allurement of others to our religion*.[22]

When a man breaketh open the jeweller's chest, by breaking an iron lock, he lays open to those present a multitude of most precious jewels. Once they are seen, every one is desirous to consider more their workmanship, glory and value at leisure. And many, on seeing them, are moved to buy them, although if they had been still under lock, no man would have regarded them. So the persecutors, by breaking the worthless locks of martyrs' bodies, lay open their faith and virtue to the sight of the world. When men see this, they fall into deeper consideration, and debate with themselves this grace and perfection. And they are moved to buy this grace though it be with loss of all their lands, liberties and lives.

O wonderful force of the Catholic faith, which above all

natural course, and beyond all reach of man's understanding, increaseth by that means by which all other things are suppressed! We have no other way to root out wickedness, sin and impiety; no means to abolish lewd behaviour and disorder among men, but only violence of torments and cruel punishments. Though sensuality and pleasure entice men with vehement incentives, yet the fear of severe chastisement maketh them bridle their affections. And if any man be executed for great enormities, when he is dead, his sin dieth with him, and seldom leaveth he any posterity that by his death is not dismayed, rather than encouraged to follow his evil example.

But in this quarrel of our faith, it happeneth quite contrary. For a good slip, grafted in a sour tree, bringeth forth nevertheless sweet fruit, agreeable to its own kind. And the sap of the same root, which in the crab is sour and bitter, in the apple of the slip is most pleasant and delightsome, and though it be loathsome in the one, it allureth in the other. So happeneth it to God's saints when they are put in the persecutor's hands. For their odious and intolerable cruelty breedeth (when it is practised upon malefactors) terror, fear and horror of the wicked fruits for which they are punished; yet in the faithful and virtuous, the same bitter torments practised upon them work the pleasant and goodly fruits of salvation, not only most acceptable unto God, but able to allure men's hearts to taste of the same.

A cunning artificer, not only of ivory or gold, but of iron or clay, can frame a proportionable image, and in a base metal or mould still shew his exquisite skill. So the true children of the Catholic Church, taught by God's spirit, shew the perfection of their virtue, not only in riches and

173

wealth, but in need and poverty, and as well in the depth of misery and in the midst of pains, as in the height of prosperity and worldly pleasure.

Thus may we understand the promise of God made by David to those that kept themselves within the walls and bounds of Jerusalem, that is, the Church: *Who giveth snow as wool, and spreadeth the mist as ashes* (Ps. 147. 16): that is, those torments which to the bad are snow-cold and unprofitable (and able to quench the natural heat that men have to follow sinful examples) are wool to the good and, in both them and others, increaseth the warmth of true faith and virtue. The rank fog of worldly disgrace, whereby the fire of heresy and sin is extinguished, are as ashes to God's servants, wherein the fire of true religion and perfect charity is preserved and strengthened. St Augustine saith: *They were imprisoned, whipped, tortured, burned, torn in pieces and murdered; and yet they were multiplied.*[23]

Philo, comparing the word of God to a coriander, reporteth that its seed hath this property, that when it is cut into little pieces, every crumb of it bringeth forth as much as the whole seed would have done.[24] So it is with the martyrs: when they are martyred, every quarter and parcel, yea every drop of blood, is able to do as much, and sometimes with more forcible effects, than the martyr himself, if he had remained alive.

Well did St Jerome say, *The passion of martyrs, and shedding blood for the name of Christ, is the triumph of God.*[25] Well may it be called the triumph of God, seeing it surpasseth all other triumphs of men. The triumphs of the Romans were wont to be solemnized in glorious chariots, drawn with lions, elephants, or goodly steeds, with applause of people, with pleasant music, with a troop of captives, with costly arches and such other monuments of victory. The banners of the foiled enemies, the rich spoils and famous prizes were carried in sight, and every thing ordered and set forth with pomp and majesty. But who ever heard of a triumph, where the conqueror was hauled and harrowed upon the ground, with his hands and feet bound, with reproach of the lookers-on, with disgrace and infamy? Who has ever heard of a triumph where the victor himself was captive; his triumphal arch was the block or the gallows; his enemies' banners, the axe or the cord; his spoils and prizes, his unbodied bowels and dismembered limbs; finally, his pomp, punishment, and his Majesty, misery? This triumph is not that which worldlings affect, neither can they conceive how torments and triumphs can agree together. And therefore did St Jerome well call it the triumph of God.

In this triumph Nabuchodonosor and Paul were captives. Justinus confesseth himself to have been converted by the constancy of martyrs. Of this triumph speaketh St Cyprian, when he saith: *So great is the force of martyrdom, that thereby even he is forced to believe with thee, that was ready to kill thee.*[26] But to prove that martyrdom is for the present disgraceful, yet in the sequel a more glorious triumph even here on earth than ever any of the Romans had, let us consider the glorious shows that set it forth. The martyrs, for their triumphal chariots, have most sumptuous and stately churches; for applause of the people, the prayers and praises of all true Christians; for their music, the solemn choirs and the instruments usual in the Church; for their triumphal arches, most rich shrines and altars; for the banners of their foiled enemies, the arms and honours of Princes, converted by their means; for their captives, Emperors, Kings and Monarchs; for their spoils and prizes, the empire, kingdoms and commonwealths; finally, for their pomp, the reverend majesty of the Catholic Church.

See now, whether our triumphs (though base in the eye) be not in effect most glorious, and whether any conquerors ever won more by killing others than the martyrs have done, by being killed themselves: St Cyprian saith: *What argueth more impotency than to be bound, condemned, whipped, tormented, killed, and to lay the head on the block at the hangman's pleasure? This sight sometimes stirreth mercy even in the most cruel tyrants. But when at the martyrs' tombs diseases are cured, the devils roar, the Monarchs tremble, miracles are wrought, idols fall down, then appeareth it how forcible the blood of martyrs is.*[27]

While the gold is yet mingled with earth in the mines, men tread it under foot, as they did the earth; but when it is tried with the fire and purified by the artificer's hand, kings themselves think it a great honour to wear it on their heads. And so the martyrs while they were alive, enwrapped in that mass of earth (I mean their corruptible bodies), were contemned and trodden on as the refuse of the world; but when their gold was severed from dross (that is, their soul from their body) by violent death in God's cause, there is no Catholic prince so haughty but that with bowed knee and stooping head is ready to adore* them and account their very ashes as chief ornaments of his crown and succours of his realm. They were not therefore subdued, for they overcame their enemies; yea and their victory was most glorious for its unusual manner.

You shall die like men, saith David, *and like one of the princes*

* *to adore*: to reverence, honour or love (Johnson's Dictionary).

shall you fall (Ps. 81. 7). You shall die like men, because your death shall seem full of human misery, but indeed like one of the princes shall you fall, that is, like one of the princes of God's people. Or, you shall die not as the sensual worldling, who *is compared to the foolish beasts, and is become like unto them* (Ps. 48. 13), but like men, judging it in reason good for your faith to die, in hope of a better life; yea, not only as men, but as princes amongst men, whose successors never fail, whose tombs are glorious, whose memory is perpetual. *Regard you not how black I am* (Cant. 1. 5), for though I be black, yet am I the fair daughter of Jerusalem.

Of all the parts of a tree, the root is, to the sight, the foulest and most ugly, and therefore nature seemeth to have hid it from the eye, that it might be no disgrace to the beauty of the other parts. But if you consider the fair flower, the sweet fruit, the pleasant leaves, the goodly branches, the very life and sap of the whole tree, you shall find that all proceedeth from that shapeless and unseemly root, which therefore ought, of all other parts, to be chiefly prized. So is it with the martyrs: they seem in their torments more miserable than all other men, covered with disgrace, infamy and reproach; but if we consider the beauty of virgins, the fruit of confessors, the leaves of temporal commodities, the branches of all nations, yea the very life and grace of the Church of God, we shall find that for all these we may thank the blood of martyrs.

Well may the martyrs be called the neats or kine of the Church, whose teats give necessary milk. Kine at all seasons, even in the foulest weather, range in the meadows, fields and pastures, and, feeding upon grass and wild herbs unfit for man's eating, by virtue of their own inward heat, turn them into sweet milk and suffer the same quietly to be drawn out of them, for the benefit of mankind. So the martyrs, even in the most stormy times of persecution, are contented to feed upon the sour and bitter pains of their enemies' rage, and, digesting all their cruelty with the inward heat of charity and zeal, turn their own afflictions to our instruction and spiritual nurture, and suffer their blood to be drawn from them, the virtue whereof hath more force to fortify our souls than the sweetest milk to strengthen our bodies. This is *the wine that breedeth virgins* (Zach. 9. 17): *the blood of grapes and mulberries provoking the elephants to the fight* (1 Mac. 6. 34), that is, Christians to spiritual battle. This is the pledge that got the privilege: *They shall judge nations and rule over people* (Wis. 3. 8): and, as Tertullian saith, *the blood of martyrs is the very key of Paradise.*[28] So that we may even of the earthly crown understand that saying of St Jerome: *The Church, increased by persecutions, was crowned by martyrdoms.*[29]

This saying, *Kings shall be thy foster fathers, and queens thy nurses* (Is. 49. 23), was verified after the death of infinite martyrs, whose very ashes the kings and monarchs have honoured, doing them as it were due homage, and acknowledging them as captains, by whom they were conquered. This Isaias foreshewed again in the following words: *With a lowly countenance they shall worship thee, and shall lick the very dust of thy feet* (Is. 49. 23). And who are the feet of the Church, but only the martyrs, apostles, and pastors, that uphold it and carry it still forward throughout all nations, of whom it is said: *How fair are the feet of the preachers of peace* (Rom. 10. 15)! *For these are they that carry my name before kings and rulers and to the very end of the world* (Ac. 9. 15). Thus we see how the words of Christ are verified. *Unless the kernel of wheat fall into the ground and die, itself remaineth alone, but if it die, it bringeth forth much fruit* (Jn 12. 24). St Ambrose noteth[30] that in the vineyards of Engaddi, a city of Jury, there is a tree that if it be pricked or cut, distilleth out most precious balm and yieldeth a most sweet savour, neither of which things it doth, being left whole. Even so happeneth it in the martyrs, whose blood gushing out from wounds is more precious, sweet and acceptable than the balm. And of this may we understand those words of the spouse: *A cluster of Cypress is my beloved unto me in the vineyards of Engaddi* (Cant. 1. 13). For, as St Jerome saith: *By this means is the savour of Christianity spread amongst the Gentiles, and this secret thought cometh to their mind, that except the Gospel were true, men would never defend it with their blood.*[31] The sweetness of the rose, if it be untouched, soon withereth away with the leaf, which today is fair and tomorrow fadeth; but put it into the still, cover it from the comfort of the sun, yea scorch it with the fire, it vapoureth out most delicate water, which may be long preserved and imparteth sweetness to whatsoever it toucheth; so that whether it be by fire or by natural course, the rose withereth. But in the first manner, both the leaf keepeth a pleasant savour and distilleth from it a most sweet liquor, whereas in the second, both the leaf is less likesome and the water lost. So fareth it with God's martyrs: while they live, they are sweet in their virtuous conversation, if they die, their example for a time doth some good; but put them in prison, keep them from worldly comforts, yea scorch them, burn them, and use them in all extremity, then do their virtues give the best savour, and their blood, wheresoever it is shed, engendereth a wonderful alteration in men's manners, making them embrace the truth, and become *a good savour of Christ* (2 Cor. 2. 15), and *an incense worthy to be odour of sweetness*: whereas in their natural death, though their example would have done good, yet neither their leaf had been so odoriferous, nor their precious liquor to such benefit of the Church. And therefore may we say with Solomon, *O how fair is a chaste generation with brightness! While it is present men do imitate it, and long after it when it is departed; it triumpheth crowned with perpetual glory, winning the rewards of their undefiled encounters.*

Personable men of comely feature, though they be by sickness or dirt disfigured, yet keep they the tokens of seemliness; yea and then their seemliness is most seen, when it is compared with some contrary deformity. And so is it in God's martyrs: even in the depth of worldly disgrace do they shew the glorious grace and beauty of their mind, and when their virtue encountereth with the persecutor's vice, then doth it shine brightest, and is unto the beholders most pleasing and amiable.

O unspeakable force of the blood of martyrs, then most powerful when it is spilt, and then most victorious when it is trodden under foot! No adamant so hard, but though it resist to the strokes of preaching, yea and to the mighty force of miracles, yet yieldeth it to the blood of innocent lambs, of which Christ speaketh, *I send you like lambs amongst wolves* (Lk. 10. 3). No leprosy is so incurable, but the blood of these infants in innocency, though not in age, in malice, though not in discretion, cannot cure. And albeit Constantine refuseth a bath of the blood of infants in age, yet doubtless had not these infants in innocency (I mean the martyrs) bathed him in theirs, God knoweth whether ever he had been rid of his spiritual leprosy. He himself in a manner acknowledged this, when he came to that famous Council of Nice. Finding there many of those fathers that had some part of their body maimed or disfigured with the torments suffered for the Catholic faith, he embraced them in humble sort, and most devoutly kissed the scars of their torments as most honourable badges of Christianity.

Three testimonies recounteth St John in this world: *There are three that give witness in earth, the spirit, water and blood* (1 Jn 5. 7). The first did St John Baptist see in the form of a dove; the second and third St John Evangelist saw coming out of Christ's side. In one sense, these three things have caused our spiritual life; in another, they maintain our corporal. Our inward man is quickened by God's spirit, cleansed by the water of baptism, redeemed with the blood of Christ; but neither would this spirit have quickened, nor the water washed, unless the blood had redeemed. The spirit soweth, the water ripeneth, the blood reapeth. The spirit appeareth in Christ's baptism, and though the heaven was opened, yet neither earth nor hell gave any sign of his coming. The water was shed when Christ wept at Lazarus' rising, and though hell was enforced to render her prey, yet neither heaven nor earth were moved at it. But when the blood came out of Christ's wounds, the heavens denied light, the earth quaked and hell delivered up the dead; and then was it fulfilled, *If I be exalted from the earth, I will draw all things unto me* (Jn 12. 32).

Our corporal life also dependeth partly upon breathing, partly on watery humours, but chiefly on blood: yet those are by natural courses tokens of life, while in the body they perform their several effects. But for our present consideration it is most important to consider that their spiritual value and force is shewn when the body is bereaved of them. No man was moved by seeing Christ draw breath, but when with a great voice he gave up his spirit and lost his breath, then did the Centurion straight cry, *In very deed, this was the Son of God* (Mt. 27. 54). While the blood and water were in his body unseen and untouched, the effect of them was never perceived; but as soon as they found passage to come out by the wound in his side, there issued also with them a fountain of grace, whereof all the sacraments take their effect.

Even so is it in the blood of martyrs: they whom their holy life nothing moved, they that by their miracles could not be converted, by their blood were mollified and brought to goodness. St Paul was obstinate for all St Stephen's preaching, he was stubborn in his opinion for all his miraculous works, he could never be won till he felt the effect of his innocent blood. For, as St Augustine saith, *Unless Stephen had thus prayed*, that is, in his bloody agony, *the Church had never had St Paul*. Of St James also it is written, that in Spain he in his life converted only eight persons; but when his blood began to work, the whole country, that regarded so little the force of his living speeches, yielded to his dead bones and relics. So likewise the city of Rome, though it had been laboured unto the truth by St Peter's and St Paul's own voices, epistles and conversation, yet it was never thoroughly converted, until it was long soaked in martyrs' blood.

Dark, saith David, *is the water in the clouds of the air* (Ps. 17. 12), and yet, that very same it is, that bringeth to light the sweet rose and fair lily, that loadeth the trees with goodly fruits and giveth pride to the stateliest plants; that is it that, though black in the clouds it seemeth, watereth the earth, and, falling upon the flowers, setteth them forth with pearls and diamonds and filleth the rivers with most clear streams. What are these clouds but martyrs, of whom it is said, *Who are these that fly like clouds, and like doves unto their windows* (Is. 60. 8)? What is the water so dark in the clouds but the blood of martyrs in their bodies while they live? But when it is once shed, it sheweth itself to be *the flood of living waters* (Jn 7. 38) that Christ promised should flow *out of his believers*, and that *voluntary rain which God hath set apart for his inheritance* (Ps. 67. 10), that falleth *like a shower upon the herbs and like drops upon the grass* (Deut. 32. 2), in whose droppings the young spring rejoiceth. From this we may understand David's prophecy: *Thou hast visited the earth*, doubtless of thy Church by persecution, *thou hast thoroughly watered it*, doubtless with the blood of martyrs, *and thou hast multiplied to enrich it* (Ps. 64. 10), with young spring of new believers. In this are the words of Isaias verified: *Since that thou art made honourable in my eyes and glorious*, by martyrdom, *I loved thee, and will give*, to my Church, *men for thee*, many for one, yea, *and whole people for thy only life* (Is. 43. 4): that of thee it may be said, as of Samson, that thou hast had a victory over more by thy death than by thy life thou hadst obtained (Jg. 16. 30).

To this effect may we refer the words of the prophet, *They shall turn their swords into cutters of ploughs and their spears into scythes* (Is. 2. 4): because since Christ's time, all the persecutors, by using their swords against the Church, have but ploughed and tilled it to prepare it for new corn, and their spears have been but scythes to reap the ripe crop, that more seed might shoot up in its place to the greater increase of God's people.

Hitherto we have experienced the performance of that promise, made to Christ's Church, *that the young growth of God's planting should to his glory shew itself to be a work of his hands, for that the least shall become a thousand, and a little one become a most strong nation* (Is. 60. 22). By the virtue of the same hands, five loaves were multiplied to be sufficient food for five thousand persons. So, for the most part, it hath been proved true in every place that *the more blood hath been shed, the more hath the multitude of the faithful flourished.*[32]

Well may the Church say unto Christ those words of Sephora, *Thou art unto me a spouse of blood* (Ex. 4. 25), seeing that he neither planted, nor increased, nor fostered her, but in blood. With blood sprouted out her first buds, as a presage and pattern of the future fruits. She was no sooner married unto Christ, but straightway the Innocents gave her notice in what grief she was to bring forth her children. Of these St Augustine speaking, saith: *They are worthily called the flowers of martyrs, which, springing in the heart of the cold of infidelity, as the first buds of the Church that shot out, a certain frost of persecution parched. Your years served you not to believe in Christ, but your flesh served you to suffer for Christ, who was afterwards to suffer for you.*[33] With their blood did the apostles, disciples and other martyrs, until our days, establish the Church's doctrines. With blood must we confirm it. In the end of the world, Enoch, Elias and other martyrs of before Christ's time must with their blood seal up the same. For, as St Cyprian well noteth, *no obligation is more infallible than that which is sealed up with the blood of so many martyrs.*[34] And therefore Christ took this course for the confirmation of his doctrine.

In the Old Testament, when Moses read the law unto the

people, he sprinkled them with blood of calves, saying: *This is the blood of the covenant which our Lord hath made with you, concerning all these speeches* (Ex. 24. 8). How much more effectually is the Church sprinkled with the blood of martyrs, as a mean to bind our hearts with insoluble covenant of belief to Christ's sayings?

The efficacy of this confirmation of our faith St Ambrose acknowledgeth as very important. *We must understand*, quoth he, *that we cannot, without great danger, dispute of the truth of that religion which we see confirmed with the blood of so many martyrs. It is a very perilous thing if, after the oracles of so many prophets, after the testimonies of the apostles, after the wounds of martyrs, thou presume to discuss the ancient faith as a novelty, and remain in thy error after so manifest guides, and contend with idle disputation after the toils of so many as have died in the cause.*[35]

Finally, how beneficial both in this, and infinite other respects, the blood of martyrs hath been unto the Church although its wondrous force no man is able sufficiently to express. Holy was the austerity and zeal of Elias and St John Baptist; godly was the estate of the old patriarchs and prophets; virtuous the life of virgins and widows; honourable the condition of confessors and religious persons: yet, as St Cyprian saith, *All must of force yield to martyrdom, whose glory is invaluable, whose measure infinite, whose victory unspotted, whose virtue honourable, whose title inestimable, whose triumph exceeding great.*[36]

To our blood the gates of heaven fly open. With our blood the fire of hell is quenched. In our blood our souls are beautified, our bodies honoured, the devil suppressed and God glorified. It is poison and death to heretics. It is restorative and comfortable to Catholics, a seed of all virtue and the bane of vice. To conclude, assure yourselves, *Of martyrdom so much may be said as may be conceived.*[37]

But now having shewed how honourable martyrdom is in itself, and how profitable to the Church, let us see how glorious it is, even in this world, unto those that suffer it. Besides the Church's triumph which, procured by its martyrs' blood, redoundeth also to their own praise, what a glory it is to the martyrs that the very prophecies about Christ are so plainly verified in themselves! It is no small conjecture how they, whose titles have so near affinity with Christ's style, resemble him also in glory. And to touch on some few of the prophecies: it is said of Christ, *He shall come up like a root out of a thirsting ground* (Is. 53. 2); and yet of this root it is also written, *It shall break out into a bud, and shall bring forth fruit* (Ez. 17. 23). And although the martyrs who are pestered in prisons, and, as it were, buried in miseries, appear like withered roots in a dry and barren soil, yet from these roots who seeth not how many buds of virtues and fruits of gained souls continually spring?

Of Christ it is said, *We have seen him, and there was no comeliness in him, yea we took him for a leper and the basest of all other men, and yet we desired him* (Is. 53. 2, 4). And how fitly agreeth this to the martyrs, whose tortured bodies and opprobrious deaths maketh you consider that there are none more abject and deformed than they? But for all this, no disfigurement or outward unhappiness could so prevail, but that they are, and ever shall be, desired, honoured and highly esteemed.

Of Christ it is said, *If he yield his soul to death, he shall see a long aged seed. And I will give him very many, and he shall divide the spoils of the strong* (Is. 53. 12). Is not this also verified in the martyrs, whose blood is seed, whose death reviveth, whose plucking up is the planting of their posterity?

Was not Joseph a principal pattern of Christ's passion, for he, like Christ, was sold and unjustly imprisoned? Were not all the sacrifices of beasts and birds types and shadows of Christ's oblation, and none of them without the shedding of blood? How perfectly therefore do martyrs resemble their Captain, since these figures and types that foreshewed him may also be aptly applied unto them?

There are only three ways that the dead can be honoured by those that be alive; first, by monuments and worthy memorials, erected for their renown; secondly, by famous writers to register their acts; thirdly, by being reverenced and generally esteemed to be of sovereign great power.

Taking the first point: though emperors and men of mark amongst the Gentiles have had divers honourable memorials yet were they for the most part of their own or others' building before they died; or if it were after their decease, it was to flatter some of their surviving friends rather than for any great care that they had of the dead parties' glory. And although there have been set up most sumptuous temples to the false gods long after their deaths, yet, with the memory of that wherein they were beneficial to the commonwealth, there was also set forth to be honoured in these memorials their brutish and unnatural wickedness, which did give to reasonable persons of good judgment more cause to abhor them for their lewdness than to honour them for their virtues. So was it a common thing to set forth the rapes of Jupiter, the adulteries of Venus, the lasciviousness of Apollo and such like, and to have them painted in the very altars and prospects of their temples. But the martyrs' monuments are so generally raised in divers countries that it cannot be deemed flattery, and of them nothing but good either hath or could be set forth, which they ever would have reckoned in their virtues, or turned to their glory. That potentates and great personages have had such remembrances is no great marvel, since they were mighty in power and had rich and wealthy posterity, who, for their own advancement as well as for the good will to the dead, were contented to renown their houses and families with such stately works. But a wonderful thing it is that common, yea abject, and base persons, such as in their life were counted the reversion and refuse of the world, such as had neither friends nor posterity to shew them any like favour, yea such as died with infamy and dishonour, devoured by beasts, and not thought worthy of so much as a place of burial in the earth, that such men, I say, should after their deaths be honoured with sumptuous churches, altars and daily solemnities, and not only in the place where they conversed but in divers distant nations and countries, where they were never known before their departure. It is a thing whereof, as there can be no natural reason, surely must needs be construed a testimony of God's mighty hand to honour his saints.

This did St Chrysostom observe, when he said: *Christ, when he was dead, drew the whole world to worship him. And why speak I of Christ, when he caused his very disciples after their decease to be glorious? Yea, and what speak I of his disciples, whose sepulchres and days he hath made to be celebrated with perpetual memory? Shew me thou the tomb of Alexander; name the day wherein he ended his life; but neither of them is notorious, they are now destroyed and quite abolished; but the sepulchres of Christ's servants are famous, advanced and honoured in the imperial city, and their days commonly known to the world, bringing with them a festival comfort. And as for Alexander's tomb, not his own neighbours know it; but those of the Saints, even the Paynims can tell of. The sepulchres of a crucified man's disciples are more glorious than king's palaces, not only in the hugeness and stateliness of the buildings (for in this also they exceed them), but that which is more, in concourse and resort of suppliants.*[38]

Theodoretus also hath the like saying: *The churches of martyrs are glorious to see, notorious for their hugeness, garnished with all kind of ornaments, and blazing abroad the pomp of their beauty. We do not frequent them only once, twice or five times in a year, but often spend in them whole days, yea many times every day do we there sing to our Lord the praises and hymns of the martyrs.*[39]

What sumptuous churches did Constantine the Great build in honour of St Peter and St Paul? What massy images of all the apostles did he make, with crowns of gold on their heads, of four score and ten pounds weight apiece, beside other passing rich ornaments, namely, two crosses of gold, one upon St Peter's, another on St Paul's tomb, of a hundred and fifty pounds weight apiece.

I omit the temple that by Gallus was built to the honour of St Mamas Martyr, mentioned by Gregory Nazianzen, and the Church of St Theodorus, which Gregory Nissen reporteth to have been most sumptuous.[40] I omit the stately, rich churches, yet extant in all places of Christendom, which are sufficient proofs to shew the martyrs of God more glorious in this behalf than the greatest monarchs that ever were. St Stephen or St Laurence hath most haughty buildings erected in their memory, not only in Rome, where their bodies are, but in France, England, Flanders, Spain, Italy, Germany and all Christendom, yea not only in every country, but almost in every chief city, and in infinite other towns.

Now taking the second point, the writers who have registered the martyrs' acts, they surpass all former potentates of the Gentiles. For how many Emperors have you, that have had Emperors to write their worthy exploits? How few (unless they were men of base calling) had their equals, or betters, to register their fame? Whereas to the martyrs, others now as famous for miracles and holiness of life as they were for their martyrdom, and as much honoured every way as they, have been the chroniclers and penners of their praises. How many martyrs doth St Cyprian, St Basil, St Chrysostom, St Jerome, St Augustine, St Bernard and others honour in their sermons and works? All men as glorious themselves in God's Church as they of whom they set forth the praises. I omit Eusebius, St Bede, Florius, Metaphrastes, Usvardus and infinite other grave authors. For what books have you written by a Christian, wherein (if the matter bear it) there is not mention made of God's martyrs? Yea, how many of the very Gentiles have registered their memories, and though they conceived them not as they should, yet speak they of them to their own confusion and the martyrs' glory?

Now, as touching the third point, which is the reverent and worthy opinion that true Christians have of the power of martyrs, it were too long to recite the particular testimonies of antiquity. For though we do not, as the heretics grossly father upon us, yield them any divine honour, or take them for gods, yet they have ever been highly esteemed of our forefathers, as they also are by us, for their wonderful power. And first, if their power in heaven be gathered by that which they had in earth, we have great cause to put confidence in it. If St Peter's shadow (Ac. 5), St Paul's handkerchiefs and girdles (*ibid.* 19), were able to cure diseases; if St Paul's prayer in the ship was able to obtain the lives of two hundred and seventy-six persons (*ibid.* 27), if St Stephen's prayer was so forcible for his persecutors as to convert a chief agent in his death (*ibid.* 7), why may we not infer with St Jerome, that they are able to do much more in heaven, where they are in more favour with God and perfected in charity towards us?[41] *When they were yet mortal,* saith St Bernard, *and sure to die, they seemed to have commandment over life and death, putting to death the quick, and raising from death the dead, and that with their only word. How much more mighty are they now, when they are advanced to such unspeakable honour, and their princedom is most assuredly established?*[42] And again, *How much more powerful are they in heaven, whose power was so great even here on earth?*[43]

Secondly, if we consider the might of the devils and the strong effects they have wrought, as by the enchanters of Pharaoh, the sudden destruction of Job's cattle, the murdering of his children by overthrowing their house and other wonderful effects that God hath permitted unto them: much more power must we presume to be in God's saints, whom in heaven we are sure he would not make inferior in might unto his enemies, over whom he gave them so great authority here in earth. And for this hath it been always a custom in the Church to go on pilgrimage to martyrs' tombs, where they have always shewed their patronage to such as come unto them for succour. Of this St Chrysostom saith, *He who is clad in purple cometh to embrace those sepulchres, and setting aside his majesty, standeth as a suppliant to those saints,*

that they would vouchsafe to pray for him; and he that goeth
adorned with his crown prayeth to a tent maker, and a fisher, and
those also dead, as to his protectors.[44] Who ever went in pilgrimage to see any king's palaces? But to enjoy the sight of
the martyrs' tombs many kings have become pilgrims.

Prudentius of this also writeth:

> *The townsmen flock to the imbrued sands,*
> *There making sure with voice, with vow, with gift:*
> *Men also came from far and foreign lands,*
> *To every coast fore-ran the fame so swift,*
> *That here the patrons of the world did lie,*
> *By whose good prayers each wight might seek supply.*[45]

St Bede also and our own chronicles make mention how
King Ceadwall and King Conrad went to Rome in pilgrimage to those holy relics of the apostles.[46] But was such
an honour ever given or so long continued to any emperor?

Moreover, the wonderful force of the martyrs is abundantly testified by the effects that have been wrought by
their very ashes, bones, garments and other things of theirs.
St Chrysostom saith that St Peter's chains, his sword and
garments wrought many miracles.[47] St Ambrose writeth,
that the relics of St Gervasius and St Protasius cured so
many diseases that the people cast their beds and garments
upon their bodies, deeming them of force to cure maladies
by the only touch of these saints.[48] The very ashes of St
Cyprian drove the devils out of the possessed, cured diseases
and gave foreknowledge of future events, as Gregory
Nazianzen writeth.[49]

St Chrysostom compareth martyrs' bodies to the emperor's own armour, the very light whereof maketh the
thieves, that is the devils, to fly, though never so eager of

prey: *For their eye aimeth not at their nature but at the secret dig-*
nity and glory of Christ, who, putting on the bodies of his martyrs,
bare them as armour in the agony of their combats.[50] What hath
been wrought by any martyr in his life, but that ordinarily
his ashes and relics have been of the like, yea and sometimes
of greater force; whether it were raising of the dead, re-
storing of the lame, giving sight to the blind, hearing to the
deaf, or speech to the dumb or what other miracle soever?

Now therefore, if David demand his old question: *Shall*
any utter thy mercy in the grave or thy truth in perdition? Shall thy
marvels be known in darkness or thy justice in the land of oblivion
(Ps. 87. 12)? we may answer, that the martyrs in their robes
extol his mercy, who by their very ashes cure diseases and
relieve many miseries. In perdition, by the loss of their lives
and shedding of their blood, they confirm and give testimony unto his truth. In darkness of infidelity and error, or
of temporal disgrace and worldly punishments, they make
the marvels of his power and majesty known. In their
graves, which are the land of oblivion, they renew a continual memory of his justice, who is so forward to afford his
reward to deservers and to crown the conquerors in his
quarrel that even he maketh their dead bones and dust
glorious in this world, before they be endued with their
final corruption.

God's Church having, to her great advancement, the
singular power of God's martyrs, hath always made an especial account of them, and had them evermore in chief
reverence. This also moved the Fathers to give them such
honourable titles. St Basil calleth them the help of Christians, the guardians of mankind, partners of our cares,
furtherers of our prayers, our ambassadors unto God, the

stars of the world, the flowers of the Church, and towers against invasion of heretics.[51] St Ambrose calleth them governors and watchers, intercessors of the world, patrons and fortresses of cities.[52] Theodoret calleth them our captains, our princes, our defenders, keepers and advocates.[53] Finally, St Chrysostom calleth them pillars, rocks, towers, lights of the Church and protectors of kings and emperors.[54]

THE TWELFTH CHAPTER

The unhappiness of the schismatics and lapsed, and comfort against their example

OH how unhappy are they, who, in order to save their goods, credit, temporal authority or other such worldly respects, forsake the glorious and divine honours and purchase a most lamentable and ignominious style! For what are they but the spoil of Christians, the destroyers of men's souls, the occasioners of our cares, hinderers of our prayer, factors of the devil, clouds of darkness, weeds of the Church and fortresses of heresy? What are they but ruins of religion, dismembered offals and limbs of Satan?

Many of them yielding before the battle and foiled before they fought, have not left themselves even the excuse of being able to say that they went to church unwillingly.* They offer themselves voluntarily, they run wittingly to their own ruin and seem rather to embrace sin as a desirable thing than to yield to an occasion that they would fain have eschewed.

But you, Catholics, did not your feet stumble, your eyes dazzle, your heart quake and your body tremble when you came into the polluted synagogue? And could Christ's servant abide to do any reverence in that place where he renounces Christ or to do any homage there to his enemy

* R. S. means Protestant services. Fines and forfeitures were exacted from Catholics who refused to attend them.

whom he had in baptism renounced? And could you come thither to offer your prayers unto God where your very presence offered your body and soul to the devil? And could Catholic ears sustain without glowing the blasphemous, reproachful and railing speeches against your true Mother the Catholic Church? Was it no pain to hear the corrupt translations, abuse and falsifyings of God's own word? Was not the law of going to church, and of being there present at what they call *Divine Service*, made and published purposely for the abolition of the Catholic Faith, for the contempt, reproof and overthrow of the true Church, for the establishment of their untrue doctrine?

Can any Catholic knowing this (for none can be ignorant thereof) deny that in obeying this law he consenteth unto the impugning of the true, and the setting up of a false, faith? Do you not remember St Paul's words: *Not only they that do such things are worthy of death, but also those that consent to such as do them* (Rom. 1. 32)? Even so is he worthy to be punished, who though in mind he favour his Prince, yet in fact cleaveth to his enemy. Moreover, was not this law made to force men to shew and profess conformity in external behaviour to this new faith? Is it not required as a sign of renouncing the true Church and approving this new form of service, sacraments and religion? To deny this is against experience. For to this is the purpose of all the penal laws and statutes. This the examinations, arraignments and executions make manifest, wherein the things still punished and condemned are: not going to the divine service (as they call it), hearing Mass, receiving priests, using the benefit of their function or acknowledging the authority of the See Apostolic. In all this, what can we think is meant but that their laws and all their endeavours tend to make us deny our belief, and accept theirs? And therefore when we obey them in these points, what do we but that which they pretend at our hands?

For if a subject should make a law that all the estates of the realm should leave the obedience of their true Queen and submit themselves only unto him; and should at the same time prescribe that in token thereof they all should come to his palace and attend there, while his servants did princely and regal homage unto him: would not their obedience to this law be a consent to his rebellion? And would not our presence at his palace be a sufficient sign of our revolt from our Sovereign? Or do we think that by forsaking our Queen, though it were through fear of her adversary, we did not fulfil the mind of his law, which was to draw all from her in order to attend upon himself, so that leaving her destitute of adherents, he might dispose of her and of her kingdom at his own pleasure? Is not this our very case? The Queen is the Catholic Church: the rebellious subject resembleth its enemies: the law commanding us from the Queen's obedience and forcing us to rebel is the penal laws terrifying us from the Catholic religion and enforcing us to the heretical service. Coming to his palace while he is honoured as king is like coming to church while heresy is set forth as true religion. Now therefore is not obedience to the law of coming to their service, whether it be for fear or love, a sufficient sign of our revolt from our Queen, that is the Catholic Church? And do we not do as much as is sufficient to fulfil the enemy's desire and intent, which is the forsaking of the open profession of service due unto her, and at the attendance upon her enemy's pleasure, so that none being left that dare openly withstand them and defend her, they may work her overthrow the better?

Surely if in a temporal cause this point should come to the scanning of any secular tribunal, the least fault for which the offenders could be condemned would be high treason. And how much greater treason is it to co-operate against Christ so directly for the overthrow of his Church, which is not only his Kingdom, but his mystical body, and he not only the Sovereign, but the head thereof whose injuries he accounteth as offered to himself, as he shewed St Paul, once a persecutor of it, when he said, *Saul, Saul, why dost thou persecute me*? (Ac. 9. 4) Neither can any protestation or other sign excuse you, for both in man's reason and God's censure you are more to be judged touching your mind by your deeds than by your words. And therefore if your deed be an establishing of their law and, consequently, an actual denial of your faith, your words excuse you no more than they should a man who, offering incense to an idol by commandment of his Prince, should say that in mind and heart he were a Christian, though all the world might see that he played the infidel. For where the action itself is contrary to the faith which in words is professed, a man's words do only argue either that he is an atheist, that careth not for religion or a Basilidian or Helckesaite, that thinketh it lawful to deny his faith, or at the least a wilful sinner, that doth wittingly against his own conscience. All these are most odious and damnable points.

And if your protestation be that you are in mind Catholic, and that you come to church only to obey the law, do you not acknowledge that this law ought to be obeyed, and that it is good and just, since obedience is due only to just laws? Do you not confess that there was in the enactors of it ecclesiastical and sufficient power to command or bind you in spiritual actions, and those such as tend to the confirmation of false doctrine and the subversion of the truth? And who does not see that this is as if you said, the law that commandeth going to church with heretics is just and temporal magistrates have spiritual authority sufficient to bind in conscience to go to their erroneous service, notwithstanding that they do it to establish misbelief and raze out the Catholic religion?

To say that going to church at such times as their service and sacraments are ministered, their doctrine preached, or the rites of their sect practised is not a spiritual but a civil action, is against all sense and reason, for it is the very principal sign of spiritual duty to be present at such things whereby religion is chiefly professed, especially when presence is commanded by a law. Indeed the known meaning of the law is to force men to a profession of a false belief, for so do the very words of being present at divine service import. I omit the scandal which you give in confirming the belief of heretics, in weakening the faith of Catholics, in overthrowing the faint-hearted and wavering schismatics. I omit the triumph you give to the Church's enemies: for they can boast of you, if not as children or voluntaries, at least as pressed men and slaves of their synagogue. I omit the danger of infection by their contagious speeches that creep like a canker, which to neglect and not to consider is wilful blindness; to consider and not to fear is tempting of God and great presumption, to fear and not to avoid is impiety towards your soul and perverse obstination.

I will not speak of your contempt of the Canon of the

Apostles and the Council of Laodicea, and divers others, forbidding to resort to the heretics' prayer of conventicles. I will not speak of the example of all antiquity, condemning the same; nor the verdict and common consent of the profoundest clerks of Christendom, and, namely, of the twelve most choice men in the last Tridentine Council, who, after sifting and examining this point, in the end found it altogether unlawful, and avouched it better to suffer all kinds of torments than to yield unto it. And although they were desired not to make this a public decree, in respect of the troubles that might arise for Catholics in England, in whose behalf the question of going to church was proposed, yet the Legate and the foresaid Fathers gave this answer, that they would have this resolution no less accounted of than if it were the censure of the whole Council.

I omit also that even divers heretics shall be witnesses against you in the day of judgment, who with letters and set treatises have by many Scriptures proved it to be unlawful for one of a true belief to frequent or repair to the service or sacraments of a false Church. Their arguments and actions in this matter will so much the more condemn you, because they were more religious in an erroneous and untrue faith, than you are in a sincere and undoubted one. Whoever should desire to peruse more at large their opinion in this matter, let him read the treatise of John Calvin, called: *Of avoiding superstitions which repugn against the sincere profession of faith*, and his book, which he wrote as an apology to false Nicodemites, who alleged in their defence the example of Nicodemus, who came to Christ by night. In this, among other points, he saith that going to the church of a contrary belief is *to part stakes between God and the Devil, assigning* *the soul to one and the body to the other.* He hath also in the like tenor written two epistles unto two of his friends. You may likewise in the same volume see the counsel of Melanchthon, Peter Martyr, Bucer, and the ministers of the Tigurine Congregation,* whose censure being by Calvin demanded, they all agreed to his opinion. Mr. Fox also recordeth divers letters of Bradford, Hullier, and others that wholly approve the same assertion. And albeit their reasons were misapplied in the particular Church to which they proved it unlawful to resort, yet are they very sufficient and forcible to confirm that the repairing to a false Church indeed is most sinful and damnable.

Therefore consider what wilful blindness you are in if you maintain a point which not only Catholics but even the very heretics themselves who carried any form or show of conscience and religion have detested as most prejudicial to the truth, offensive to God and pernicious to yourselves. You are not merely content to offer your own souls to sacrifice your faith, to make an host† to the devil of your eternal salvation and your portion in heaven; but you carry also with you your seely innocents and force your children to the like impiety, as though it were not enough for you to perish alone. Shall not they, as St Cyprian noteth,[1] cry out against you in the day of judgment? They will say: We of ourselves have done nothing. We did not of our own accord leave the meat and cup of God to run to profane infections. The infidelity of others hath cast us away. We felt our own

* *the Tigurine Congregation*: the followers of Zwingli at Zurich. *Tigurinus pagus* was a district of ancient Helvetia, generally identified with modern Zurich.

† *host*: a victim for sacrifice.

parents our murderers; they denied us the Church for our Mother, and God for our Father, and have revived the old sin of the Jews and Gentiles. *They offered up their sons and their daughters to devils* (Ps. 105. 37). Oh, how cruel and how unnatural a thing you commit in thus training your little ones in so impious a way! You gave them but a temporal life, and you take from them a spiritual. You bred their body, and you are the bane of their soul. You brought them forth for heaven, and you guide them the way to hell. Was this the fruit of your painful labour, to bring into the world one who through your education should curse the father that begot him and the mother that bred him and the hour of his birth, and wish that the womb had been his tomb, his nativity his decease, and his beginning his ending?

Oh, how much better did that good mother of the Machabees, who exhorted her children to martyrdom, rather than to offend God by saving their lives (2 Mac. 7)! Much better did St Felicity, who in the time of persecution was as desirous to send her children before her to heaven, as other mothers are to leave theirs after them here on earth. She confirmed them in spirit, whose bodies she had borne, and was their mother in their birth to God as well as in their nativity towards the world. And, as St Gregory saith,[2] seeing her seven dear pledges martyred before her, she was in a sort martyred in them all; and though she were the eighth in place, yet from the first to the last she was always in pain, and her own killing was not the beginning but the end of her martyrdom.

The like examples we read of St Symphorosa, and St Sophia, who, as they were mothers in affection, so were they also in care of their children's souls, exhorting them to constancy and giving example of the same. Alas, how contrarily do the parents of our days, who, as though their children were nothing but flesh and blood and bodies without souls, pamper them in all sinful delight, and do not fear whether their souls be in a state of grace and members of the Catholic Church? Such as are cruel to themselves, how can they be merciful to others? And such as are themselves fallen from God, how can they either exhort or uphold others in God's service? Oh, blindness and dullness of heart! Had you rather have God than man for your enemy? Had you rather be the devil's than God's prisoners? Had you rather live captives here in earth than die to be saints in heaven? What are your riches as you use them but gyves to chain you and fetter you in sin? Are they not most straight and strong bolts, by which, as St Cyprian saith, *both virtue is slacked and faith suppressed and the mind overcome and the soul imprisoned*?[3] Yea and besides this, do not these chains bring with them a most cruel keeper, that is the love of money? And this keeper, once he hath gotten a man, does not suffer him to depart the prison, but holds him sure with a thousand bands, locks and doors, and casting him into an inward hold, makes him take pleasure in his bondage. Oh, what a miserable exchange do you make! You sell with Esau your heavenly inheritance for a little broth (Gen. 25). You sell your soul that cost no less than the life and blood of God himself for the short use of a few riches. You sell God and all he is worth for a small revenue of a few years. Nor can the fear of temporal loss excuse you. You must not be unwilling to forgo for God what he gave you. It is folly to think that God can allow as an excuse the loss of a little pelf* when the soul which he bought

* *pelf*: money, wealth, riches.

with his own blood is lost for the saving of it. Clement of Alexandria reporteth that Apelles, seeing one of his scholars painting Helena, and limning her image with much gold, said unto him that, since he was not able to paint her fair, he meant at the least to make her rich.[4] These words we may well use to those that allege their riches as a cause of their revolt. Since their fault is so palpable that they cannot paint an image with any seemly shape of virtue, they seek at the least to gild it and make it seem tolerable with the pomp of their riches, as though where true beauty and grace wanteth, there heavenly Apelles could be blinded from espying the deformity of their image by the glittering of their gold. No, no, well seeth God your gross error and the folly of your bargain. *They who change the Kingdom of heaven for money*, saith St Chrysostom, *are like unto him that, being dispossessed of a large kingdom, should glory in a heap of dung*.[5] They that desire to gain, he saith elsewhere,[6] seek in putting forth their money such as will give them greatest usury and take their money thankfully at their hands. But you seem to take a quite contrary course; you forsake God, who offereth not the hundred part, but the hundredfold gain, and put your money on such as cannot so much as restore the principal. What can your belly return you, which consumeth most part of your riches, but dung and corruption? What can your vain pomp and glory return but malice and envy? What can your unchastity return but hell and the worm of conscience? And yet have you chosen these for your debtors. And the return for the usury and loan of your wealth will be present evils and future punishments.

What comfort can your wealth give you, for, howsoever richly you are attired, without Christ you are naked? With whatsoever jewels or ornaments you are set forth, without Christ's beauty you are deformed? Howsoever your face is painted and your beauty blazed, without grace you are ugly and monstrous. And (alas) how can you take any pleasure in these vanities considering that you have lost yourself, and that you carry about you your own funeral, while your body is a filthy tomb of a more filthy soul, not only dead but almost rotten in sin?

And will you thus lend your riches to your own revenge, and not rather put them out to Christ, who offereth heaven and life everlasting for your loan? If the time of his payment seem somewhat long, and that withhold you, remember that you are bidden, *Seek first the Kingdom of God, and for necessaries you shall not want* (Mt. 6. 33). Remember the longer he keepeth it, the more gain he hath to return for it. You not only bear but wish for this delay in your usury with men; have you so little confidence in God, and such fear he should become bankrupt, that you dare not trust him so long as you would an ordinary merchant?

Consider with yourselves that the articles of your faith are no fables; the words and contents of the Scriptures, no poets' fictions but undoubted truths that shall assuredly be verified. Christ saith, whosoever loveth father, mother, riches, wife, or children more than him is not worthy of him (Mt. 10. 37). And whoso gathereth not with Christ, scattereth; and he that is not with him is against him (Mt. 12. 30). Such as deny him here, shall be denied by him in the next world (Mt. 10. 33). And whosoever confesseth him here, shall be acknowledged of him in the day of judgment (Lk. 12. 8). And both these sayings being of equal truth and credit, then (as St Cyprian saith): *If the faith that conquereth be crowned, then must the foiled perfidiousness be chastised.*[7] Wherefore whosoever hath fallen, let him now rise. If he have shewed himself a man in sinning, let him not shew himself a devil in obstinately pursuing his fault. So many delights as you have to leave, then so many sacrifices you have to appease God. Your number of vices may you turn into a number of virtues, employing all that you abused to the contempt of God in your wickedness to serve God in your repentance.[8]

Fly out of the midst of Babylon, saith St Bernard, *and save your souls. Fly unto the city of refuge, where you may do penance for that which is past, obtain grace for the present, and expect the comforts that are to come.*[9]

Let not the burden of your conscience withhold you, for where sin hath much abounded there aboundeth also God's grace in repentance. Let not the fear of difficulties and rigour dismay you. *The passions of this world are not condign*, neither to the past sins, which are released, nor to the present sweetness of grace, which is restored, nor to the future glory, wherewith they shall be rewarded (Rom. 8. 18).

If you believe not words, believe examples of so many. How many have you in prison, both by nature and custom very dainty and tender? Nothing is impossible to true believers, nothing sharp to true lovers, nothing hard to the meek, and nothing rough to the humble, to whom grace affordeth help and devout obedience easeth the weight of God's commandments.

Remember what judgments God hath shewed on those that denied him. One, as soon as he had denied Christ, was presently stricken dumb, and so began his punishment in that in which his fault began.[10] Another woman, having committed the like crime, was suddenly in the baths seized on by an evil spirit and tore off her tongue, by which she had renounced her Faith, with her own teeth; thus she was made the revenger of her own offence and within a little space, extremely tormented with wringing in her bowels, she gave up the ghost. Harken what St Cyprian saith of those that in his time were guilty of this revolt: *How many are every day fraught with foul fiends? How many waxing witless fools are in the end shaken with a furious madness? Neither need I go over the particular ends of every one, seeing that in the manifold ruins and revolts through the world, the punishments of their sins are as various as the multitude of offenders is great.*[11]

Let every one of you consider what he himself hath deserved as well as what others have suffered. Let no man flatter himself in the adjourning of his chastisement; yea let him rather fear the more, seeing God reserveth his sin to an eternal revenge. Be not moved with their example, that either through reckless error or dullness of faith run headlong forward in their wilful blindness. Go not you to perdition with them for company. Do not think it better to go to hell with many than to heaven with a few. Join your prayers with ours, that daily pray for you. Be not slack in your own cause to which so many co-operate; and laugh not you in your misery, which so many rue.

God is ready again to receive you. He openeth unto you the gate of his mercy. He calleth you, inviteth you with fatherly pity. Oh, ungratefulness! Why stick you? Why stand you? What stayeth you from coming? Your soul lyeth upon it; your eternal weal or woe is in the balance. Take mercy while you may, enter while you have access, lest the gate be shut, and your knocking not heard, and your last answer be, *I know you not.*

And you on the other side, most constant Confessors, continue your course. Persevere in your commenced enterprise. Let not the example of those that fall make you the weaker: *If they had been of us they would have stayed with us* (1 Jn 2. 19). *We should rejoice,* saith St Cyprian, *when wolves and beasts are sequestered from the Church, lest with their cruel and venomous infection they prey upon the doves and sheep of Christ.*[12] How can the sweet stand together with the sour, darkness with light, the calm with the tempest? *Let no man imagine that the good go out of the Church. The wind carryeth not away the wheat, neither doth the storm overthrow the trees that are strong rooted. The light chaff is tossed with every tempest, and the weak trees with every blast are blown down.*[13]

The pillar in a building, if it stand right, the more weight that is laid upon it, the more firm and immovable it standeth; but if it lean to either side, any weight maketh it fall quite down and break asunder. So those that walk uprightly in this spiritual building of the Church, framing their behaviour agreeably to the integrity of their faith, are rather strengthened and confirmed by the poise of persecution; but such as are of loose demeanour and evil life and lean to the liberty of this wicked time fall in schism with every little weight of adversity, and are broken off from the members of Christ's mystical body.

When the sun shineth, asks St Augustine, is it the palm that withereth or the cedar that is parched? Is it not rather the wearish* hay that suddenly fadeth with the heat?[14] Though you see some Saul of a prophet become a prophet's

* *wearish*: destitute of savour, sickly, shrivelled.

persecutor (1 Kgs 19), some Judas of Christ's apostle become his betrayer (Mt. 26. 14), some Nicolas of a deacon become an archheretic (Apoc. 2. 6 and 15), yet be not you moved. What marvel if the beam lose the light when it is severed from the sun, if the bough wither when it is cut off from the tree, or if the book quite dry up when it is parted from the headspring? This cannot any way prejudice but rather profit the Church, whose purity is increased when it voideth out of it such ordure and corruption. For, as St Gregory saith, *No man in the Church doth more harm than he that, living perversely, beareth the name and degree of piety. For such a one no man presumeth to reprove: and a great deal more apparently turneth the fault to evil example when, for reverence of the order, the offender must have his honour.*[15] Better therefore it is that they should go out of it, who within it be a disgrace unto it, and without it honour it as a ground that cannot brook such rank and poisoned weeds.

Condemn not the pearl because the swine tread upon it, despise not the light because the evil-doers hate it, think not worse of the Church if the wicked forsake it. It were a folly in the Egyptians to condemn their river Nile that fatteth their soil and causeth all their abundance or to refuse to eat the fruits which it engendereth by watering the earth because therein the crocodile breedeth or because sometimes it casteth out an ugly viper. So were it much more madness to condemn the Church or her sacraments, because some poisoned worms have bred and fed in them and afterwards impiously revolted from them.

It is not much to see some cockle in God's field so long as the enemy may sow it. Look you upon the wheat, for the Angels shall bind the cockle in bundles and throw them into unquenchable fire (Mt. 13). The net is not yet drawn to shore for the fisher to cast out the evil fish (Mt. 13). The good-man of the house hath not yet sorted his vessels, nor severed the vessels of reproach from the vessels of honour (Rom. 9. 21). *When he taketh his time, he will judge justice itself* (Ps 74. 3); how much more their impiety?

In the meanwhile though some of the bad sever themselves from Christ's body, we must rather think it a happiness than a novelty. For so hath it been always heretofore, and so will it be always hereafter, until such time as *the Angels shall come and sever the bad from amongst the just* (Mt. 13. 49), and allot everyone to his deserved home. *It is better for us to be humbled with the meek than to divide spoils with the proud* (Prov. 16. 19). Better it is to be a wounded and tormented member in the body than a member clad in gold and cut off from the same.

It were great folly in one that seeing a horse fair to the eye, of a good colour, of a proper make, and set forth with a gorgeous furniture, would straight buy it at an unreasonable price, neither considering its pace, courage, force or soundness. So were it extreme madness to buy the advancements of this world with loss of eternal joy, only for the fair show and flattering delights, not weighing the slipperiness, the vanity and the danger of them.

If they think worldly pleasure so great felicity as to take it at this rate with the loss of their souls, let us not imitate or like their bargain. Children seeing the stage-players in costly attire think them happier than the rich gentleman who goeth plain, because neither consider they the players' base condition otherwise nor their shameful profession, but only their feigned glory. So let us not be so childish as to

make the like account of worldly gluttons, who have revolted from God to gorge, knowing that though they are
clad in purple and every day pampered with magnificent
banquets, yet end with this miserable conclusion: *The rich
man died and was buried in hell* (Lk. 16. 22).

Who is so mad as to admire his might, saith Eusebius
Emissenus, that is only mighty to do himself mischief? Who
could deem him happy that had a strong hand for no purpose
but to cut his own throat? Who would praise his swiftness
that runneth hastily to his own perdition or marvel at his
high ascent whose mounting is only to his great ruin? Such
felicity is much like theirs who, having taken the poisoned
juice of certain herbs, are by the operation thereof brought
to die with excessive laughter.[16] And what felicity is it,
said St Chrysostom, for one sick of the dropsy to have choice
of pleasant drinks, which the more they allure him to taste
them, the more they forward him towards his death.[17]

Let them triumph in their imaginary happiness and true
misery. Let them rejoice in their wickedness and glory in
their destruction. Let us comfort ourselves in our passions
and afflictions for Christ, which we know will advance us
to an eternal reward, and to those glorious titles before
mentioned which undoubtedly are due unto the martyrs in
our cause and to no other.

THE THIRTEENTH CHAPTER

That heretics cannot be Martyrs

ALTHOUGH it has been the property of heretics to vaunt of such as died for their religion and to term them martyrs because they held steadfastly to their heresy: yet in fine it has always appeared that as their doctrine was heresy, so their death was desperation. Eusebius[1] writes that the Cataphrygians, being driven to an exigent, had no other way to maintain their doctrine but to flee to their martyrs; to whom Apollinaris well answered that so had the Marcionists and other heretics done: but *how* (saith he) *is it possible for them that want the truth of Christ to have the truth of martyrdom?*

The manna, when it was used agreeably to the precept of God, had all kind of delightsome tastes and was fit to nourish and very pleasant to eat; but when his commandment was not observed in the use thereof, that most comfortable viand rotted and turned into worms. So though martyrdom (if it be well used) be an act of singular virtue, yea of all virtues together, and turns to the incomparable glory of the martyr: yet when it is not taken for a right cause and in a due sort, it is to the sufferer but a beginning of an eternal corruption and breeds an everlasting worm of conscience. And upon such alights that curse of God mentioned in Deuteronomy: *They shall sow much food and reap little corn because the locust shall devour it; they shall plant and dig a vineyard but never drink the wine thereof because the worms shall destroy it; they shall have olive trees in all their grounds and yet not be anointed with the oil because the olives shall fall and perish* (Deut. 28. 38–40). And so, whatever torturing the wicked or heretics suffer, it shall avail them nothing but pain. For if all were martyrs that die for their religion, then many heresies, both contrary amongst themselves and repugnant to the evident doctrine of Christ, would be truths: which is impossible.

He can be no martyr, said Cyprian, *that is not in the Church: he cannot achieve the Kingdom that forsakes her that shall be Queen: they can make no abode with God that refuse to be peaceable in his Church. Well may they broil in flames and, being thrown into the fire or whirled to wild beasts, cast away their lives. It shall be no crown of their faith but a punishment of their perfidiousness: it will not be a glorious end of their religious virtue but a death of desperation. Well may such a one be killed, but he cannot be crowned: he so professes himself to be a Christian as the Devil falsely feigns to be Christ: as the Lord forewarned us, saying, "Many shall come in my name, saying, I am Christ, and shall deceive many"* (Mt. 24. 5).[2]

In the same fire, saith St Augustine,[3] the gold shines and the straw smokes. Under the same flail the corn is purged and the husks broken. Neither is the oil and dregs confounded together because they are both under the weight of the same press. Even so the same violence that proves, purifies and cleanses the good, damns, wastes and spoils the bad; and in the same affliction the wicked curse and blaspheme God, and the good praise him and pray unto him; it matters not what things but in what state and cause every one suffers. For when the mire is stirred it breathes out a horrible stench, but when sweet ointment is stirred it breathes out a delightsome favour. The Red Sea of martyrdom, though to the true Israelite (Wis. 16) it yielded dry way without impediment, yet Pharao and the false Egyptians (Ex. 14) are drowned therein and sink to the bottom like stones. Who were ever more ready to die for their religion than the Donatists? They did not only die obstinately when they were condemned but provoked men to kill them for their religion. Have we not seen the same furious spirit likewise in the Anabaptists? For though they deny the Scripture and the humanity of Christ, though they stick only to their own dreams and revelations, though they permit such brutish community and plurality of wives, and marriage of sister and brother together: yet they die in defence of these damnable paradoxes, and with such pertinacity as though they had bodies of steel that felt no pain or torment. But let not this move anyone to think the truth on their side.

Even to this day do the Jews die in defence of the fables of their Talmud, which is to them as the Bible is to us. Wherein notwithstanding (besides the denial of the coming of Christ) there are very many ridiculous things: such as that God spends three hours in the day in reading their law; other certain hours he weeps and afflicts himself for suffering the Temple to be destroyed and the Jews brought into bondage; that he appointed certain sacrifices every new moon to be offered for his sin in giving the sun that light which wrongfully he had taken away from the moon; and other fables of like folly. And yet childish things as these be, there want not to this day Jews that will die in defence of their religion.

And not many years since a renegade Christian becoming a Jew was burnt for this fond doctrine. Neither is this a marvel when the Gentiles themselves, even unto this day, have also their martyrs. For as may be seen in the epistles and stories of India, it is thought a very laudable thing among them, putting themselves and their goods into an unfurnished ship, new built for that purpose, to bore the ship through, and to sacrifice themselves to their false gods by drowning in the sight of their friends and the people. Others also during their great and high solemnities used to lie flat in the thresholds of the doors of the temples, when the press and throng of people is most, and so suffer themselves to be trampled to death, and are thereby accounted saints.

I omit Decius, Scaevola, Leocorius, Leonides and others of older date whose facts may easily avouch St Augustine's saying that *the cause, not the punishment, makes the martyr*. [4] And therefore they are mad (saith he) that divide the members of Christ, abolish the sacraments, and yet glory in their persecution because they are forbidden to do these things by the Emperor's laws, which were enacted for the unity of God's Church, and boast guilefully of their innocence, seeking at men's hands the glory of martyrdom, which at our Lord's they cannot have. But the true martyrs are those of whom our Lord said, *Blessed are they that suffer persecution for justice' sake*. And not they that suffer for their own iniquity or for the impious breach of Christian unity but they who suffer persecution for righteousness are indeed the true martyrs: *And, O faction of Donatus, if thou hast suffered corporal persecution of the Catholic Church, thou hast suffered as Agar of Sara; return therefore unto thy mistress.*

Whom have you amongst all ancient authors that doth register as martyrs these many hundreds of heretics who have been put to death in former ages for their heresies, yea, that condemns them not for obstinate heretics? Where have you any of their festival days, their glorious tombs, their honour and memories celebrated, mentioned or known? We see that the true martyrs' days, names, acts and ashes are still famous, though they were straight after Christ's time and have passed the storms of so many and great persecutions. They are mentioned by all antiquity, honoured with the style of as great saints as themselves, *and their memory shall be blessed* (Ecclus. 45. 1). But not all Arius' posterity, not all the races of other heretics could maintain their doctrine or their martyrs' credit long, but it befell unto them, and will do unto Foxe's Martyrs, as David prophesied: *I have seen the wicked exultant, yea, lifting himself up like the cedar of Lebanon. I passed by and lo, he was not, I sought him and he was not to be found* (Ps. 36. 35). For a while they were honoured as saints and had the glory of the Cedars of Lebanon given unto them; but in the end they are found to have been barren trees and thrown into unquenchable fire, and their place was no longer found amongst saints.

Martyrdom cannot be the just punishment of sin but the crown of virtue. Whosoever is justly executed for a true offence, saint he may be (if he repents of his fault and takes his death as his just desert) but martyr he cannot be, though he endure never so many deaths or torments. For as one that on a hot summer's day walking in a dry and barren field, and being sore parched with the sun and extremely thirsty, though he settled himself to paint or grave in the earth most pleasant fountains or delightsome and shadowy bowers, he would nevertheless be as much annoyed by the heat as before and his thirst as little eased: so they that walk in the fruitless field of heresy, in which it is impossible that either the fountain of grace should spring or the arbours of glory

grow, however much they may, in the heat of their just persecution and thirst of comfort in their punishments, feed
their imagination with a vain presumption of future joys:
yet in truth all their hope is like a painted fountain that
rather increases than diminishes their pain. And therefore
in yielding themselves so rashly to torments for their heresies they are like a poor wretch lying asleep on the edge of a
high and steep rock, who, dreaming that he were made a
king with a glorious train of nobility to attend him, sumptuous palaces to lodge him in and the commodities of a
whole kingdom at his command, should upon the sudden
starting up and leaping for joy fall down from the rock and
in lieu of all his imaginary solaces kill himself and lose that
little comfort which he had in his miserable life. For in
truth, as St Paul saith, *Though I deliver my body to be burned,
and have no charity*, and union with God and his true Church,
it availeth me nothing (1 Cor. 13. 3).

And for this would Christ have his first martyrs Innocents,
and, as St Cyprian saith: *The age unable for the combat was apt
for the crown, and that it might appear that those who die for
Christ are innocents, innocent infancy was first for his name put to
death.*[5] David seemed to insinuate this when he said: *Keep
innocency and behold equity, because they are relics for the peaceable man* (Ps. 36. 37). But where this innocency wanteth
and this equity faileth, this peaceableness with God's Church
is not observed. Well saith St Cyprian: *If any such be appre-
hended, he need not flatter himself as though he were a confessor of
Christ's name: seeing it is manifest that if any such be killed, it is no
crown of his faith but a penalty of his faithlessness.*[6]

And therefore if any of their acts be committed to writing, it is not a report of their praises but a rehearsal of their

iniquities. For, as David foretold, *Their memory vanished with a sound* (Ps. 9. 7): and again, *The unjust shall perish and their very relics be quite extinguished* (Ps. 36. 38).

Wherefore to you only and to your predecessors who suffer in this glorious cause of the Catholic Faith, and whose only quarrel (as before is proved) is the true quarrel of religion: to you (I say), and to no other, appertaineth the glory of martyrs in this world and the unspeakable felicity prepared for them in the world to come.

THE FOURTEENTH CHAPTER
The glory due unto Martyrs in the next world

How great is their glory may easily be conjectured. For if their dead bodies are so highly honoured here on earth and held in such estimation, what may we think of the majesty of their souls in heaven? For first all the comforts, joys and delights that are here scattered in divers creatures and countries, all the beauty and comeliness that any worldly thing here hath, shall be there united and joined together in every saint and they shall be without any of these imperfections wherewithal they are here coped.

Would we not think a man happy who with a word might have all the wealth and treasure, solace and comfort that this world is able to afford; if he might be beloved of whom and as much as he would, honoured of all and partner of every man's joy as much as themselves, and have everything in what time, place and manner that it pleased him to appoint? We see how much any one pleasure is prized. Some will venture to any peril to please their state; others to content their eye; many to satisfy their ear; infinite to fulfil their sensuality. And yet what are all the contentments of these senses but shadows and dreams of delight, neither sufficient to quench sorrow, nor able to continue long, nor won without hazard, nor ended without fear, nor lost without grief? But in heaven all the senses are evermore and without fear of loss fully satisfied with their several pleasures and drowned in the depth of unspeakable delight.

How glorious is the place may be guessed by St John's description (Apoc. 21) of heavenly Jerusalem, whose walls are precious stone; whose gates, pearls; whose porters, angels; whose streets are paved with gold and interlaced with crystal rivers, the banks whereof are set with the trees of life, whose fruit reneweth and whose leaves preserve from all kinds of sickness. God is their sun that ever shineth, their temple that is ever open: for their day never endeth, their felicity never decayeth, and their state never altereth. This description, though set forth with the most precious things of this world, the better to resemble the glory of that place, yet in truth it hath little comparison to the thing itself. But because we are ruled by our senses, more than by our understanding, we conceive not spiritual matters except by the similitude of earthly things; but let this for the glory of the place suffice: that all the ornaments, delights and inventions that either nature hath bred, or art devised or man imagined shall there meet to the furniture of these rooms; and whatsoever hath been, is or shall be of rare beauty to set forth anything shall there be present; and all this in a thousandfold more delicious and exquisite manner than ever hath been seen or conceived in this world.

Now range with your inward eye in the sumptuous palaces and stately buildings of monarchs and emperors. See what you can and think a thousand times more than you see; it is but a fancy in respect of that with which heaven is garnished. Now for your company: you must not think that because the lame, blind, poor and despised objects of this world are those that go to heaven, whilst on the other side the princes, peers and potentates for the most part are those that sink into hell, therefore all the best company is banished from heaven and only the rejects of mankind left to fill up the seats of the fallen angels.

For first, all those of all estates and degrees whose company shall be grateful shall be there present. But such as were unworthy of their earthly preferment and abused it to their damnation, as most do, are much less worthy of heavenly glory, and their company we shall utterly detest and therefore never be troubled with it.

Secondly, if God can make such mighty emperors and worthies, as we read to have been in times past, from a child that cometh naked out of his mother's womb and hath no more to help himself than the poorest brat that is born in the world, how much more able is he to advance the most impotent wretch to a greater dignity in heaven? God esteemeth not the toys that men account of, his judgment only searcheth every man's deserts. On the death of a prince and the accession of a new one, they that were in authority are then deposed; those that were base and abject before are then advanced; and the prince that is newly created regardeth little whom his predecessor favoured, but who seemeth to him best worthy of preferment: even so when we die little esteemeth God what account the world hath made of us, but how well we have deserved to be well thought of, and worthily rewarded.

Besides men, we shall have the company of many choirs of angels, of our Blessed Lady, Christ and the most Blessed Trinity; and these so beautiful to see and so amiable and loving to converse with that we shall have no less joy of our company than of our own glory. Of this Anselm speaketh thus: *Whosoever deserveth to come thither, whatsoever he would wish shall be, and what he will not shall not be, neither in heaven nor earth. For such is the love of God to his saints, and of them amongst themselves, that all love God more than themselves, and none will have but what God will have; and that which one will have, all will have, and that which one or all will have, God also will have it so to be:*[1] so that everyone's wish shall be fulfilled in himself, in all other creatures, yea and in almighty God. And so shall all be absolute kings, because everyone's pleasure and will shall be fully accomplished.

Finally, in the sight of God we shall have the fullness of felicity, which neither eye hath seen, nor ear heard, nor man's heart achieved. The understanding shall be without error, the memory without forgetfulness, the will without evil desires, the thoughts pure and comfortable, the affection ordinate and measurable, all the passions governed by reason and settled in a perfect calm. No fear shall affright us, no presumption puff us up, no love disquiet us, no anger incense us, no envy gnaw us, no pusillanimity quail us: but courage, constancy, charity, peace and security shall replenish and establish our hearts. It shall be lawful to love whatsoever we like, and whatsoever we love we shall perfectly enjoy; and not only love, but be also loved so much as we ourselves will desire. Our knowledge shall comprise whatsoever may be to our comfort, not only one thing at once but all things together: so that the multitude of the objects shall delight us, not confound us; fill our desire of knowledge, not hinder the perfect intelligence of them all.

And for our bodies, they shall be of most comely and gracious feature: beauteous and lovely, healthful without all weakness, always in youth, flower and prime of their force, personable of shape, as nimble as our thought, subject to no penal impression, incapable of grief, as clear as crystal, as bright as the sun, and as able to find passage through heaven, earth or any other material stop as is the liquid and yielding air.

Our sight shall feed on the most glorious and eyesome* majesty of the place and on the glory and beauty of the company. The ear shall always be solaced with most sweet and angelical harmony. The smelling shall be delighted with heavenly scents and odours. The taste shall be pleased with incomparable sweetness. The feeling shall be satisfied with a perpetual and unknown pleasure. Finally, every parcel, joint, sinew, vein and member of our body shall have his several and peculiar delights. Which though they be most diverse in quality and so vehement that the least of them were more than our mortal body would bear in respect of the excessive joy that it would cause in us, yet the presence of the one shall not diminish the full comfort of the other, but every one increase the pleasure of the others so that we have a several contentment both of every one by itself and of them altogether.

There, plenty cloyeth not. There, satiety offendeth not. There, continuance annoyeth not. There, hunger is satisfied yet not diminished. There, desire is accomplished but not sated: so that their mind is quieted by having their desire, and annoyance avoided by desiring what they have. Neither is their joy contained in their own persons. For, as Hugo saith, *each by loving others as himself, delighteth in others' joy as much as in his own; and what he hath not in himself he possesseth in his company:*[2] so that he hath as many joys as fellows in

---

* *eyesome*; cf. note, p. xx. This sentence is cited in Murray's *New English Dictionary* (Oxford, 1897) as the latest known example of the use of this obsolete adjective.

223

felicity, and the several joys of all are of as great comfort to every saint as his own peculiar joys: and because all love God more than themselves, they take more pleasure in his bliss than in all their joys besides.

O how glorious will it then be for God's martyrs, when in security they shall recount their conquests of Satan and his instruments through patience and constancy! When they shall have an eternal triumph for a short victory! When they shall look down upon their glorious spoils of souls converted by their blood, and shall see their enemies either confounded by God's justice or reclaimed by his mercy! What a singular joy shall they conceive by considering the torments avoided, which the lapsed shall endure, and the glorious change that they find in themselves? For their prison they shall have a paradise of delights; for their reproach and shame, honour and reverence; for the railing against them, everlasting praise and titles of renown; from the rage of enemies they shall pass to the league of saints. O how glorious will the scars of their wounds and the tokens of their agonies then shew! These (as St Augustine saith) they shall bear about them as perpetual testimonies of their victories: *For there shall be in them no deformity but dignity: and a certain beauty shall shine, though in the body, yet not of the body, but of virtue.*[3] So saith St Chrysostom: *It is a glory to a courageous soldier to bring home with victory a torn and hacked buckler and to shew his wounds.*[4] And in another place he saith that they shall not only be after the resurrection badges of triumph, but are also now very forcible motives to obtain their petitions, and to pray confidently for us: *For as soldiers shewing their King the wounds received in his quarrel speak confidently unto him: so they, carrying and bringing in presence their heads chopped off, may obtain of the King of Heaven whatsoever they will.*[5] The same doth St Jerome insinuate,[6] saying that the Martyrs keep the marks of the pulling out of their eyes, the slitting of their nose and such like maims for God's cause.

In testimony whereof we see that Christ, the pattern of our resurrection, did bear with him into heaven the prints of his wounds (as St Bede noteth) to the confusion of his enemies and shame of the Synagogue as eternal testimonies of his love towards us, as glorious proofs of his obedience to his Father and as perpetual discharge of our ransom: *O sinner*, saith St Bernard, *securely mayest thou come to the Father, where thou hast the Mother to intercede before the Son and the Son before his Father. The Son sheweth his Father his side and his wounds, the Mother her breast to her Son, neither can there be any repulse where there plead so many marks and tokens of charity.*[7] O how terrible will these wounds of Christ be to the Synagogue when they shall be verified in the day of doom: *They shall look on him whom they have pierced* (Jn 19. 37)!

O how comfortable these wounds of Christ's are to all saints but especially to martyrs, who shall not only rejoice in them as assurances of their salvation, as certificates of Christ's love towards them and as pledges of perpetuity in bliss, but also in that they themselves are scarred in like manner and have a more particular resemblance to that glory! They also with their wounds shall terrify their tormentors; and every stripe and hurt that they have received shall be so inevitable an accuser and witness of their persecutors' impiety that they would rather (if they might) hide their heads in hell fire than see those prints and stripes of their barbarous cruelty. This doth St Leo signify in his sermon upon St Laurence: *What*, saith he, *hath not thy wisdom found out to the glory of the conqueror, when the very instruments of his torments are turned to the honour of his triumph?*[8] For so indeed they are, while it pleaseth God to make the prints thereof principal ornaments of glory. And as Goliath's sword, which he meant to have imbrued in David's blood, was first his own bane, and afterwards a perpetual ornament of David's victory against him: so the tormentors' holes and wounds, that they make in the bodies of martyrs, will turn to their condemnation, and to the martyrs' endless comfort. And therefore St Ambrose, honouring the scars of martyrs, and shewing the glory of their very ashes yet in their graves, giveth us notice how much more glorious they shall be, when they are raised to their felicity: *I honour*, saith he, *in the flesh of the martyr, the scars of the wounds received for the name of Christ. I honour the memory of his life in the perpetuity of his virtue. I honour his very ashes sanctified by the confession of God. I honour in his ashes the seeds of eternity. I honour the body that sheweth me how to love Our Lord, that teacheth me not to fear death for our Lord. And why should not the faithful honour that body, which the very devils reverence and which though they afflicted in torments yet they glorify in the tomb? I honour therefore that body which Christ hath honoured by the sword and which with Christ shall reign in heaven.*[9] By which words we may gather how honourable these scars will be in heaven, that deserve so much honour here in earth; how glorious the revived body, when the dead ashes thereof are of such price; how high a growth of all happiness will be in the saint, when the seeds of eternity spring so high in his only dust; what a whetstone he will be of the love of Christ; what a comfort to them that contemned death for Christ: how much honoured of other Saints; what a terror to the devils; finally, how highly esteemed of God in his glory, seeing that all these prerogatives are so forcibly expressed even in his dead bones and relics. And this is the effect of that especial crown peculiar and proper unto martyrs, which is nothing else but a singular comfort and contentment of mind, expressed in particular signs of glory in the body for having suffered constantly death in defence of the faith. And although the like crown, by the divines and fathers called aureola, be also a privilege of virgins and doctors, yet as the combat of martyrdom is more violent, hard and victorious than that of virgins against the rebellions of the flesh or of the doctors against the devil's subtleties, wherewith he endeavoureth to subvert souls: so hath the crown of martyrs a pre-eminence before them both. Finally, how unspeakable the reward of martyrs is, may be gathered by the manner of Christ's speech, who assigning in all other beatitudes a particular reward, limited the guerdon of martyrs to no certain joy, but said in general, *Your reward is very great in heaven* (Mt. 5. 12): to shew the abundant fullness of their felicity. Neither must we think them only to achieve this triumph, who by apparent violence, by wounds or effusion of blood conclude their life: but all they, though never so unknown, whose days by imprisonment, banishment or any other oppression, are abridged in defence of the Catholic Faith. For we have example in St Marcellus, who, being condemned to keep beasts and put to extreme drudgery, after many years spent in that unsavoury office departed without any other forcible violence, and yet hath always been esteemed a martyr, and for such a one is honoured of the Church.

THE FIFTEENTH CHAPTER

A warning to the persecutors

CONSIDER now, O you that persecute us, what harm you do us: yea to what titles and glory you advance us, by putting us to death. You see, when you condemn us, you crown us; when you kill us, you increase us. *Our number increaseth so often as you reap us, and seed is the blood of Christians*.[1] The more the children of Israel were oppressed, the more they increased: and so is it with Catholics, as St Augustine saith, *The resurrection of immortality sprung more fertility, when it was sown in the blood of Martyrs*.[2] Our palms grow higher with weight; our flame waxeth the hotter with suppressing; and our spice yieldeth the better scent by pounding.

When you persecute us, you do but sow seeds that will spring with a more plentiful harvest. You think it is the seminary priest that enlargeth the Catholic faith, whereas indeed you yourselves make the chief seminary,* in which Catholics do grow, according to that saying of St Jerome: *The blood of the martyrs is the seminary of the churches*. The Pope and his bishops make them priests, but it is you that make them seminaries. Though their voice does somewhat, yet, alas, it doth but little in comparison. *The voice of the blood of your murdered brethren crieth out of the earth against you* (Gen. 4. 10) and this voice is it that so forcibly worketh.

* R. S. is here playing on the word "seminary", using it in three senses: (i) a seeding ground, (ii) a training college for priests, (iii) a priest trained there.

The bishops speak what books teach them, but, as Tertullian saith, *their words find not so many disciples as Christians do teaching by their deeds*. Our constancy forceth men to look more into our cause, and then by seeking they find, by finding they believe, and by believing are as ready to die as we ourselves. Our prisons preach, our punishments convert, our dead quarters and bones confound your heresy. You have laboured to suppress us this thirty years; and yet from our ashes spring others and our dead bones, as Ezechiel prophesied, are come to be *a huge army* (Ez. 37. 10).

By your thundering the cloud of error is dissolved, the enclosed light of truth displayed and the earth watered with profitable showers to the ripening of God's corn. New slips are ever engrafted when the old bough is cut off; and the virtue of the root that the bough releaseth, the slip enjoyeth. You cut open our fruit and shed the kernel on the earth, where for one that you spoil, many will spring up from it.

We are the wheat of Christ, as St Ignatius said, and are ready, if you will, to be ground with the teeth of wild beasts, or if you will not suffer that, with the mill-stones of your heavy persecution, that we may become pure and clean bread in the fight of Christ. The cross is our inheritance, as St Ambrose saith, and therefore if you bring us to the cross or, which is all one in effect, to the gallows, we may say with St Andrew: *O good cross, take me from men and restore me to my Master, that by thee he may receive me, why by thee hath redeemed me* (antiphon for Matins, feast of St Andrew, Apostle, 30 November). For in this quarrel, not *accursed* but blessed *is the man that hung upon a tree* (Deut. 21. 23). And therefore: *Go on, you good Magistrates, so much the better in the people's eyes if you sacrifice Catholics unto them; rack us, torture us, condemn us, yea grind us; your iniquity is a proof of our faith.*[3] You open us the way to our desired felicity; you give us an absolute acquittance from endless misery; you wash away the uncleaness of our iniquity and deliver us from the assaults of our eternal enemy.

Peradventure you will say: "Why then complain you of our persecution if you desire to suffer? You should surely love those by whom your desire is fulfilled. If we give you pleasure, thank us; and if we be so beneficial unto you, we cannot do but well in continuing our course." We answer you to this with our Saviour's words, who said: *With desire I have desired to eat this Pasch with you* (Lk. 22. 15): and yet it stood well with this saying, to say also: *Woe be unto him by whom the Son of Man shall be betrayed, better it had been for him if he had never been born* (Mt. 26. 24).

Being soldiers by profession, we are glad to have so just occasion to fight in defence of the truth, and yet are heartily sorry to see you bid us battle, by impugning and persecuting the same. Howsoever it go with us, we are sure of victory, for if we have the upper hand, we have won Satan and chased him out of his haunt to the confusion of heresy; and if we be oppressed and murdered for our faith, then we win a heavenly reward for ourselves and a confirmation of our religion for our posterity. Therefore small is the hurt that you do unto us, and unspeakable the benefit; but, alas, unknown is the misery that you work unto yourselves. For though you mark it not, or will not see it, that saying, *Let their sword enter into their own hearts* (Ps. 36. 15), shall be verified in all persecutors.

The rooting out of Catholics from amongst you is the sure

way to procure your ruin. For you pluck up the flowers, and leave the weeds. You cut off the fruitful branches, and let the withered alone. You burn the corn, and spare the stubble. You put Noah into the ark (Gen. 7), whose presence amongst you kept you from the deluge. You thrust Lot out of Sodom, who kept the city from burning up (Gen. 19). You oppress Moses (Ex. 32), who should wrestle with God's anger and keep it from you. And therefore putting Catholics to death, you dig your own graves, and cut off the shot-anchors that should save you from shipwreck.

It were but a folly for a king that desired peace, first to abuse, disgrace and torment the ambassadors, and all the servants of a monarch mightier than himself, and then to send them home thus cruelly treated, to utter their wrongs and to call upon their sovereign to revenge their injuries. Yet is this the extreme folly of all persecutors, who think it necessary for their peace, first to impoverish, spoil and torment God's servants, and by barbarously martyring them, to send them to heaven, there to be continual solicitors with God for revenge against their murderers. The effect of their prayers you partly prove; and if God's mercy be not the greater, more shall you prove hereafter.

When the red hot iron is put into the water, it maketh a great noise and seemeth to do the water great harm, whereas in the end we find that the fire thereof is quenched, the force of burning lost and the water little the worse. Like this is your triumph over us; for though you imbrue your bloody fists in our bleeding wounds and make to the eye a great show of victory, yet when it cometh to the proof, God will shew you by rueful experience that all the noise that you made was but the sound of your own quenching, fall and ruin; and that the Martyrs' estate was not hurt, but abettered by your severity.

Do but consider even at this present the wonderful straits into which your temporal state is fallen. And if this scourge seem not enough, consider what reward hath been given to such as persecuted God's flock, and how heavy his hand hath been in revenge of his servants' quarrel. For, as St Cyprian saith, *never doth the impiety of the wicked rage against us, but straight God's heavy revenge doth accompany their wickedness.*[4]

Nero, the ring-leader of your dance, fell from killing Christians to be his own butcher and, murdering himself, he ended his life with these words: *Filthily have I lived, and more filthily do I die.* Domitian was stabbed to death by his own servants. Maximinus was slain together with his children, his murderers crying out: *Of so lewd a race, not so much as a whelp ought to be left alive.* Decius tasted of the same cup, seeing his children slain and himself with them. Valerianus, being taken at seventy years of age by Sapor, King of the Persians, was kept like a beast in iron grates, and in the end being fleeced, miserably ended his life. Diocletian, after many diseases, in the end consuming away, fell mad and killed himself, and his house was burnt up with fire from heaven. Antiochus, president under Aurelian while St Agapitus was in martyring, cried that he burned within and suddenly gave up the ghost.[5] Flaccus, the Prefect, after the martyrdom of Gregory, Bishop of Spoleto, was stricken by an Angel and did vomit out his entrails. Dioscorus, St Barbara's father, was burnt up with fire from heaven for his butchery of his daughter for her faith. The night on which St Chrysostom was exiled, the city of Constantinople, and especially that part where the Emperor's palace stood, was so shaken with an earthquake, that they were glad to call him back again. When Valens, the Arian Emperor, would have chased the Catholics out of the same city, there fell such a hail of stones that it had like to have destroyed it. I omit the horrible ends of Antiochus, Herod and Julian the Apostate, of which the first two were eaten up with vermin; the third was stricken miraculously with an arrow from heaven, and the earth opened and, breaking out with fiery flames, swallowed him quick into hell, as Gregory Nazianzen writeth.

Therefore, you that persecute Catholics in England, consider how easy it is for God to practise the like punishments upon you, as these examples have sufficiently given you warning. Remember the sudden and horrible death of one Younge, an apostate and pursuivant, who pursuing a Catholic at Lambeth fell down on the sudden, ere he could lay hands on him that he persecuted, and foaming at the mouth, presently died.

Remember Justice Bromley, who after he had condemned a Catholic schoolmaster in Wales, called Richard Gwyn, became bedridden and childish, and never sat in judgment after, but remained so to his dying day. Even most of the members of the jury that condemned him died soon after, and the Clerk of the Assizes was so stricken in his eyes that he could not read the indictment.

Consider the death of Norton,* your rack-master, who upon his death-bed, in desperate manner, cried out that he was racked more cruelly than ever he racked any: not to

---

* Thomas Norton, 1532–84, tortured Edmund Campion and Alexander Briant.

mention what befell his son and his wife, to the more apparent revenge of his cruelty.

Consider the accident that befell Blyth, a man of special authority in the Council of York. He spoke in derision thereof very unreverent words when a priest, coming to the bar, made the sign of the cross, and within a few hours he fell down a large pair of stairs in the President's house, and lived not many days after.

Remember the just revenge of God against Cheek and Hurlestone, notorious enemies of Catholics and the chief agents in the apprehension, condemnation and execution of Mr Ingleby, the Priest. The first survived not long after. The second, going to speak with the Bishop at his house without York, sent a messenger in to advertise him of his coming. When the messenger returned, he found the man dead, and with so intolerable a savour that the very ground where he lay (as it is credibly reported) retaineth the stench, and they were fain to draw him away with long ropes at a boat's tail on the river, for they were unable to endure him in the boat, for the extreme bad scent that came from him.

I omit Judge Alliffe, who, staying in place when the other judge retired, while the jury consulted about the condemnation of Father Campion and his company, pulled off his glove and found all his hand and his seal of arms bloody, without any token of wrong, pricking or hurt. Dismayed therewith, because with wiping it went not away but still returned, he shewed it to the gentlemen that sat before him, who can be witnesses of it till this day and have (some of them) upon their faiths and credits avouched it to be true.*

* R. S. is here quoting verbatim from a contemporary account. Cf. Richard Simpson, *Edmund Campion*, London 1896, p. 433.

Yea and he himself soon after was cut off by death from so bloodily occupying the room any longer.

I omit the strange and sudden deaths of the chief knights and gentlemen in Devonshire, who, presently upon their cruel and unjust handling and traducing certain Catholic strangers, by God's justice soon died, and to the terror of others were appaid with their due revenge.

I omit the wonderful stay and standing of the Thames on the day that Father Campion and his company were martyred, to the great marvel of the citizens and mariners. I omit the like stay of the river Trent about the same time. Although some will impute these accidents to other causes, yet as they happened at such special times when so open and unnatural injustice was done, they cannot but be interpreted as tokens of God's indignation.

God hath as much care of his servants now as he had in former ages. He is as much the enemy of wickedness now as then he was, and no less able to revenge what he disliketh than heretofore he hath been, as the rehearsed examples may give you proof. We speak not this in way of daring. For as Tertullian said to Scapula: *We fright you not, for we fear you not; but our desire is to help all to salvation, and to warn them not to declare battle on God.*

The priests and Catholics whom you persecute are stones that God throweth at you, to make you, by their example and exhortation, stop feeding on the carrion of sin and heresy. But, like enraged hounds, you break your teeth upon the stone, not considering the hand that threw it. As for us, our accounts are cast and our reckoning down, and this only I speak to warn you of your error. If God suffer you, while you break your own teeth, to worry us also and to

R

butcher our bodies, we know he doth it not for our harm. But St Chrysostom well said that, as the cunning artificer, to better an image, doth first melt and dissolve it, in order to cast it afterwards in a more perfect mould: so God permitteth our flesh by you to be mangled, to make it more glorious in the second casting. [6]

A cunning embroiderer, having a piece of torn or fretted velvet for his ground, so contriveth and draweth his work that, as the fretted places are wrought over with curious knots or flowers, they far excel in show the other whole parts of the velvet. So God working upon the ground of our bodies, by you so rent and dismembered, will cover with unspeakable glory the ruptures, breaches and wounds which you have made.

The paperer of old rotten shreds, oftentimes gathered out of unclean dunghills, maketh by his industry fine, white and clean paper, fit to receive any curious drawings, painting or limning. So our scattered parts, by you cast into dunghills, he will restore to such purity and perfection that they shall be more capable of his glorious ornaments than they were before. And this is that which St Paul said: *He shall reform the body of our humility configured unto the body of his brightness* (Phil. 3. 21), a phrase of speech which argueth that the more the body is humbled for him in torments, the more shall it be partaker of his brightness in glory.

Otherwise will it be in the bodies of the wicked here pampered in all kinds of pride. For though the hawks, while they are alive, are highly prized, daintily fed and honoured upon great persons' fists, yet when they are once dead, their bodies serve for nothing but to be thrown unto the dung-hill. The partridge, however, whose flesh hath been torn with the hawk's talons, is notwithstanding served on a silver plate at the king's own table. So the wicked, who in this life are cherished with all kind of solaces and set forth with great pomp, after their death are only fit for hell-fire; whereas the bodies of God's martyrs are both on earth oftentimes honoured by open miracles, and in heaven are preferred to the king's table, not to be eaten themselves, but to feed upon the repast of angels.

Cease therefore to abuse and condemn what God esteemeth. Cease to pursue those whom God defendeth. Hear his gentle warnings lest he pour upon you more intolerable scourges. He beginneth to give a taste of his anger already; and therefore if you love not us, consider at the least your own welfare. If you also neglect that, at the least have care of the commonwealth, lest the offence of magistrates bring the whole nation into the compass of God's heavy revenge.

Alas, why should you use these extremities against us? Why should you pain and waste us with such lingering torments? We say with St Cyprian: to be a Catholic is either a capital crime or not. If it be, we acknowledge that we have this fault, and will never forsake it. Why then do you not forthwith put us to death for it? If it be no such fault, why do you persecute innocents and put the undeserving to death, torments and prison? Tormenting is for those that acknowledge not the accusation; but we do not only not deny or conceal our faith from you but are ready, if you will, to preach it in your most public assemblies. And if all those were to suffer for our faith that believe it to be the best, I will not only say, as Tertullian did to Scapula of Carthage: *What shall Carthage suffer if it should be tithed (tenthed) by thee?*

but, *What shall England suffer if it should be thirded by your cruelty?*

St Cyprian saith to a persecutor: *Why dost thou turn thee to the frailty of our bodies? Why striveth thou with the weakness of our flesh? Encounter the force of our mind; impugn the stoutness of our reason; disprove our faith; overcome us by disputation if thou canst; overcome us by argument.*[7] This is not the way of Christian charity. You should first sufficiently inform us of the truth, by putting us to silence and convincing the learned on our side of error, before you proceed to punish us for not embracing it. We have read your books. We find them full of wilful corruptions, both of Scriptures and Fathers, purposely wrested from their true meaning. Private conference is to small purpose, for it commonly endeth in only railing against us. The way of God's Church hath always in such cases been to give free liberty to the very heretics, to have public disputation before sufficient judges, and if they were there convicted or refused to come, they have been subject (and that worthily) to temporal punishment. But hitherto could we never have any equal conditions of disputation granted, unless it be equal for a man to be brought from the rack to dispute. And yet that very disputation was so little to the advantage of your cause that many of your belief were since then less friendly to your faith, and others became altogether Catholics.

But if you will needs keep on your violent course against us and prolong your iniquity, we will say: *The Lord is our aider, and we will not fear what man can do unto us* (Ps. 117. 6). The martyrs in St Cyprian's time digested the like miseries with joyful hearts saying: *We are not only not in fear of the enemies of truth, but we challenge them. In not yielding to God's adversaries, we have overcome them and mastered their wicked laws against the truth. And though as yet we have not shed our blood, we are prepared, if need requires, to shed it at any time.*[8]

If you shew us worldly honours, thereby to entice us unto you, you shew the lion hay for which he careth not. If you threaten us with torments, thereby to enforce us, you shew the salamander fire, with which she is not harmed. For neither can your pleasures profit us, nor your punishments hurt us, and therefore equally we condemn them both. The worst you can do unto us is our best. Though temporally you oppress us, you cannot hinder our spiritual advancement. Though you spoil us of our worldly goods, you cannot bereave us of our heavenly inheritance. However heavily you affright us, you shall never be able to suppress our religion. Though the upper heavens violently turn the lower from east to west, yet have they their peculiar and proper course from west to east. And well may you use violence to our bodies to remove us from the east of God's Church (where the sun of truth riseth) to the west of heresy (where the light thereof goeth down), but you shall never make us leave our natural motion from the error of all false doctrine to the east of true religion.

If God will permit you, we refuse not to endure and stay his pleasure; if he will, he is able to help us; if he will not, he will make us able to sustain you. If it please him, the frogs, the gnats, the flies, the grasshoppers are armies strong enough to enforce you from molesting us, as they did Pharaoh from molesting the people of Israel (Ex. 8 and 9). But if he thinks it better for us to have the number of our brethren made up, before he revenge our injuries, we will content ourselves with his divine appointment.

It were no delight to us to see you in the misery that we ourselves desire to be rid of. Your scourges could not avail us. We envy not your prosperity so much that we desire your overthrow. To your hatred we render goodwill; for your punishments, prayers; and we would willingly purchase your salvation with our dearest blood. But how well soever we be affected towards you, take heed that the earth that receiveth our blood cry not out against you, according to Genesis: *The voice of thy brother's blood crieth out of the earth* (Gen. 4. 10). Upon which St Ambrose noteth that God said not, it crieth not out of thy brother's body, but, out of the earth. *For though thy brother forgive thee, yet the earth forgiveth thee not: though thy brother say nothing, the earth condemneth thee. It is against thee both a witness and a judge. It is a more earnest witness, that reeketh with the blood of thy unnatural murder; a more severe judge, that was defiled with so heinous a crime and received thy brother's blood at thy hands.*[9]

For ourselves, we from our hearts forgive your injuries towards us, and only pity your abuse of God's benefits, that you should offend him with his own gifts, and for his favours towards you persecute his flock, and hinder the course of his religion, and even endeavour to abolish the name of his Catholic Church. Alas, your labour is in vain, inestimable your offence. *The Spouse of Christ cannot play the adultress, she is undefiled and chaste, she knoweth but one house, and with unstained integrity keepeth the sanctity of one only chamber.*[10] And we have no doubt that God will give us grace to be loyal and true children to so pure and chaste a mother and to die rather than degenerate from the profession of our faith.

We are children of her brood [the Church], we are fostered with her milk, we are quickened with her spirit. She preserveth us for

God, and she assigneth to a kingdom the offspring that she hath brought forth.[11] Heretofore she hath been as fiercely assaulted, when in one Christmas day she had twenty thousand of her children martyred, and yet was never overcome.* And she is, as St Augustine saith,[12] like a die, which, howsoever you let it fall and throw it, it evermore lieth on a flat side and can never fall amiss. She is a sure ship, and wrought so cunningly by our heavenly shipwright that, *howmuchsoever the sea rage and the winds beat upon it, howmuchsoever this ship be tossed amongst the waves, it is kept from sinking and it runneth on.* And doubtless sink it cannot, having at the stern him of whom it is said, *the sea and the winds obey him* (Mt. 8. 27).

Your idol Dagon must needs fall before God's ark, and bewray† his own impotency by broken hands and feet (1 Kgs 5. 3–5). Though you rip your veins and sacrifice your blood, yes, your souls unto Baal, when he once cometh to strive for the upper hand with almighty God he must needs be dumb and deaf. If your scribes and pharisees seek with slanders and obloquies to deface Christ's doctrine, he can make the devils confound their own imps, and if there should want any to defend it, the very stones would cry out and your own children's mouths be instruments to perfect the praise thereof.

It was not without cause that St John Baptist called your predecessors *a generation of vipers.* Their nature, as Eusebius Emissenus writeth,[13] is such that, after the female hath mated the male, she killeth him, and when she groweth big with young, she also is murdered by her own brood. For

---

* This is a reference to the martyrdom of St Ursula and her virgins.
† *bewray*; reveal prejudicially or show up.

they, refusing to stay the ordinary course of coming forth, gnaw themselves a passage through the sides of the dam, and with their birth work her death. Thus fareth it with persecutors of true pastors, who deliver unto you the seed of Catholic doctrine, and you most ungratefully murder them for their pains. But for all you can do, this seed breedeth young in your own bowels and your very brood will eat themselves out of your impious womb, and leave in the end your adulterous synagogue, dead and consumed, as hitherto it hath happened in all other heresies.

Return you therefore to the Church, acknowledge with us your Mother whom you now afflict. *Believe you and live you, and though you now persecute us here for a time, yet rejoice with us for ever.*[14] But if you continue still in this rigorous course, how many souls have you to answer for, who through your severity have no means either to hear or embrace the truth? You have enough in hell already that curse the day that ever you were born, through whose cruelty they find themselves fallen into unspeakable torments. O how heavily will our blood weigh upon you! You will think every drop a load of lead. What will you answer for the spoil of Catholics, whose damages, if you repent not, you shall repay in eternal torments? Remember what the Scripture saith. This saith our Lord: *You who feed in blood, and lift up your eyes to your uncleanness, and shed innocent blood: think you to possess the land by inheritance?* (Ez. 33. 25) Nay rather, *I will deliver thee over unto blood, and blood shall persecute thee, and since thou hast hated blood, even blood shall pursue thee* (Ez. 35. 6). And *woe be unto them that make unjust laws and, writing, have written injustice that they might oppress in judgment the poor and do violence to the cause of the humble of my people, that the widows might be their prey and they might spoil the orphans. Whither will you flee in the day of visitation and calamity that cometh afar off? To whose aid will you make recourse and where will you leave your glory, that you be not bowed down unto the chain, and fall not with those that are slain* (Is. 10. 1–4). *Because you spoiled the poor, and took away the choicest prey from him, you shall build houses of square stone, and shall not inhabit them. You shall plant most pleasant vineyards, and shall not drink the wine thereof* (Am. 5. 11). For this reason God saith: *Those whom you have oppressed shall cry unto me and I will hear their cries, and my fury shall take indignation, and I will strike you with the sword, and your wives shall be widows, and your children orphans* (Ex. 22. 23, 24). Yea, *and I will feed the enemies* of my Church *with their own flesh, and they shall be drunken with their own blood, as it were with new wines* (Is. 49. 26).

Remember what is said in the Book of Wisdom: *One just man dead condemneth many wicked yet alive* (4. 10): Solomon saith: *They shall see the end of the wise man, and shall not understand what God hath determined of him, and why the Lord did protect him. They shall see and shall condemn him, but the Lord shall laugh them to scorn. And after these things they shall fall without honour, and be a reproach among the dead for ever. For he shall burst them puffed up and speechless, he shall move them from the very foundations, and shall bring them to utter desolation, and they shall groan, and their memory shall perish* (Wis. 4. 17–19). Thus hath it happened to persecutors of former times, who have (as is shewn) even with their posterity been rooted out for their cruelty shewn to their Mother, the Church. Neither can such step-children ever prosper, according to that saying of Christ: *Every plant that my heavenly Father hath not planted shall be rooted up* (Mt 15. 13), and that of Solomon: *All planting that my Father hath not planted shall be rooted up, and bastard slips shall never take deep root, nor be settled in any staid surety* (Wis. 4. 3). Remember that he who speaketh these things is able to perform them, and doubtless wi do it if you will not cease to deserve it.

THE SIXTEENTH CHAPTER

Conclusion

Bᴜᴛ now to return to you, most glorious confessors. Remember who said unto you, *Fear not, thou little flock* (Lk. 12. 32). *For the adversaries of the Lord shall be afraid of him*, more than you of them, *and he will thunder from heaven upon them* (1 Kgs 2. 10). *He will turn their lightnings into rain* (Ps. 134. 7) of consolation. And if here he *measure the waters* of your short miseries *with his closed fist* (Is. 40. 12), heaven and his eternal rewards he will measure unto you with his open span. If here *he hath made darkness his secret place* (Ps. 17. 12), he will afterwards shew himself unto you, *clothed with light as with a garment* (Ps. 103. 2), and *will make the comfortless desert* wherein you now dwell *a place of delights, and the wilderness of your desolation as the garden of the Lord* (Is. 51. 3).

In the meantime you must be contented to say with Job, *I have been a brother unto dragons, and a fellow of ostriches* (Job 30. 29), taking well their evil usage and requiting dragons' spite with brotherly charity, and the unnaturalness of the ostrich (that, as the Scripture saith, *is hardened against her younglings, as though they were not hers* [Job 39. 16]) with friendly demeanour and dutiful subjection. Remember what St Gregory saith: *Abel he cannot be, that is not exercised by the malice of Cain, and the rose whose pleasant savour delighteth groweth with a stalk whose prickle woundeth.*[1] God will not be angry for ever, neither will he always contain in wrath his mercies (Ps. 76). *Yet a little while and a very short space, and my wrath* (saith he) *shall be consummated and my rage also upon the enormity of mine enemies* (Is. 10. 25). *The day of their destruction is near, and the times hasten to hand* (Deut. 32. 35). *And then shall the burden be taken from your shoulders, and the yoke from your neck* (Is. 10. 27). *Then shall God afford you a crown of glory, instead of the ashes of your disgrace; oil of joy for your mourning and a garment of praise for the spirit of heaviness* (Is. 61. 3).

Happy therefore is he that drinketh in the way of the torrent of martyrdom, *for he shall lift up his head to an unspeakable crown* (Ps. 109. 7). Happy is he that is *like a firebrand snatched out of the flame* (Am. 4. 11) of persecution, because with a most fortunate violence he is carried bright with an enflamed charity to the presence of God. Happy is he that *sucketh honey out of this rock, and oil of this most hard stone* (Deut. 32. 13). For by the taste of this honey shall his eyes be opened, as it happened to Jonathan (1 Kgs 14) and he shall see *the yoke* of all misery *rot away in the face of this oil* (Is. 10. 27). Finally, blessed is he that with David can say, *My mouth said in my tribulation, I will offer up unto thee holocausts full of marrow* (Ps. 65. 14–15), yielding himself with Isaac as a perfect sacrifice, rather than our Mother the Church should want living hosts (even of her own children) to offer when God shall appoint it, for the confirmation of his truth. *For with such hosts is God's favour earned* (Heb. 13. 16).

Persecution in God's cause is a sign that you are Satan's enemies, since he thus pursueth you; a sign that you are God's children, since he thus chastiseth you. You have Christ's example to encourage you; the necessary miseries of this world to make you willing; the avoiding of greater pains due unto your sins to comfort you. Your cause is good.

The estate of the persecuted is honourable in God's Church, imprisonment glorious, martyrdom precious in itself, profitable to the Church and beneficial to the sufferers, your final reward ample and great. Therefore it remaineth but for you to rejoice in so many titles of consolation and happily to continue that which you have fortunately begun. For as St Cyprian saith : *It is a small matter to have been able to get a thing; more it is to be able to keep it, when it is once got.*[2]

This is the time that many of your forefathers have desired to live in, so that they might not only profit the Church by example of their life and by virtue of their preaching, but also (which they counted most to be desired) by the effusion of their blood. When England was Catholic it had many glorious confessors. It is now for the honour and benefit of our country that it be also well stored with numbers of martyrs; and we have (God be thanked) such martyr-quellers now in authority, as mean (if they may have their will) to make saints enough to furnish all our churches with treasure, when it shall please God to restore them to their true honours. I doubt not but either they, or their posterity shall see the very prisons and places of execution, places of reverence and great devotion, and the scattered bones of those that suffered in this cause, which are now thought unworthy of Christian burial, shrined in gold, when the profane carcasses of heretics, now so costly embalmed, shall be esteemed more worthy of the martyrs' present disgrace and far more unworthy of such funeral solemnities. So is the example manifest in other countries, where places of martyrs' executions and torments are frequented by kings, princes and great potentates, though their own predecessors had been the chief persecutors.

Let us, in the meantime, take this occasion of so great preferment in God's court, and be as careful in this age to aspire unto this present dignity of watering God's Church with our blood, as our forefathers have been to guide it and further it by their virtuous example and glory of good works. *The Church*, said St Cyprian, *was heretofore white with the works of our brethren; it is now purple in the blood of martyrs. For amongst the Church's flowers neither roses are wanting nor lilies. Let every one therefore now endeavour to attain to the most ample dignity of each honour that they may receive crowns, either white for their good works or purple for their blood.*[3] *Look up unto the rock out of which you are hewn*, that is the martyred body of our Saviour, *and to the cave of the lake out of which you are cut* (Is. 51. 1), that is the deep and wide wound of his blessed side. Consider from whence you came, that you may shew yourselves worthy stones of so noble a quarry, and not unworthy metal of so honourable a mine. Remember your day-penny, and you will easily bear *the heat and weight of your toil* (Mt. 20. 12). Let your *rock* be struck, that *water* of life may issue out; and be contented to sit upon earth (Ps. 77. 15, 16) and on the *dung* of worldly disgrace, the better to be placed with the *princes of God's people* (Ps. 112, 7, 8).

The Kingdom of heaven, saith St Augustine, *requireth no other price but thy self. It is worth all thou art; give thyself and thou shalt have it.*[4] O thrice happy are you that are now in the last step to this glory! Joy in your happiness, and pray that God may accept us also to the like comfort, always remembering that *this light and momentary tribulation will work in you an eternal poise of glory* (2 Cor 4. 17), and confirming yourselves with these comfortable words: *Whether we live,*

248

unto our Lord we live; whether we die, unto our Lord we die; whether we live or die, our Lord's we are (Rom. 14. 18).

Finally, to conclude with St Bernard's words: *What now remaineth (my dearest) but that you be warned of perseverance, which only deserveth renown to men and reward to their virtues. For without perseverance neither getteth the champion the conquest, nor the conqueror his crown. The accomplishing of virtue is the virtue of courage, nurse to our merits and mediatrix to our need. It is the sister of patience, the daughter of constancy, the lover of peace, the knot of friendship, the band of agreement, the bulwark of godliness.*[5] Take away perseverance, no service hath any pay, no good turn any thanks, no prowess any praise. In sum, not he who beginneth, but he who persevereth unto the end, shall be saved.

By him that highly reverenceth your prisons, beareth most dutiful affection to your persons, and humbly craveth part in your prayers.

Ro. Southwell

THE AUTHOR'S REFERENCES TO THE FATHERS

PREFACE

1 Tertull. l. ad Mart.

2 Tertull. l. de patient.

THE FIRST CHAPTER

1 Cyp. ep. x. ad Cornel.
2 Chrysost. hom. 18 ad Heb.
3 Bern. Serm. de nativitate Joan. Baptist.
4 Basil in aliquot scrip. loc. hom. 21.
5 August. in Psal. 83.
6 Chrys. lib. 2 de Prov. Dei.

7 Origen l. 7 cont. Celsum.
8 Cypr. ep. 66.
9 Greg. hom 2. in Evang.
10 Chrys. hom. 31 in Gen.
11 Hom. 1 ad Pop. Antioch.
12 Chrys. hom. 25 in Mat.
13 Hom. 5 in Matt.

THE SECOND CHAPTER

1 Greg. lib. 21 moral.
2 Basil. in c. 5 Esa.
3 Aug. in Psal. 99.
4 Greg. lib. 21 moral.
5 August. in Ps. 72.
6 Chrys. Hom. i de resur.
7 August. in Psal. 93.
8 August. ibid.
9 Greg. in Ezech.
10 Cle. Alex. l. 2. Pedag. cap. 2.
11 August. in Psal. 91.
12 August. l. de Virginit.

13 August. Serm. 59 de verb. Domin.
14 Chrys. ho. 14 ex variis in Mat. loc.
15 Euse. Emiss. ho. 3 de Epiph.
16 Euseb. Emiss. ibid.
17 Basil. in ho. *Non esse adhaerendum rebus saecularibus.*
18 Chrys. de Avar. tom. 5.
19 Chrys. ho. 4 ad Pop. Antioch.
20 Hilar. in Ps. 2.
21 Macar. hom. 26.
22 August. in Ps. 61.

THE THIRD CHAPTER

1 August. de vita Chri.
2 Hier. in vit. Paul. Eremi.
3 Ansel. in meditat.
4 Bern. Ep. 2.
5 Cypr. de zelo et livore.
6 Greg. in moral.
7 Cypr. lib. de mortal.

8 August. in soliloq.
9 August. in Psal. 26.
10 August. l. 13. Confess.
11 Bern. de diligen. Deo.
12 August. de catechiz. rudib.
13 Bernard. in quodam serm.
14 Ibidem.

15 Cassiod. in Psal. 50.
16 August. de catechis. rudib.

17 Cypr. lib. de opere at elemosina.

THE FOURTH CHAPTER

1 Damascen. hist. de Barlaam et Josephat.
2 Bern. c. 15 meditat.
3 Cypr. in l. de morte.
4 August. l. de singul. clericor.
5 Bern. in serm.

6 August. in confess.
7 Greg. lib. 8 Moral.
8 Bas. in Gordian. Mart.
9 August. super Joan.
10 August. in Ps. 138.
11 Greg. in mort.

THE FIFTH CHAPTER

1 Tertull. de patient. et alibi.
2 Tertull. in Apologet.
3 Ansel. lib. de cas. diab.
4 Bern. in quod. serm.
5 Vide Egesippum et Josephum.
6 Oros. lib. 5. cap. 1.
7 Diodo. lib. 15. Strab. lib. 8.
8 Euseb. in chron.
9 Xiphilinus in Trajano.
10 Orosi. lib. 1. cap. 7.
11 Orosi. lib. 3. cap. 3. l. 4. cap. 13.
12 August. de civit. Dei, l. 7. c. 20.
13 Liv. lib. 7.
14 August. de civit. 1. 18.
15 Orosi. lib. 7. cap. 1.
16 Diodo. 1. 2.

17 Orosi. lib. 4. c. 11. de Tiber.
18 Orosi. l. 3. cap. 4.
19 Jul. Obsequens. Oros. l. 4. cap. 4.
20 Orosi lib. 3. cap. 3.
21 Orosi. lib. 4. cap. 4.
22 Idem. c. 11.
23 Idem. lib. 4. cap. 4.
24 Orosi. lib. 5. cap. 10.
25 Diod. lib. 4. cap. 3.
26 Plato in Timeo. Orosi. lib. 1. cap. 11.
27 Ciril. in orat. de exitu animae.
28 Cassian. in conf. Theo. par. 3.
29 Isidor. lib. 1. de summo bono, cap. 31.
30 Greg. l. 9. mor. cap. 48.

THE SIXTH CHAPTER

1 Cypr. lib. 1. Ep. 3.
2 Hier. lib. 3. Apolog. con. Ruff.
3 Cyril. apud D. Thom. in cat.
4 Theod. Epist. ad Renat. Pres. Roman.

5 Rufin. in expos. Symboli.
6 Greg. Nazian. in car. de vita sua.
7 Lactant. lib. 4. cap. 30. Hier. cont. Luciferian. in fine.
8 August. lib. cont. Ep. Fun. cap. 4.

252

9 Tertull. lib. de praescri. Optatus lib. 2. contra Parmen. Aug. lib. 3. contra Dona. c.2.

10 Leo ser. de SS. Petro et Paulo.

11 Amb. ser. 90.

12 Pallad. in hist. Lausiac. Damas. in vita Barlaam et Josaphat.

13 Iren. l. 1. c. 21, l. 2. c. 5.

14 Aug. l. 1. de bap. c. 6. l. de 50 haeres. haer. 46.

15 Epiph. l. 1. cont. haere. tom 3. l. 2. tom. 1.

16 Rufin. l. 10. hist. c. 25.

17 Hilar. l. ad Constant.

18 Evag. l. 3. et 4. hist.

19 Orig. hom. 4 in Cantic.

20 Chrys. hom. in 4 Cor.

21 Iren. lib. 1. cap. 1.

22 Origen, l. 10. in ep. ad Rom. cap. 14.

23 Hilar. lib. 2. de Trinit.

24 Iren. lib. 3. cap. 5.

25 Hieron. in continu. chron. Euseb. Epiph. haer. 27. Aug. Ep. 165.

26 Basil. de Spiritu Sancto. Greg. in vita ejus. Hier de viris Illust. in vitis eorum.

27 Greg. lib. 3. cap. 23.

28 Greg. lib. 9. ep. 58. Bed. lib. 1 hist. c. 31.

29 Bede, lib. 3, 4, 5 hist.

30 Ber. in vita Malachiae.

31 Plin. 2. lib. 10. Ep.

THE SEVENTH CHAPTER

1 Cypr. de mortalite.

2 Ambr. serm. de Passio.

3 Maxim. serm. de Mart.

4 Tertull. Apol. cap. 30.

5 Tertull. de fuga in persecut.

6 Chrys. hom. 29 in Ep. ad Rom.

THE EIGHTH CHAPTER

1 Cypr. ep. 4.

2 Cypr. ibid.

3 Cypr. ep. 89.

4 Cypr. ep. 65.

5 Chrys. in c. 4 ad Ephes.

6 Chrys. ibid.

7 Chrys. ibid.

8 Basil. hom. 7 de jejunio.

9 Chris. hom. 18 in 1 ep. ad Tim.

10 Cypr. ep. 4.

11 Cypr. ep. 89.

12 Cypr. ibid.

13 Cypr. ep. 6.

14 Tertull. lib. ad Mart.

15 Cypr. ep. 16.

THE NINTH CHAPTER

1 Cypr. ep. 63.

2 Chrys. hom. 46. in Matth.

3 Bern. ad milites Templar.

4 Chrys. hom. 7 in Ep. ad Heb.

5 August. in sententiis a Prosp. collectis, sententia ultima.

6 Chrys. hom. 24 in ep. ad Rom.

7 Chrys. ep. 6.

8 Ibid. hom. 2 ep. ad Coloss.
9 Gregor. Naz. in oratione de pauperibus amandis.
10 Basil. in Psal. 1.
11 Greg. lib. 11. mor. c. 26.
12 Innoc. 3. l. 1. de contemptu mundi, c. 24. vel secundum alios, c. 20.
13 Chrys. hom. 20. in Mat.

14 Chrys. ep. 7. ad Eutro.
15 Hier. in vita Hilarion.
16 Possidon. in vita S. August. cap. 7.
17 Ibidem.
18 Cypr. lib. de mortal.
19 Ibidem.
20 Amb. lib. de bono mortis cap. 7.

THE TENTH CHAPTER

1 Tertull. ad Mart.
2 Cypr. ad Donat.
3 Cypr. ep. 2. ad Demetrium.
4 Idem. ep. 6.
5 Arnob. l. 2. cont. gent. in fine.
6 Apologet.
7 Tertull. ad. Mart.
8 Tertull. l. ad Mart.
9 Tertull. de fug. in persecut.

10 Tertull. in Scorp.
11 Tertull. ibidem.
12 Cypr. ep. 63.
13 Cypr. ep. 63.
14 Tertull. in Scorp.
15 Tertull. ibid.
16 Tertull. ibidem.
17 Chrys. hom. 4 in Matt.
18 Tert. Apolog. c. 6.
19 Cypr. l. de mortal.

THE ELEVENTH CHAPTER

1 Aug. 1. de Virgin. c. 46. tom. 6.
2 Aug. ad Fortu. l. de Eccles. dogmat. cap 74. tom. 3.
3 Cypr. de singu. clerico. versus finem.
4 Tertull. in Scorp.
5 Epiph. haer. 78.
6 Cypr. de laudibus mart.
7 Chrys. ep. ad Neoph.
8 Aug. de verbis Apost.
9 Aug. in Enchirid. cap 64.
10 Aug. tract. 22. in cap. 5. Joan.
11 Origen. l. 3. in Job, in illud, *Pereat dies in quo natus sum.*

12 Chrysolog. serm 129.
13 Cypr. l. de mortal.
14 Aut alius ejus nomine, in editione Gagnei Hom. 50 de Genesio.
15 Chrys. ser. de Iuvent. et Max. mart.
16 Cypr. de laudibus martyr.
17 Theod. serm. 9. de cur. Graecor. affect.
18 Hilar. de Trin. 1. 4.
19 Epiph. in anchorat.
20 Ambros. ser. 92. de Nazario et Celso.
21 Cypr. de laud. mar.
22 Tertull. ad Scapulam.

23 Aug. 22. de ci. cap 6.
24 Philo. lib. 2. 10. Allegor.
25 Hieron. q. 11. ad Hedib.
26 Cypr. de laudibus martyrii.
27 Cypr. aut alius eius nomine de duplici Martyrio.
28 Tertull. l. de anima cap. 32.
29 Hieron. in vita Malach.
30 Ambr. ser. 3. in psal. *Beati immaculati in via*
31 Hieron. q. 11. ad Hedib.
32 Cypr. aut alius ejus nomine de duplici Martyrio.
33 Aug. Ser. de Epiphania.
34 Cypr. de duplici Martyrio.
35 Ambr. ser. 92. de Nazario et Celso.
36 Cypr. de laudibus Mart.
37 Ibid.
38 Chrys. ho. 66. ad populum Antioch.
39 Theodor. l. 5. de cur. Graecor. affect.
40 Dama. Papa in vita Silvestri. Greg. Nazian. orat. in Julia. 1.
41 Hieron. cont. Vigil.
42 Bern. ser. 2. de Pet. et Paul.
43 Ser. in vig. Petri et Pauli.
44 Chrys. ho. 66. ad popu. Antio.
45 Prudent. hymno 1 in Hemiter. et Chelidon. Martyr.
46 Beda. l. 5. histo. c. 7. et 20.
47 Chrys. ser. in adora. vener. caten. Petr.
48 Ambr. ep. 85. ad sororem.
49 Greg. Nazia. orat. in laudibus Cypr.
50 Chrys. hom. de nati. 7 Macha.
51 Basil. hom. 20. in 40 Mart. Basil. ibidem.
52 Ambr. ep. 85. et ser. 93. in Nazar. et Cels.
53 Theod. l. 6. Graec. affect. cur.
54 Chrys. ser. in Juvent. et Max. mart. ser. 66. ad populum Antioch.

THE TWELFTH CHAPTER

1 Cypr. de lapsis.
2 Greg. hom. 3 in Evangel.
3 Cypr. de lapsis.
4 Clem. Alexan. l. 2. pedag. c. 11.
5 Chrys. hom. 64 in Matt.
6 Chrys. hom. 33 ad popu. Antio.
7 Cypr. de lapsis.
8 Greg. hom. 13 Evang.
9 Bernar. in quod. ser.
10 Cypr. de lapsis.
11 Ibidem.
12 Cypr. de unitate Ecclesiae.
13 Cypr. de simpliciate prelatorum.
14 Aug. in Psal. 93.
15 Greg. in pastora.
16 Euseb. Emis. de SS. Epiphod. et Alexandro.
17 Chrys. hom. 3 de Lazar.

AN EPISTLE OF COMFORT

THE THIRTEENTH CHAPTER

1 Euseb. lib. 5. hist. c. 15. 16.
2 Cyp. l. de simplicitate prelatorum.
3 Aug. l. 1. de civitate Dei cap. 8.

4 Aug. l. 3. de civit. Dei. Idem ep. 50.
5 Cypr. ep. 24.
6 Cypr. ep. 16.

THE FOURTEENTH CHAPTER

1 Ansel. ep. 2 ad Hugonem.
2 Hugo l. 4. de anima c. 15.
3 Aug. l. 22. de civitate cap. 20.
4 Chrys. in 24 cap. Matt.
5 Ser. de SS. Iuven. et Max.

6 Epist. ad Hedib.
7 Bern. in Cant.
8 S. Leo ser. in Laur.
9 Amb. ser. 93 de Nazario et Celso.

THE FIFTEENTH CHAPTER

1 Tertull. apol. c. ult.
2 Aug. 22. de civit. cap. 7.
3 Tertull. apol. c. ult.
4 Cypr. Epist. 2.
5 Hen. de haer. lib. 6. cap. 29.
6 Chrys. in id *de dormientibus nolumus vos ignorare.*
7 Ep. ad Demetrium.
8 Moses et Maxi. Cyprian.

9 Ambr. l. 2. de Cain et Abel cap. 9.
10 Cypr. de simp. prae.
11 Nic. lib. 7. cap. 6.
12 Aug. qu. 57 ad Orosium.
13 Euseb. Emiss. hom. in nativit. S. Steph.
14 Cypr. ad Demetr.

THE SIXTEENTH CHAPTER

1 Greg. in moral in id *Frater fui Draconum et socius struthionum.*
2 Epist. 24 ad Reg.

3 Cypr. ep. 4.
4 Aug. ser. 37. de SS.
5 Bern. ep. 129 ad Ianuenses.